Sovereignty 2035: The India Equation

Sandeep Chavan

Published by Gyrus Vision, 2025.

SOVEREIGNTY 2035: THE INDIA EQUATION

First edition. December 8, 2025.

ISBN: 978-81-995414-9-8

Written by Sandeep Chavan.

Table of Contents

Part I — The Age Of Compute ... 1
Chapter 1 — The Collapse of Old Power Models ... 2
Chapter 2 — Compute as Sovereignty ... 10
Chapter 3 — The Architecture Wars ... 19
Chapter 4 — The Global Dependency Ladders ... 28
Closing Reflection — Part I ... 38
Part II — India's Reality ... 40
Chapter 5 — The Ambition–Capability Gap ... 41
Chapter 6 — Internal Chaos as a Strategic Tax ... 51
Chapter 7 — The Illusion of Strength ... 61
Chapter 8 — The Talent Paradox ... 71
Chapter 9 — India's Architectural Deficit ... 82
Closing Reflection — Part II ... 94
Part III — The Tightrope ... 97
Chapter 10 — The U.S. Dilemma ... 98
Chapter 11 — The China Window ... 108
Chapter 12 — The Russian Lesson ... 118
Chapter 13 — Multialignment in the Compute Century ... 127
Closing Reflection — Part III ... 137
Part IV — The India Equation ... 139
Chapter 14 — The Core Doctrine ... 140
Chapter 15 — The Building Blocks of Modern Sovereignty ... 155
Chapter 16 — The Stability Equation ... 172
Chapter 17 — The Integration Equation ... 182
Chapter 18 — The 2035 Moment ... 197
Closing Reflection — Part V ... 212
Part V — The Architecture of a Sovereign India ... 214
Chapter 19 — India's Institutional Rebuild ... 216
Chapter 20 — Leadership Architecture for a Billion People ... 224
Chapter 21 — Economic Architecture for Compute Power ... 233
Chapter 22 — The Talent Infrastructure of the Future ... 244

Chapter 23 — Security, Intelligence, and the Digital State ...253
Closing Reflection — Part V ...264
Part VI: The Two Futures ...266
Chapter 24 — Future A: The Ascending India ...267
Chapter 25 — Future B: The Dependent India ...276
Chapter 26 — The Point of No Return ...284
Chapter 27 — Resetting India's Trajectory ...292
Final Chapter — Sovereignty as Alignment ...301
Epilogue ...309
Appendices ...314
Appendix A — ICDI ...315
Appendix B — CIIS ...320
Appendix C — India's Talent Leakage Map ...326
Appendix D — 10 Scenarios for India 2025–2035 ...332
Appendix E — Glossary of New Sovereignty Terms ...338
References and Further Reading ...343
Quote Bank from the Book ...348
Closing Note ...352
Acknowledgements ...354
About the Author ...356
Also by Sandeep Chavan ...358

To every student who dreams in spite of the system,and to every citizen who still believes India can build what it deserves.This book is for the India that must be designed—not imagined.

"Nations do not rise through emotion—they rise through architecture.2035 is not destiny. It is a deadline."

— S.C.

Disclaimer and Statement of Originality

Disclaimer

This book is a work of independent analysis, research, and interpretation. It does not represent the views of any government, institution, organization, or employer. All assessments of national capability, geopolitical strategy, institutional performance, and policy architecture are based on publicly available information, observed patterns, and the author's own analytical framework.

The scenarios, indices, models, and equations presented in this book— including the India Compute Dependency Index (ICDI), the Chavanian Institutional Integrity Scale (CIIS), and the Talent Leakage Map—are conceptual tools designed for intellectual exploration. They are not predictive guarantees, official metrics, or substitutes for professional policy analysis.

Although every effort has been made to ensure accuracy, the fast-changing nature of technology, geopolitics, and economic systems means that some data points may evolve over time. The author and publisher assume no responsibility for decisions made based on the contents of this book.

This book is intended for educational, analytical, and discussion purposes only.

Statement of Originality

This work is an original intellectual creation by **Sandeep Chavan**. All models, frameworks, strategic equations, indices, architectural concepts, and narrative interpretations— including *National Power = Capability × Stability × Integration*, architecture sovereignty models, dependency ladders, scenario frameworks, and the Chavanian terminology used throughout—have been independently developed by the author.

Any resemblance to existing theories or publications is coincidental or arises from universal analytical reasoning applied to public phenomena. No portion of this work has been copied, reproduced, or adapted from other sources without appropriate attribution.

The writings, arguments, structures, and perspectives presented in this book reflect the author's lived experience as an educator, researcher, and analyst, and represent his original contribution to the discourse on India's strategic future.

Opening Note

Sovereignty 2035: The India Equation

India stands at an extraordinary threshold in its civilizational journey—a moment that demands clarity over comfort, architecture over emotion, and execution over narrative. For the first time since independence, the forces shaping India's rise are not political, territorial, or ideological. They are structural. They are technological. And they are brutally indifferent to our internal debates. In the age of compute, a nation is not judged by its speeches, slogans, or elections, but by its capability, stability, and integration. Every country is now defined by the architecture beneath it—its chips, its cloud, its talent, its institutions, and the coherence of its society. Power is no longer what a nation declares; it is what its systems can sustain.

India's story is unique. We are not Russia, locked in forced isolation. We are not China, shielded by insulation. We are not the United States, architect of the global digital empire. We are a rising but chaotic plural society attempting something no nation has attempted at this scale—to grow, stabilize, modernize, democratize, and globalize, all at once, without collapsing under our own contradictions. This book does not flatter our ambitions, nor does it criticize governments. It maps the decade in front of us with honesty. 2035 is India's last window to choose its trajectory: a future of acceleration, or a future of dependency. A future where India becomes a pillar of the world order, or a future where it becomes a geopolitical consumer in an age that rewards creators.

This is not a book of predictions; it is a book of consequences. A blueprint that dissects the tightrope India is walking between the gravitational pulls of the U.S. and China, between domestic aspiration and institutional weakness, between global opportunity and internal entropy. If India succeeds, it will be because we built capability faster than chaos. If India fails, it will be because we allowed narrative to substitute for execution. This book is my attempt to articulate India's real equation—without sentiment, without fear, and without ideological baggage. It is written for policymakers, thinkers, students, and every citizen who believes India deserves a future built on clarity, coherence, and capability.

The world will not wait for us. 2035 will not negotiate. And sovereignty, in the age of AI, will belong only to those who build it. Let us decode what India must do before time decides for us.

Executive Summary

India stands at the edge of a rare decade—one that will determine its position in the global hierarchy for the next hundred years.

Between 2025 and 2035, the world will reorganize around compute, capability, and institutional strength. Nations will rise or fall not by GDP or military display, but by their ability to build and sustain new architectural power.

This book provides a clear doctrine for understanding that shift:

National Power = Capability × Stability × Integration.

If even one variable collapses, the entire equation collapses.

1. The Global Operating System Has Changed

Traditional power models—military strength, GDP growth, demographic size—no longer guarantee influence. Chips, cloud, algorithms, and institutional coherence shape modern sovereignty. Nations that command these architectures dominate global systems; those that rent them remain strategically vulnerable.

2. India's Reality Is a Gap Between Ambition and Capability

India carries extraordinary aspiration but operates on outdated systems: weak institutional capacity, talent leakage, architectural fragmentation, and chronic domestic chaos. Internal dysfunction acts as a strategic tax that slows national acceleration and weakens global positioning.

3. India Walks a Tightrope Between the U.S. and China

The U.S. offers integration but risks dependency. China sets the benchmark but cannot be replicated. Russia provides the cautionary tale of sovereignty through isolation. India's path forward demands a multialignment strategy driven by architecture—not ideology.

4. The Equation of National Power

India's rise depends on three mutually reinforcing variables:

- **Capability:** compute, talent, research, industry, execution systems.
- **Stability:** social harmony, predictable policy, strong institutions, political maturity.
- **Integration:** diversified global partnerships, resilient supply chains, compute alliances.

Success requires strengthening all three simultaneously. Any weakness reduces national power to zero.

5. The Architecture India Must Build

India's transition to a sovereign power requires an institutional rebuild:

- modern courts, empowered regulators, autonomous research bodies;
- leadership teams instead of personality-driven governance;
- economic engines anchored in semiconductors, AI, manufacturing depth, and innovation;
- a talent architecture that converts brain drain into brain networks;

- a national security framework that integrates digital, intelligence, and physical domains.

6. The 2035 Moment: A Window That Will Not Reopen

By 2035, India will face one of two futures:

Acceleration: India builds capability, stabilizes internally, integrates globally, and becomes a central pillar of the compute century.

Dependency: Internal chaos persists, capability gaps widen, institutions stagnate, and India becomes a large consumer market shaped by the architectures of others.

This book argues that India's destiny is not predetermined. It is architectural. It is actionable. And it is time-bound.

If India gets the next decade right, the world will reorganize around it. If not, the world will reorganize without it.

Preface

India is entering a decade unlike any other in its history. Not because of politics, not because of geopolitics, and not because of the usual stories we tell ourselves about growth or destiny. This decade is different because the world itself has changed its operating system. Power is no longer determined by territory or GDP, but by compute, capability, institutional strength, and the ability to stay stable in a world defined by acceleration.

For years, I have watched India move with extraordinary ambition while standing on fragile foundations. I have seen students with world-class intelligence lose their way in systems that were never designed for their scale. I have seen institutions stretched to their limits, governments celebrating narratives rather than outcomes, and a nation trying to sprint while its internal architecture drags behind.

This book was born from a simple realisation: **India is not weak—but it is unprepared.** Not for lack of talent, or spirit, or opportunity, but because we have misunderstood the nature of modern power.

As an educator, I see the aspiration of young India every day. As an independent researcher, I see the structural gaps that prevent that aspiration from converting into capability. As a student of geopolitics, I see how nations rise or fall not through ideology, but through architecture. And as a citizen, I see a country standing at a rare convergence of possibility and risk.

Sovereignty 2035: The India Equation is not a prediction—it is a blueprint. A clear-eyed examination of:

- what India possesses,
- what India lacks,
- what India must fix,
- and what India must resist.

It is not a book of flattery. It is not a book of despair. It is a book of consequences.

Every chapter attempts to decode the structural forces shaping India's trajectory—forces often invisible beneath political drama and national emotion. This is a book about equations, not ideologies; architecture, not narratives; sovereignty, not sentiment.

If India strengthens capability, stability, and integration together, the next decade becomes a launch window. If even one variable remains weak, the world will quietly outpace us—and 2035 will become the year we look back on with regret.

I have written this book for thinkers, policymakers, entrepreneurs, educators, students, and every Indian who understands that national rise is not a miracle—it is a design.

The window is open, but not forever. Now is the moment to decide what India must become.

— **Sandeep Chavan**

Author, Educator, Independent Researcher

How to Read This Book

This is not a book of opinions. It is a structural map. A way of seeing India through the lenses that define modern power—compute, capability, stability, and integration. To get the most value from this book, read it as a strategic manual, not as commentary.

1. Begin with the architecture of the world.

Part I reframes global power in the compute century. It shows why old measures—GDP, population, military size—no longer define national strength. This part prepares your mind to think in systems, not slogans.

2. Then turn the lens inward.

Part II examines India's internal contradictions: the ambition–capability gap, institutional fatigue, talent leakage, and the tax of internal chaos. These chapters are uncomfortable, but necessary. They reveal why India often runs hard without moving far.

3. Understand the tightrope India walks.

Part III places India between the gravitational pulls of the U.S., China, and Russia. This is not geopolitics as you know it—it is architecture politics. It explains why alliances can empower India or quietly limit it.

4. Discover the formula that defines national rise.

Part IV introduces the core doctrine of this book:

National Power = Capability × Stability × Integration.

Every country's rise or decline can be understood through this equation. Including India's.

5. Move toward solutions, not sentiment.

Part V outlines the architecture India must build—institutions, leadership frameworks, economic engines, talent systems, and national security redesigns. These are not wishful reforms; they are structural necessities.

6. Treat the appendices as strategic tools.

The indices, maps, scenarios, and glossary are not add-ons. They help policymakers, researchers, entrepreneurs, and students measure where India stands—and what must change.

7. Read slowly, think deeply, and revisit often.

This book is designed for reflection, not consumption. The ideas compound with each chapter. By the end, you will see India—and the world—through an entirely new architecture.

Above all, read this book with one question in mind:

If India continues on its current path, what will 2035 look like—and what must we change today to avoid the cost of doing nothing? The answers are not emotional. They are structural.

Prologue

The Tightrope Nation

Why India cannot follow Russia, China, or the U.S.—and why the next decade will define the next hundred years

India has always been a puzzle to the world, but in the age of compute, it has become a puzzle even to itself. A billion people rising with ambition, energy, and momentum, yet suspended over a landscape of contradictions, structural defects, and unresolved questions. India is not a nation marching confidently toward a single destiny; it is a nation walking a tightrope stretched across history, technology, geopolitics, and its own internal chaos. That tightrope defines everything.

To one side lies the gravitational pull of the United States—offering integration, innovation, geopolitical comfort, and access to the world's most advanced compute architecture. To the other side lies China—offering competition, manufacturing scale, strategic pressure, and the constant reminder that global power respects only capability, not intention. Behind us lies Russia—an ancient friend, a cautionary tale, and a mirror reflecting what happens when sovereignty is pursued without architecture. India cannot follow any of these models.

We cannot copy Russia, because sovereignty through isolation would break our economy, fracture our society, and collapse our technological aspirations. We cannot copy China, because a command-and-control state cannot function in a democracy as diverse and chaotic as ours. We cannot copy the United States, because we lack the institutional depth, the innovation culture, and the historical momentum of a knowledge economy that has compounded for a century. India must create its own architecture—and the runway for doing so is frighteningly short.

The world is entering an age where power is measured not in borders or armies, but in compute, capability, and coherence. Nations are no longer competing over territory; they are competing over algorithms, supply chains, infrastructure, talent mobility, and integration. In this new landscape, India stands in a position no major country has ever stood in: too deeply dependent to claim sovereignty, too large to be ignored, too diverse to centralize, too young to stabilize, and too ambitious to remain a follower. This contradiction is no longer philosophical; it is existential.

If India builds the right architecture—of technology, institutions, leadership, and social stability—it will rise as one of the world's primary pillars. If it stumbles, delays, or allows internal chaos to outrun capability, it will become a geopolitical dependency in a world that rewards only those who can execute at scale. This is the decade that will define the next hundred years. Not because of elections. Not because of ideology. But because the architecture of power is rewriting itself, and India is standing at the exact intersection where nations either rise decisively or drift permanently.

This book is written from that tightrope—from the vantage point where India's opportunities and vulnerabilities are both visible with uncomfortable clarity. It does not argue for optimism or pessimism. It argues for alignment, for execution, for capability, for stability, for integration—the three forces that will decide whether India becomes a creator of global power or a consumer in someone else's world order.

In the chapters ahead, we will decode what India must build before 2035, because once this decade passes, the window closes, and the future will no longer be a choice. It will become a consequence.

Welcome to the truth of India's tightrope. The world's largest democracy is about to enter the most defining ten years of its modern existence—and how we walk this line will decide everything that follows.

Part I — The Age Of Compute

The New Geopolitical Map

"Nations once fought for land and oil. Today, they fight for the architecture that shapes reality. Power no longer belongs to the strongest army but to the system that everyone else depends on."
— S.C.

Overview

This part reframes the world through the lens of compute—chips, cloud, data, algorithms, and the invisible architectures that now decide sovereignty. Traditional power maps collapse, replaced by supply chains, infrastructure dependencies, and digital empires. Here, we decode why the U.S. leads without occupying, why China rises without conquering, and why Russia falls despite resisting. This section builds the foundation to understand India's place in a world where control of compute—not geography—defines the new world order.

Chapter 1 — The Collapse of Old Power Models

Why military power, GDP power, and population power have lost dominance.

The Day the Old Powers Went Silent

It begins in three different rooms, in three different capitals, on the same quiet morning. In the first room, a military chief stands before a giant digital map glowing with red and blue markers. He taps a region, zooms in on battalions, updates radar sweeps. His face is stern, confident—he believes power is measured in tanks, fleets, and missile ranges. He believes that if war ever comes, he will decide the outcome. In the second room, a finance minister flips through a report showing the country's GDP climbing like a proud mountain. Graphs spike upward. Foreign reserves look strong. Exports are stable. He smiles, convinced that numbers this large can buy respect, stability, and global leverage. In the third room, a politician boasts to his advisors about the nation's population—"the youngest workforce in the world," he repeats like a mantra. He imagines factories, innovation corridors, demographic dividends turning into unstoppable national momentum. Three rooms. Three models of power. All valid—once.

And yet, outside their walls, something is shifting. Quietly. Invisibly. Without a single explosion or election or protest, the world is upgrading its operating system, moving away from the old metrics they worship. Tanks matter less than chips. GDP means nothing without compute. Population becomes a burden without capability. A nation without cloud sovereignty cannot claim independence, no matter how loud its speeches. By the time these leaders realize the truth, the map, the graph, and the demographic boast will have lost their magic. Power did not disappear. It simply moved. And none of them noticed when the world went silent and switched to the age of architecture.

1.1 — Military Strength: The Illusion of Hard Power

For most of the 20th century, military strength was the ultimate currency. Nations measured their status by the weight of their tanks, the range of their missiles, and the size of their armies. Leaders assumed that whoever owned the biggest arsenal controlled the world. It was simple, visible, and comforting—power you could touch, parade, and point at. But the 21st century quietly broke that illusion.

Look at Ukraine. A country with a modest military, outnumbered and outgunned, should have collapsed in weeks according to every 20th-century model. Yet wars are no longer fought on the ground alone; they are fought in the invisible layers above it—satellite intelligence, cyber networks, drone swarms, supply chain resilience, and compute-driven battlefield awareness. Ukraine survived not just because of courage, but because of architecture. Real-time data flows, global cloud integration, precision logistics, and drone economies reshaped every assumption of old warfare. Tanks suddenly looked slow, missiles looked dumb, and military parades looked outdated—ceremonies for a world that no longer exists.

Or look at the Middle East, where non-state actors use $500 drones to neutralize multi-billion-dollar defense systems. You don't need a tank division to create disruption; you need a laptop, a signal jammer, and a few off-the-shelf components. Warfare has become asymmetric because the architecture behind the weapon now matters more than the weapon itself.

Cyberwar takes this even further. A country can shut down another nation's power grid, banking system, or transportation network without moving a single soldier. No flags raised, no announcements, no negotiations—just silence, chaos, and a hard truth: software can now wound a nation more effectively than steel. Suddenly, military size becomes irrelevant if your digital infrastructure can be breached by a group of teenagers in a basement or a well-funded intelligence team halfway across the world.

Even the strongest militaries now depend on chips manufactured elsewhere, communication systems routed through foreign clouds, and supply chains they do not control. A nation might have the best fighter jets, but what happens when someone cuts off the chips inside their control systems? Or their satellite feeds? Or the rare earths in their engines? A modern army is not a fortress; it is a network—and networks collapse when even one node fails.

This is the uncomfortable truth: nations with big armies but weak architecture are spectators, not players. You can have a thousand tanks, but if you cannot secure your data, protect your cloud, or sustain your supply chains, you are not a military power—you are a museum of old strength.

In today's world, the battlefield is shaped long before the first shot is fired. Compute, intelligence, integration, and resilience decide outcomes. Hard power still matters, but only when it is plugged into the right architecture. Without that, military might is just noise—loud, impressive, and strategically irrelevant.

1.2 — GDP: The Most Overrated Number in Modern History

For decades, GDP has enjoyed a celebrity status it never deserved. Economists worshipped it, politicians flaunted it, and news channels displayed it like a national scoreboard—as if the higher the number, the stronger the country. Yet GDP, in reality, is like a selfie taken from the perfect angle: flattering, selective, and not a reliable indicator of real strength.

Let's be honest—GDP measures activity, not capability. It counts what you sell and what you buy, but it cannot reveal whether you control the architecture that makes your economy function. In an age where nations depend on chips they don't produce, cloud they don't own, and supply chains they don't influence, GDP becomes an inflated number floating above a hollow foundation.

Think of countries with massive GDPs but no technological sovereignty. They are like wealthy individuals living in rented mansions: great lifestyle, impressive photographs, but the moment the landlord raises the rent or changes the rules, everything collapses. There is prosperity, yes—but there is no power.

Consider a country with a trillion-dollar economy yet fully dependent on foreign cloud providers. One policy change in a headquarters thousands of miles away can alter its banking security, government records, and corporate operations. It doesn't matter how big the GDP is. If the digital spine belongs to someone else, the sovereignty does too.

Or imagine a nation with booming consumption, growing exports, and flashy infrastructure—but with semiconductor dependence so deep that even a minor global disruption halts its manufacturing, defense production, and medical supply chains. What does GDP mean then? It becomes an illusion of stability, masking a structural vulnerability.

This is the modern truth policymakers avoid: GDP is not a power metric; it is an activity metric. And activity without architecture is noise. Even within countries, GDP often celebrates things that weaken a nation—import dependence, consumption bubbles, speculative finance, and low-value outsourcing. It rewards volume, not depth. It rewards movement, not mastery. It tells you how much your economy dances, not whether it can stand on its own feet.

A high GDP without technological sovereignty is like a mansion built on sand—beautiful until the tide arrives. And that tide is arriving in the form of AI, compute dependency, supply chain weaponization, and digital geopolitics. The nations that will dominate are not those with the biggest GDP numbers flashing on television, but those with the deepest control over chips, cloud, code, capital flow, and coherence.

This is why GDP, once a respected indicator, now feels like a polite joke—a number that impresses guests but does nothing for long-term survival. Prosperity without sovereignty is temporary. Economic size without internal capability is decoration. In the age of compute, architecture—not GDP—is the real scoreboard. The rest is accounting.

1.3 — Population: The Burden Disguised as Strength

For years, countries with large populations proudly declared it a "demographic dividend," as if the world owed them greatness simply because they had more people. More workers, more consumers, more innovation, more youth—it sounded like an advantage written into destiny. But destiny, as always, has a sense of humour. In the age of compute, population is no longer an asset by default; it is a responsibility that must be managed, trained, aligned, and equipped. Otherwise, the so-called dividend quickly mutates into a liability with compound interest.

Imagine a vast crowd standing at the entrance of a global stadium where the future is being played. The doors open—but only for those who have the right skillset, the right education, and the right technological alignment. The rest remain outside, not because they lack ambition, but because the system behind them failed to convert numbers into capability. That is the silent tragedy of population-first thinking: numbers create pressure, not power.

A large population demands world-class institutions, resilient infrastructure, and a talent engine firing at full capacity. Without them, what you have is not a demographic dividend—it is a demographic demand for jobs, services, housing, stability, and opportunity. A demand that grows faster than the nation's ability to supply. When capability does not keep pace with numbers, the future does not accelerate; it strains.

We often forget that population advantage is conditional. It works only when every additional citizen becomes a contributor to national capability, not a casualty of institutional weakness. A million engineers mean nothing if they are trained in outdated systems. A massive youth population is useless if only a fraction has access to quality education. And a large workforce becomes irrelevant if global industries migrate toward automation, AI, and high-skill compute economies that reward depth, not volume.

There is a paradox here: the world respects countries with fewer people but higher capability more than those with many people but limited alignment. A small, highly skilled population can outperform a large, poorly trained population by orders of magnitude. The size of your population matters far less than the strength of your talent architecture. In fact, every additional citizen without matching capability quietly increases national fragility.

And yet, many nations continue to celebrate their numbers as if the world has not changed. They call population a source of power—but the truth is simpler and more uncomfortable:

population is power only when supported by capability; otherwise, it is pressure disguised as pride.

This is the new geopolitical reality. Demographics do not decide a nation's strength. Capability does. And in a world driven by compute, the real dividend is not how many people a country has—it is how many of them can build, think, innovate, and integrate with the architecture of the future.

1.4 — The Silent Rise of Architecture Power

Some shifts in history arrive with noise—revolutions, wars, collapses. But the most important shifts arrive quietly, without headlines or fireworks. They slip into the world through upgrades, infrastructure logs, server rooms, supply chains, fiber cables, and silent policy decisions. And before anyone realizes it, the structure of global power has already changed.

Welcome to the age of architecture power.

This is the power no general can parade, no politician can simplify, and no economist can capture in a single metric. It is the power built beneath the surface: compute capability, semiconductor pipelines, cloud infrastructure, energy resilience, data governance, institutional depth, and the coherence of systems. Nations rise today not because they have more troops, more money, or more citizens—but because they can build, secure, and sustain the architecture that everyone else relies upon.

Look at the United States. Its real power is not its military or GDP—it is the architecture it owns. The chips the world depends on. The software everyone uses. The global cloud networks that run economies. The institutional alignment that allows continuous innovation. This architecture creates gravitational pull—nations integrate with the U.S. not out of loyalty, but out of necessity.

Consider China. Its strength does not come from its population; it comes from the manufacturing and supply chain architecture it spent decades constructing. Entire industries orbit around Chinese factories, logistics networks, and production ecosystems. Architecture—not ideology—built China's influence.

Even smaller nations—Taiwan, South Korea, Japan, Israel—punch far above their demographic or military weight because they mastered architecture. They built semiconductor ecosystems, industrial clusters, research institutions, and supply chain nodes that the world cannot function without. Power flows toward indispensability.

This is the new reality: if you control architecture, you shape the world. If you depend on architecture, the world shapes you. In this frame, traditional strengths are only multipliers. An army without compute is slow. A large GDP without supply chain control is fragile. A big population without institutional alignment is a burden. Power today is less about how loudly a nation speaks, and more about how deeply its systems run.

And the most remarkable part? This transformation happened without a war, without a coup, without a crisis dramatic enough to make global headlines. The old world did not fall; it was simply overwritten—one algorithm, one server rack, one supply chain redesign at a time.

The world didn't change with a bang. It changed with a quiet system update. And most nations didn't even notice when the loading bar completed.

Chapter 2 — Compute as Sovereignty

The new currency: chips, cloud, algorithms, alignment

The Kingdoms Built on Sand

Walk through any modern capital city and you'll see the same spectacle: gleaming skyscrapers piercing the sky, glassy airports humming with traffic, highways stretched like metallic rivers, and digital billboards announcing GDP triumphs as if the future were already secured. Nations love this view of themselves—clean, confident, and upward-looking. It is the official portrait of progress, carefully framed and proudly displayed. But progress, like a photograph, can hide the shadows beneath its shine.

Behind the glittering façade of these new-age kingdoms lies a foundation far less solid than the roads and buildings suggest. Their entire infrastructure—financial systems, hospitals, metros, energy grids, logistics networks, even their governments—runs on chips they do not manufacture, cloud they do not own, and software they do not control. Algorithms written in distant cities shape what their citizens see, buy, believe, and fear. Their data travels across borders without passports. Their digital identity rests in servers they will never touch. It is a strange kind of sovereignty: proudly displayed on the ground, quietly borrowed in the cloud.

Imagine a nation boasting about its sprawling airports, unaware that even the aircraft navigation systems depend on foreign chips.

Picture a government announcing digital governance reforms while its core data sits inside a corporate server farm owned by someone else. Think of a country celebrating its booming digital economy while the algorithms that drive its markets come from laboratories beyond its borders. These are the kingdoms built on sand—beautiful to look at, fragile to depend on.

The old symbols of strength—steel, concrete, GDP—still dominate political speeches. But the real foundation of modern power is invisible: the compute architecture a nation controls. The pipelines of semiconductors, the sovereignty of cloud infrastructure, the ownership of code, the depth of data governance, the alignment of institutions with technology. Without these, even the largest economies become tenants in a house someone else designed.

And here lies the uncomfortable question no nation wants to answer aloud: can a country truly call itself sovereign if another country—or another company—controls the foundation of its digital life? This is not a philosophical question. It is a geopolitical one. Because in the age of compute, borders are not drawn on maps—they are drawn in silicon, servers, and software. Nations rise or fall not by the size of their armies or the height of their skyscrapers, but by the architecture beneath them.

The world that looks stable from above is trembling below. And most kingdoms have not yet realized that their foundations are shifting.

2.1 — Chips: The New Oil, The New Oxygen

If the 20th century was powered by oil, the 21st century runs on something far smaller, far lighter, and infinitely more decisive: the semiconductor chip. These tiny slivers of silicon—so small they disappear between your fingertips—now carry more geopolitical weight than entire oil fields once did. Everything that breathes, moves, computes, or connects in the modern world inhales through chips. They are the new oxygen. And yet, most nations treat them as invisible.

Think of any sector you can name. Defense? Missiles, satellites, radar systems, drones—all chip-dependent. Agriculture? Smart irrigation, tracking systems, climate prediction, supply chain logistics—chips again. Finance? Every transaction, algorithmic trade, fraud detection model—chips. Healthcare? Medical devices, diagnostics, genomics, hospital systems—chips. Transport? Cars, trains, aviation, logistics—nothing runs without semiconductors. Even governance has become a silicon enterprise: digital identity, tax systems, welfare delivery, public surveillance, smart cities—chips everywhere.

We have built an entire civilization on the assumption that chips will always be available, always be cheap, always be accessible. But that assumption is now crackling like a voltage spike in an overloaded circuit. Here's the humorous but painful truth: if oil stopped flowing, we would panic; if chips stopped flowing, we would suffocate. A modern superpower without semiconductor capability is like an athlete with world-class muscles but no lungs—powerful in theory, breathless in practice.

And designing chips is only half the challenge. Manufacturing them is where the real nightmare begins. Only a handful of countries on Earth can produce advanced chips, and even they depend on supply chains stretched across dozens of nations. One country makes the machines. Another mines the minerals. Another produces the chemicals. Another fabricates the wafers. Another handles packaging and testing. It is a global ballet where the slightest misstep—a factory fire, an export ban, a political tantrum—can bring entire industries to a halt.

We saw this recently. A small disruption in Taiwan or a policy change in the Netherlands can send shockwaves through automakers in Europe, smartphone companies in China, and defense contractors in the United States. That is how fragile the world's digital oxygen supply has become. Nations that lack semiconductor sovereignty face a quiet but constant vulnerability. They may have large militaries, strong GDPs, and massive populations—but all of it stands on silicon foundations they do not control. Their missiles fly only if someone else's chips cooperate. Their banks function only if someone else's fabs stay open. Their digital dreams exist at the mercy of global supply chains they cannot influence.

And this is the strange irony of our time: countries shout loudly about borders, but whisper timidly about chips. They brag about GDP, but avoid talking about where their semiconductors come from. They show off skyscrapers, but never show their supply chain maps. Because deep down, every nation knows the truth: power today flows through silicon. And without chips, sovereignty becomes a slogan, not a reality.

2.2 — Cloud: The Invisible Empire Above Nations

For centuries, nations fought over land—borders, rivers, mountains, islands. Territory was power because everything important lived on the ground. But somewhere in the last fifteen years, something astonishing happened: the center of national life quietly floated upward, slipped past the skylines, and settled into a layer of reality no one can see. Today, the most valuable territory a country depends on is not on Earth—it is in the cloud.

And the cloud, inconveniently, does not belong to nations. It belongs to corporations.

This is the new geopolitical map: governments may own the soil, but corporations control the sky—where data lives, where computation happens, where intelligence flows. Citizens walk on national ground, but their digital selves float in private empires above the nation-state.

If this sounds dramatic, let's bring it down to daily life. Your banks run on cloud. Your hospitals run on cloud. Your education platforms, digital payments, public welfare systems, startup ecosystems, tax databases, identity infrastructure—all run on cloud. A single cloud outage can pause a country more effectively than a natural disaster. A single policy shift in a corporate boardroom can force a government to rewrite its digital strategy. A single cyber incident inside a cloud environment can expose millions of citizens more thoroughly than any physical breach ever could.

And here is the quiet vulnerability: most countries do not own the clouds they rely on. Their national security strategies sit inside someone else's server racks. Their intelligence agencies store data on infrastructures they cannot inspect. Their "digital sovereignty" depends on Service-Level Agreements written by lawyers in another jurisdiction. It is the most elegant form of dependence ever created—soft, silent, convenient.

Consider the irony: a government may spend billions securing its borders, yet its voter data lives on hardware it has never seen. It may run a powerful military, but its defense software updates come from servers in another time zone. It may have the world's fastest-growing digital economy, yet the backbone of that economy is rented, not owned.

And countries accept this arrangement because the cloud is addictive. It is convenient, scalable, fast, and cost-effective. It simplifies governance, speeds up innovation, and fuels entire industries. But convenience is the tax collector of sovereignty—what it gives in the short term, it quietly takes back in the long term.

The bold question we avoid asking is simple: how sovereign is a nation whose digital nervous system sits inside the infrastructure of a private corporation? Most leaders never say this aloud, perhaps because the answer is uncomfortable. But the truth remains: the future of nations will be decided not just on land or sea, but in the invisible cloud empires that now hold the world together.

And unless countries build, own, or at least strategically shape these digital skies, they remain tenants in someone else's future.

2.3 — Algorithms: The Silent Governors of Modern Life

If you want to understand power in the 21st century, don't look at parliaments, armies, or stock exchanges. Look at the code running quietly on servers across the world—algorithms, those invisible governors of modern life. They never give speeches, never appear on ballots, never attend diplomatic summits, and yet they shape everything from daily decisions to global events with a precision no king or prime minister ever commanded.

Take a simple morning routine. You wake up, open your phone, and your day is already being negotiated by algorithms. They decide the first news you read, the ads you see, the friends you hear from, the trends you think matter. By the time you finish your coffee, algorithms have already influenced what you believe the world looks like. And the unsettling part? You didn't vote for any of them.

Move beyond personal life and the picture becomes even more dramatic. Markets rise or fall based on algorithmic trades executed in microseconds. Supply chains are optimized or disrupted based on predictive models. Hospitals allocate resources because machine learning forecasts demand. Police departments deploy patrol units because algorithms predict hotspots for crime. Militaries simulate war strategies based on AI analysis. Political campaigns target voters using algorithmic micro-profiling that can shift entire elections without a single loudspeaker on the street.

And yet, through all of this, most nations are not building these algorithms—they are consuming them. This is the asymmetry of our age: those who write the rules shape the world; those who follow the rules surrender sovereignty.

The countries that design algorithms control what the world sees, buys, fears, trusts, and aspires to. They control how global markets behave, how narratives spread, how societies react, and how governments respond. They can tilt public opinion, sway political outcomes, influence consumer behavior, and strategically guide entire populations—all from behind the curtain of code.

Meanwhile, nations that only consume algorithms live in a world designed by someone else. Their public discourse becomes vulnerable to manipulation. Their markets respond to foreign intelligence. Their citizens are studied more closely by external companies than by their own governments. Their military strategies depend on predictive models developed in distant labs. Their youth grow up with a worldview shaped quietly by recommendation engines.

This is power without borders. Influence without armies. Control without conquest.

The great irony is that traditional geopolitics still obsesses over territory and treaties, while the real struggle for power is happening in lines of code. Whoever controls the algorithms controls the flow of global intelligence. And whoever controls global intelligence controls the future.

In an age where algorithms decide so much, sovereignty is no longer just a matter of land, law, or economy—it is the ability to write your own code. The nations that fail to develop their own algorithmic architecture will not merely fall behind; they will fall under someone else's influence—silently, seamlessly, and without resistance.

2.4 — Alignment: The Unseen Architecture of Power

Chips matter. Cloud matters. Algorithms matter. But none of them matter alone.

Every nation now tries to collect these components like trophies—buying chips, renting cloud, importing algorithms, hiring consultants, launching digital missions. On the surface, it looks like progress. Ministers cut ribbons, CEOs sign partnerships, newspapers print headlines. Yet these components, by themselves, do not create power. They are simply tools. And tools without alignment are nothing more than expensive decorations.

Real power does not come from possessing technology—it comes from integrating it. This is the part of sovereignty nobody likes to talk about, because it demands discipline rather than drama. Alignment is not as glamorous as a semiconductor fab or as loud as a new defense contract. It is slow, systemic, foundational work. It is the quiet synchronization between institutions, talent, policy, and national vision. And yet, this hidden alignment is what separates digital superpowers from digital dependents.

Consider chips. A nation can buy billions of dollars' worth of semiconductors every year. But if its industries cannot design with them, its universities cannot innovate with them, its defense systems cannot secure them, its supply chains cannot sustain them, and its leaders cannot strategize with them, then chips remain mere imports—not instruments of power.

Or take cloud. Every government now uses cloud infrastructure. But if the nation's regulatory framework is weak, its cybersecurity fragmented, its data strategy unclear, its agencies disorganized, and its local industries disconnected, then cloud becomes not a strength, but a dependency disguised as convenience.

Even algorithms, the most powerful force of the digital age, are useless without aligned institutional capacity. A country may purchase the world's most advanced analytics platforms, but if its bureaucracy cannot understand them, its education system cannot produce talent for them, and its politics cannot manage them responsibly, then the algorithms do not elevate the nation—they overwhelm it.

This is the uncomfortable truth: a country may own the tools of power, but without alignment, it cannot convert them into sovereignty. Alignment is the unseen architecture that gives technology meaning. It is the invisible thread connecting silicon to policy, cloud to governance, algorithms to institutions, and citizens to opportunity. When alignment exists, nations accelerate effortlessly. When alignment collapses, even the most ambitious countries stumble.

Look at the world today. The nations rising the fastest are not the largest, richest, or most populous. They are the most aligned. Their institutions speak to each other. Their regulations match their ambitions. Their talent pipeline is coherent. Their national strategies are unified. They move like a well-practiced orchestra, not a crowd improvising in chaos.

And that is the philosophical shift this book now invites the reader to see: sovereignty is not a possession. It is a coordination. A nation becomes powerful not when it owns technology, but when it aligns with it.

The next chapter will build on this foundation—and reveal why the future belongs to countries that master alignment, not accumulation.

Chapter 3 — The Architecture Wars

U.S. narrative control, China's insulation strategy, Russia's forced isolation

Three Empires, Three Strategies, One Battlefield

On a quiet evening, three capitals—Washington, Beijing, and Moscow—watch the same world unfold, each through a window shaped by its own fears, ambitions, and strategies. The world looks identical from above: the same satellites orbiting the Earth, the same shipping lanes glowing on maps, the same digital networks pulsing with data. And yet, each capital sees a different battle, a different threat, a different opportunity—because each is preparing for a different kind of war.

In Washington, the strategy room glows with dashboards tracking global cloud usage, software adoption, AI research clusters, chip supply lines, and data flows. America's empire is not built with armies; it is built with infrastructure. Its power lies not in conquest but in influence—structuring how the world communicates, computes, learns, transacts, and entertains itself. Silicon Valley writes the tools. Hollywood writes the stories. The cloud hosts the world. Washington doesn't force anyone to follow; it simply builds platforms everyone willingly climbs onto. This is narrative control—not as propaganda, but as architecture.

Thousands of miles away in Beijing, the atmosphere feels entirely different. Here, screens display internal ecosystems: domestic chip programs, proprietary operating systems, closed networks, state-supervised AI, and parallel platforms mirroring global ones—but with Chinese characteristics. China is not seeking to dominate the world through openness; it is seeking to protect its rise through insulation. Its firewall is not just a digital barrier—it is a strategy, a worldview, a shield. China builds an empire inward first, ensuring that its vulnerabilities are sealed, its dependencies reduced, and its sovereignty guarded fiercely. It is a nation constructing a parallel universe—one where outside influence is minimized, and internal control is maximized.

And then there is Moscow. The room here is darker, quieter, almost heavy with consequence. Screens show sanctions, blocked supply chains, isolated financial channels, and shrinking technological access. Unlike the U.S. or China, Russia did not choose its architecture; it inherited it through conflict. Cut off from the global digital ecosystem, with limited access to advanced compute, chips, and Western technology, Russia operates in survival mode. It improvises, repurposes, and isolates because it must—not because it wants to. It is an empire pushed to the edge of the digital map, fighting to remain relevant in a world that has already moved past its old strengths.

Three capitals. Three architectures. Three visions of sovereignty. And yet, despite their differences, they share one battlefield: the global architecture of power. Geopolitics is no longer defined by ideology or territory; it is defined by the systems a nation builds, the dependencies it chooses, and the digital gravity it creates around itself.

This is the age of architecture wars—silent, systemic, and far more consequential than any conflict fought with borders and flags. The world is no longer choosing alliances; it is choosing operating systems. And every nation—knowingly or not—is being pulled into one of these three gravitational fields.

In this emerging order, the question isn't who has more power. It is: whose architecture will the world run on?

3.1 — The United States: Winning Through Narrative and Infrastructure

If great empires of the past expanded through conquest, the United States mastered a far more elegant strategy: it builds what the world cannot live without. No armies marching, no flags planted, no borders redrawn—just infrastructure, quietly, consistently, irresistibly shaping global behavior. The U.S. does not need to occupy territory; it occupies the global operating system.

Think of how your day begins. You search for something—you use an American platform. You send an email—it travels through an American protocol. You watch a movie, check a map, store a file, run your business, attend an online class—every layer rests on American digital rails. The most remarkable part? No one forced you. No treaty required you. You simply chose what worked best.

This is the genius of American architecture: voluntary domination. Cloud platforms run the digital nervous systems of governments across continents. American chips power the world's most advanced technologies, from smartphones to missile systems. Operating systems built in California run billions of devices. The global financial system clears through rails designed in New York. Even the world's scientific imagination is shaped by American universities and research networks.

Step back and the picture becomes clear: the United States did not build an empire of land—it built an empire of infrastructure. This is where the idea of "narrative control" is often misunderstood. People hear the phrase and imagine propaganda, manipulation, or some grand media conspiracy. But America's narrative power is not a marketing trick; it is structural dominance. When the world uses your platforms, your standards, your technologies, your scientific frameworks, and your cultural ecosystems, the narrative naturally flows through your architecture.

It's not that the U.S. tells the world what to think. It's that the world sees the world through tools the U.S. built. And that creates a subtle but profound gravitational pull. Countries can disagree with American policies but still depend on American infrastructure. They can criticize American culture but still consume it daily. They can worry about American tech dominance but still build their economies on it. This is not coercion—it is convenience married to capability.

Even when rivals try to build alternatives, they struggle to match the scale, polish, and global interconnectedness of U.S. systems. American infrastructure becomes the default option, not because it is forced upon anyone, but because it works—and because switching away is painfully expensive.

This is America's true superpower: influence without invasion, dominance without force, leadership without asking for permission. In the architecture wars, the U.S. doesn't play the game—it designed the board. And in a world where the most powerful tools are used willingly, not imposed, the nation that builds the most trusted infrastructure shapes the future more quietly and more deeply than any traditional empire ever could.

3.2 — China: The Great Insulation Experiment

While the United States built an empire of open rails that the world eagerly climbed onto, China chose a different path—one less about expansion and more about containment. China's philosophy of power is not "connect to dominate," but "insulate to survive." To understand China's strategy, you must imagine a nation creating an entire digital universe inside a massive, carefully guarded dome.

Inside this dome, China has built almost everything it needs: its own chips (or at least an aggressive roadmap toward them), its own cloud, its own social platforms, its own search engines, its own messaging systems, its own e-commerce giants, its own operating environments, and, of course, its own governance model for data and algorithms. What seems like isolation from the outside is seen as sovereignty from the inside.

Walk through this parallel universe and you'll see something remarkable. People use apps no one outside China has heard of. Payments run through networks entirely domestic. Social engagement lives on platforms that never touch American servers. AI models are trained on data that never leaves Chinese borders. Even internet traffic flows through highly controlled routes, monitored and optimized to maintain the integrity of the dome.

This is architecture as a shield—not a bridge.

China's reasoning is straightforward: if you control the entire ecosystem, you eliminate dependency, reduce vulnerability, and achieve long-term resilience. No foreign cloud outage can bring the country to a halt. No external algorithm can influence social stability. No geopolitical tension can choke the data flow of the world's second-largest economy. In a turbulent global environment, China has chosen predictability over permeability.

But insulation comes with a cost—and it is not a technical cost, but a strategic one. By sealing itself off, China protects its internal stability but limits its global gravitational pull. While American platforms dominate worldwide, Chinese platforms rarely escape the dome. While U.S. cloud providers serve the world, China's remain largely domestic. While American standards set the global rules, China's remain self-referential. The architecture that gives China its strength at home restricts its influence abroad.

It is a paradox at the heart of China's rise: the more self-sufficient China becomes, the less universal it becomes. And this is what makes

China's strategy both fascinating and fragile. It has built an alternative digital civilization that runs parallel to the world, yet remains disconnected from it. A system designed for internal resilience may not scale well into external dominance. China may not fall behind—but it may not pull others forward either.

Standing outside the dome, the world sees China as a formidable power. Standing inside, China sees itself as fortified. Both are true. Both are incomplete.

China's experiment raises the question that will shape the rest of the century: can a nation become a global superpower through insulation, or does influence require openness? The dome protects—but it also contains.

3.3 — Russia: Isolation by Force, Not Choice

If the United States is shaping the world through infrastructure, and China is fortifying itself through insulation, Russia is navigating a very different reality—one it never intended to design. Russia's digital and economic architecture is not the result of long-term planning, strategic vision, or technological philosophy. It is the architecture of consequence—an ecosystem formed not by ambition, but by isolation. Not by choice, but by force.

To understand Russia today, imagine a vast nation with centuries of power, culture, and resilience—suddenly cut off from the very systems that define modern strength. Global supply chains withdraw. Critical technologies become inaccessible. Semiconductors essential to modern warfare, healthcare, transportation, and industry vanish overnight. Financial channels freeze. Platforms disconnect. Partnerships dissolve. Entire industries must reinvent themselves in real time.

Russia did not fall into a digital blackout—it fell into a digital narrowing. Its engineers scramble to replace chips they once imported. Its companies repurpose old technologies to mimic modern systems. Its military adapts whatever hardware is available. Its economy shifts inward, relying on parallel networks that provide survival, not superiority. The country becomes an improviser—resourceful, persistent, relentless—but always operating with fewer tools, fewer pathways, fewer choices.

This is not narrative control like the United States. This is not insulation like China. This is survival architecture—an architecture stitched together under pressure.

Russia's strategy today resembles a craftsman repairing a broken machine with whatever parts remain on the table. Innovation exists, but within shrinking boundaries. Sovereignty exists, but in a diminished form. Power exists, but increasingly as memory rather than momentum. Even Russia's considerable natural resources and military arsenal cannot compensate for the vacuum created by technological exile.

This is the tragic irony: Russia possesses nuclear weapons but lacks semiconductor sovereignty. It commands territory the size of continents but has limited access to global cloud ecosystems. It controls energy pipelines but remains dependent on foreign compute. The world once feared Russia's tanks; today, Russia fears the absence of chips inside those tanks.

This is not weakness of spirit—Russia's resilience is legendary. It is weakness of architecture. And in the modern age, architectural weakness quietly neutralizes traditional strengths.

This section is not a criticism of Russia—it is a lesson. A lesson about how fragile even great powers become when they lose access to critical technologies. A lesson about how sovereignty today is not defended at borders, but at supply chains. A lesson about how nations can possess strength on paper yet face vulnerability in practice.

If Russia teaches the world anything, it is this: a nation can have weapons, borders, and pride—but without architecture sovereignty, it stands on unstable ground. Russia's story is not about decline. It is about the harsh price of dependency—a price no country, especially rising ones, can afford to ignore.

3.4 — The Real Battlefield: Competing Operating Systems of Power

Step back for a moment and look at the world not as a map of nations, but as a map of architectures. Suddenly, the patterns become clearer—and far more unsettling. The United States, China, and Russia are not merely pursuing different geopolitical strategies; they are offering the world three competing operating systems of power.

The U.S. offers integration as dominance. Join its platforms, use its cloud, adopt its standards, learn in its universities, build on its software, trade on its financial rails—and you enter an ecosystem that rewards participation with opportunity. The more you integrate, the more influence the U.S. gains. It is empire through adoption.

China offers insulation as power. Build inside its walls, follow its protocols, accept its governance model, and operate within a parallel universe designed for control and continuity. It does not ask the world to join; it expects the world to adjust. Power here comes not from openness, but from self-contained stability.

Russia offers isolation as consequence. It never sought to lead by architecture—it simply lost access to the global one. Its operating system is forged under pressure, marked by improvisation and necessity. It signals to the world not a model to imitate but a warning of what happens when a nation becomes structurally excluded.

These three forces—integration, insulation, isolation—are the gravitational fields shaping the global order. Not because armies move, but because architecture moves. Not because treaties are signed, but because systems interlock. Nations do not align by ideology anymore; they align by technological dependence.

A country that builds on American cloud infrastructure is inevitably pulled toward Washington's ecosystem. A country that adopts Chinese digital governance finds itself orbiting Beijing's architecture. A country locked out of advanced compute drifts toward Russia's improvisational model, whether it intends to or not.

Coercion is no longer necessary. Architecture is the new gravity.

And here lies the real revelation: the 21st century will not be defined by wars between nations, but by wars between operating systems. Wars between supply chains. Wars between cloud empires. Wars between competing visions of digital sovereignty. Wars waged not on borders, but in silicon, software, and alignment.

Every nation—big or small, wealthy or struggling—is being pulled into one of these architectures, often without realizing it. The choices appear technical, but the consequences are geopolitical. This is the silent battle that will decide the future balance of power.

And India, more than any other rising nation, stands at the crossroads. India cannot blindly integrate like U.S. allies. It cannot insulate like China. It cannot afford the isolation Russia endured.

India must build its own operating system of power—its own architecture, its own ecosystem, its own alignment. Because in the world emerging before us, sovereignty will not belong to the loudest nation, the largest nation, or the richest nation. It will belong to the nation that builds an architecture strong enough to stand on its own—and deep enough to pull others into its orbit.

This is the battlefield India must choose wisely. The age of architecture wars has begun.

Chapter 4 — The Global Dependency Ladders

Where nations sit in cloud, semiconductor, and AI supply chains

The World Built on Borrowed Ladders

Imagine a country standing proudly at the base of a towering structure called "Digital Sovereignty." Its leaders point upward and declare, *"We are climbing toward the future."* They pose for cameras, announce new initiatives, launch digital missions, and unveil sleek dashboards filled with progress indicators. From a distance, it looks confident—ambitious, even unstoppable.

But look closer. The ladder the country is climbing does not belong to it. The rungs of the ladder—its cloud, its chips, its AI—are all built elsewhere. Each step depends on someone else's decisions, someone else's technology, someone else's resilience. The country climbs higher, but with every meter, the dependency deepens. The ladder becomes both the pathway and the vulnerability.

The cloud rung is hosted in another nation's data center. The chip rung is manufactured in a factory thousands of miles away. The AI rung is trained on models created by companies that don't speak the country's language—literally or philosophically.

It is a strange picture: a sovereign nation suspended mid-air, ascending confidently on borrowed infrastructure. And the unsettling truth is that almost every country is climbing the same ladder—some carefully, some desperately, some without even realizing the ladder is not theirs.

Look at Europe: a powerful region standing on U.S. cloud rails. Look at Japan and South Korea: technological giants still dependent on American chip architecture. Look at Africa and Latin America: entire digital ecosystems balanced on foreign platforms. Even China, despite its insulation, still relies on foreign lithography equipment. And the United States itself depends on Taiwan's fabs like a climber trusting a single rung made of glass.

Some ladders are stable, some shaky, some quietly cracking—but none are fully owned. The world likes to believe each nation stands on solid ground. But in reality, almost everyone is climbing someone else's infrastructure, leaning on someone else's supply chain, depending on someone else's algorithms. Geopolitics today is a landscape of climbers, not owners.

And here's the quiet irony: countries boast about "digital independence" while their data lives abroad. They celebrate "technological breakthroughs" built on imported chips. They claim "AI leadership" while using models trained in California or Shenzhen. The speeches are sovereign. The systems are not.

This is the new global condition—an age where sovereignty is less about flags and borders, and more about who owns the ladder you climb. The higher a nation climbs on borrowed infrastructure, the more impressive it looks—and the more vulnerable it becomes.

There is no solid ground anymore. Only ladders—some owned, most borrowed. And the hierarchy of nations is now defined by one question: are you building the ladder, renting it, or clinging to whatever rung is still within reach?

This chapter explores the truth behind global dependency—and why countries that do not build their own ladders eventually find themselves stuck on someone else's terms.

4.1 — The Cloud Ladder: Who Owns the Digital Sky?

If land was the battlefield of the 20th century, the sky is the battlefield of the 21st—but not the sky filled with aircraft and satellites. This is the digital sky, the invisible realm where data lives, decisions are processed, intelligence flows, and national life increasingly operates. Governments talk about cloud as if it were a neutral utility—just another service, like electricity or water. But the cloud is not neutral. It is owned.

And the unsettling truth is that only a handful of corporations—mostly headquartered in one country—operate the majority of the world's digital infrastructure. Nations proudly announce they are "going digital," "building e-governance," or "modernizing public systems," without realizing they are stepping onto a ladder whose top rung someone else controls.

This creates a global hierarchy—a ladder with three tiers:

Tier 1: Cloud Owners — The United States: The U.S. doesn't just lead cloud technology; it dominates it. AWS, Microsoft Azure, Google Cloud—these platforms form the digital backbone of governments, banks, universities, startups, militaries, and corporations across the world. When a country moves to the cloud, it is often moving into American architecture. And this dominance gives the U.S. something extraordinary: soft, structural influence. Not because it demands it, but because everyone depends on it.

Tier 2: Cloud Builders — China: The China doesn't want to rely on foreign infrastructure, so it builds its own clouds—Huawei Cloud, Alibaba Cloud, Tencent Cloud. These clouds primarily serve the domestic market and a few partner nations, forming a parallel sky, separate and self-contained. China's cloud strategy, like everything else in its architecture, favors insulation over global adoption. It is a walled sky—but a powerful one.

Tier 3: Cloud Renters — Everyone Else: The Europe rents. India rents. Africa rents. Latin America rents. Even developed nations rent. They don't own the infrastructure that powers their digital economies; they subscribe to it. Their national security architecture sits inside private data centers. Their banking systems run on servers they do not control. Their elections rely on platforms whose backend lives abroad. Their public services operate in a sky owned by someone else.

This is not dependency by force—it's dependency by convenience. Nations love cloud because it is cheap, fast, scalable, and reliable. But convenience is always the first step toward dependence. A country that cannot store, process, secure, or compute its own data is like a nation that keeps its gold in another country's vault. Safe, yes—until it isn't.

And here comes the gently provocative question: if your entire digital ecosystem lives in someone else's cloud, who really governs your country—your parliament, or your platform provider? The answer is not literal, but it is structural.

Cloud is not just infrastructure—it is sovereignty. And in a world where the digital sky is controlled by a few, nations must decide whether they want to climb the ladder forever or start building one of their own.

4.2 — The Semiconductor Ladder: The Most Fragile Supply Chain on Earth

If cloud is the digital sky, semiconductors are the heartbeat of the modern world—tiny silicon squares that quietly run everything from national security systems to your electric toothbrush. And yet, the global chip ecosystem is not a smooth highway. It is a ladder—an absurdly tall, narrow, overengineered ladder with too many owners, too many fragile steps, and too many nations clinging to it without a safety net.

To understand global power today, you must first understand this ladder.

The Top Rung: Design Power — The United States At the very top sits the U.S., not because it manufactures chips, but because it designs them. Firms like NVIDIA, Intel, AMD, and Qualcomm write the blueprints that the rest of the world depends on. These designs are so advanced that a single miscalculation in their logic can cascade through global supply chains. The genius is American. The factories are not.

The Rungs Below: Equipment Power — The Netherlands & Japan: To build the chips designed in the U.S., you need machines—machines so complex they make space rockets look like household appliances. Only a few companies in the world—ASML in the Netherlands, Nikon and Tokyo Electron in Japan—know how to produce them. If one of these firms sneezes, the global semiconductor industry catches a fever.

The Middle of the Ladder: Manufacturing Power — Taiwan & South Korea: Here sits the true bottleneck of the modern world. Taiwan's TSMC and South Korea's Samsung manufacture nearly all advanced chips used in AI systems, smartphones, servers, defense technology, and industrial machinery. These tiny islands of silicon power hold more geopolitical leverage than oil kingdoms ever did. One earthquake, one blockade, one political miscalculation—and the world goes dark.

The Bottom Foundations: Mineral Power — Australia & China: Chips begin as minerals—rare earths, quartz, cobalt, gallium. Australia mines key minerals. China controls processing at scale. Without minerals, there is no wafer. Without wafers, there is no chip. Without chips, there is no modern civilization.

It is the most interdependent ladder in human history—and the most fragile.

Most Nations Sit Far Below: Countries loudly celebrating their "digital transformation" often stand near the very bottom of this ladder. They buy chips but do not design them. They import machines but cannot repair them. They rely on minerals processed elsewhere. They depend on manufacturing concentrated in two geographically tense regions. And yet they speak of sovereignty.

Here's the humorous but painfully accurate summary: the semiconductor ladder has too many owners, too few steps, and absolutely no room for error. A disruption at any rung—be it U.S. export bans, Dutch equipment delays, a Taiwanese blackout, or Chinese mineral controls—shakes the entire world.

The Silent Truth: A nation's true economic and military capability is not defined by GDP or army size. It is defined by how high it stands on the chip ladder—and how firmly it grips each rung. In the age of compute, sovereignty is measured in nanometers. And most countries are still climbing with borrowed hands.

4.3 — The AI Ladder: Who Builds Intelligence, Who Consumes It

If semiconductors are the heartbeat of the modern world, AI is the brain rapidly learning to run it. And like every brain, it comes with hierarchy—some nations create intelligence, some shape it, and most simply consume it without fully understanding how it works. This is the AI Ladder, and where a country stands on it quietly determines its future competitiveness, security, and sovereignty.

Let's climb it step by step.

Top of the Ladder: Creators of AI — The U.S., China, and a Select Few: At the highest rung sit the nations that do not just use AI—they invent it. They build the core models, the architectures, the algorithms, the training frameworks, the hardware accelerators, the regulatory philosophies, and the ethical boundaries. They decide what "intelligence" means in the digital era.

Silicon Valley and Shenzhen aren't merely tech hubs—they are laboratories where the world's cognitive future is written. Their models power everything: search, commerce, defense, entertainment, governance, finance, logistics, and scientific discovery. Nations on this rung are not just shaping markets—they are shaping reality.

Creating AI means controlling the direction of intelligence. Everyone else, knowingly or not, follows their lead.

Middle of the Ladder: Shapers of AI — Nations With Talent But Limited Infrastructure: This rung is filled with countries that have brilliant minds, strong engineering cultures, and vibrant tech ecosystems, but lack the deep compute infrastructure, semiconductor sovereignty, or capital intensity required to train frontier AI models.

They don't create AI from scratch—but they adapt it, fine-tune it, localize it, regulate it, and apply it creatively. These are the AI artisans of the global system—skilled, resourceful, imaginative, but limited by the constraints of architecture. They can shape intelligence but cannot define it.

This rung includes regions with strong academic talent but limited cloud resources, economies capable of innovation but dependent on foreign chips, and governments that want AI sovereignty but lack the infrastructure to achieve it. They contribute meaningfully, but the foundational rules are still written above them.

Bottom of the Ladder: Consumers of AI — Everyone Else: This is the largest group by far. These nations use AI the way people use electricity—without knowing how it's generated, who controls it, or what vulnerabilities lie beneath it.

They adopt foreign AI models, integrate external APIs, rely on imported analytics engines, and outsource algorithmic decision-making to platforms they cannot inspect. These nations may think they are "modernizing," but what they are actually doing is delegating intelligence. And delegation, in geopolitics, is dependency with a smiling face.

Here lies the structural weakness: if you don't build the model, you can't shape the model. If you can't shape the model, the model will shape you.

From digital governance to political narratives, from financial risk scoring to job markets, from healthcare predictions to national security assessments—imported AI quietly becomes the lens through which societies interpret themselves. And that is not just a technological vulnerability. It is a sovereignty vulnerability.

The Strategic Punchline: AI is not a tool—it is an operating system for the future. Nations that build intelligence will lead the century. Nations that only consume it will be led by those who do.

The AI Ladder is not merely about capability. It is about destiny.

4.4 — Dependency as Destiny: The Hidden Hierarchy of the Compute Century

For centuries, power was imagined horizontally—maps with borders, colors, armies, and alliances. Nations were lined up side by side, competing across land and sea, measuring strength through territory, GDP, or the size of their populations. But in the compute century, that map is obsolete. The real world power structure is not horizontal at all—it is vertical.

A ladder.

A global ladder of dependency.

At the top stand the owners of architecture—nations that design chips, build cloud infrastructure, train frontier AI models, and set the world's digital standards. They are the architects of the modern world, shaping global behavior without needing approval, treaties, or coercion. They do not just lead markets; they define the rules by which markets operate.

Below them stand the renters of architecture—countries that participate in the digital economy but depend on others for chips, cloud, algorithms, and compute. They climb the ladder because it offers convenience, growth, and opportunity. But they do not own the rungs they stand on. Their ascent is limited by architecture they cannot control.

And at the very bottom, clinging to whatever steps remain, are the dependents—nations that consume technology they neither understand nor influence. They rely on borrowed intelligence, imported infrastructure, and foreign systems. Their sovereignty is symbolic, not structural.

This vertical distribution of power is the hidden hierarchy of the 21st century.

And the most striking part? Most nations still think they are competing on the old horizontal map. They proudly point to their population size, GDP rank, military budget, or growth rate—without realizing these metrics matter less than the rung they occupy on the compute ladder.

Because in the age of architecture:

- Territory does not guarantee sovereignty.
- GDP does not guarantee capability.
- Population does not guarantee power.

Only architecture does.

Countries that own the ladder rise effortlessly, pulling talent, capital, innovation, and influence upward with them. Countries that rent the ladder can stabilize and grow—but only on someone else's terms. Countries that cling to the bottom remain perpetually vulnerable, forever reacting to architectures shaped elsewhere.

This ladder defines everything:

- economic resilience
- military readiness
- technological competitiveness
- national security
- global influence

And now comes the softly ominous truth that frames the rest of this book:

India stands at a critical rung.

Too high to fall without consequence. Too low to claim leadership. Too dependent to be comfortable. Too ambitious to remain where it is.

India's future will not be decided by intentions, ideology, or inspirational slogans—but by whether it climbs this ladder, stabilizes on it, or slips downward while others rise.

Dependency has become destiny. But destiny can be rewritten—only by those who build the architecture of their own ascent.

Closing Reflection — Part I

When the Map Changed and No One Noticed

Part I ends where the world began to shift—not loudly, not violently, but silently through servers, silicon, and systems. The old power map we inherited—armies, economies, populations—no longer explains the world we live in. Something deeper, quieter, and far more consequential has taken its place.

We now see nations not as colors on paper but as climbers on ladders—cloud ladders, semiconductor ladders, AI ladders—each rung defining their resilience, capability, and vulnerability. Sovereignty has drifted upward from land to architecture. And without noticing, we entered an era where power is decided by alignment, not ambition.

In this new world:

- The U.S. leads without occupying.
- China hardens without expanding.
- Russia resists without influencing.
- And the rest of the world borrows ladders without building any of their own.

The architecture wars are not futuristic—they are already underway. We have simply been looking at the wrong battlefield.

Yet the greatest silence in this story is India's silence. A rising power standing at the edge of transformation, watching the tectonic plates shift beneath the global order, but unsure which path to choose—and which path will close forever if it waits too long.

Part I exposed the mechanics of modern power. Part II asks a harder question:

Where does India actually stand in this new world—and why is its rise threatened more by internal unpreparedness than by external competition?

As we step into Part II, the lens turns inward. The global models are clear. Now we examine India's reality—its strengths, illusions, dependencies, and the fragile architecture holding everything together.

The world has changed. Now India must ask whether it has changed with it—or whether it is still standing on a map that no longer exists.

Let's begin.

Part II — India's Reality

Power Without Preparation

"A nation does not rise on desire; it rises on design. Dreams create momentum—architecture creates destiny."

Overview

Part II turns the mirror inward. After mapping global power, we confront India's hardest truth: ambition has outpaced capability. Potential is constrained by outdated systems, fragmented institutions, and an execution engine unfit for the compute century.

India's rise is limited not by talent, but by architecture—the silent forces shaping how the nation thinks, organizes, and builds. This section examines India's strategic taxes: internal chaos, institutional fatigue, political illusions, and the widening ambition–capability gap.

Chapter 5 — The Ambition–Capability Gap

A billion dreams running on outdated architecture.

The Country Running Faster Than Its Legs Can Carry

Picture a nation sprinting at full speed. Not walking, not jogging—sprinting. Its lungs bursting with ambition, its heart pounding with possibility, its eyes locked on a future it believes it deserves. This is India today: a country overflowing with youth, energy, dreams, startups, innovations, aspirations, slogans, and relentless optimism. A billion people are in motion, all at once, all surging forward as if the world will open its doors simply because India is running toward them.

But look down at the road beneath its feet.

It is not the road of the present. It is a narrow, cracked, uneven road built decades ago—patched, repainted, repaired, and repurposed so many times that it no longer matches the sprinting speed above it. Institutions designed for the 1970s. Processes born in the 1980s. Governance models still carrying the habits of the 1990s. Digital infrastructure expanding faster than the physical infrastructure can absorb. Systems optimized for survival, not for acceleration.

You don't need an economist or a strategist to see the mismatch. You can see it in the long queues outside government offices, in students memorizing outdated textbooks, in startups stuck navigating paper-based approvals, in world-class talent trapped inside archaic systems, in innovators forced to slow down because the machinery around them is built for a different era.

India is a young athlete wearing the shoes of an elderly marathoner.

And the irony is almost poetic: we call ourselves the world's fastest-growing major economy, the largest democracy, the biggest talent pool, the next global superpower. And all of this may well be true. But beneath the surface, the country is running faster than its legs can carry—not because its people lack strength, but because its architecture lacks speed.

This is not a criticism. It is an observation. Not a complaint. A reality check. India does not have a shortage of ambition—it has a shortage of systems designed to fulfill ambition.

The dreams of a billion are traveling at 5G speed; the architecture managing those dreams is still buffering at 2G.

This is the heart of the Ambition–Capability Gap: the space between what India wants to become and what India's current architecture is capable of delivering. A space filled with friction, bottlenecks, inefficiencies, frustrations, missed opportunities—and yet, paradoxically, also filled with hope. Because if a nation can run this fast with outdated architecture, imagine what it could achieve with an upgraded one.

Part II begins here—with the recognition that India's momentum is real, but its scaffolding isn't ready to hold the weight of its aspirations. Before India can rise in the new global order, it must first strengthen the legs that carry its dreams.

5.1 — The Velocity of Dreams vs. the Speed of Systems

Walk through any Indian city today and you can feel the velocity of dreams in the air. It vibrates in crowded coaching classes at 6 a.m., where teenagers chase careers that didn't exist ten years ago. It hums inside cafés filled with young founders pitching ideas with global confidence. It pulses through middle-class households where parents, once content with stability, now demand transformation for their children. And it flickers brightly on millions of smartphone screens—India's new window to the world—where inspiration is just a swipe away.

This is a country convinced it can rise, convinced it deserves to rise, convinced that the world will make space simply because its ambition burns hotter than ever before. Ambition is no longer a luxury here; it is a national mood.

But then you step into the systems meant to carry these dreams forward—and the contrast hits you like a wall.

Inside universities, brilliant students sit memorizing answers for exams designed decades ago. Laboratories with great potential struggle with outdated equipment. Professors with global exposure fight bureaucratic webs just to introduce a single new course. The world outside is sprinting into quantum computing and gene editing; the world inside is still arguing about attendance registers.

In the startup ecosystem, founders with world-class ideas find themselves slowed not by competition or innovation challenges, but by paperwork, compliance delays, unpredictable regulations, and institutional inertia. Their minds move at the speed of Silicon Valley, but their approvals move at the speed of a government file traveling between desks. It's a race car stuck in traffic.

Researchers face their own contradictions—global talent on local ground, operating inside structures not designed for them.

They collaborate with labs abroad but wrestle with procurement rules at home. They imagine breakthroughs but spend months waiting for permissions, funding, or basic resources. Their minds stretch toward the future; their environment pulls them backward.

Even the financial system—one of India's proudest modern achievements—still ties entrepreneurs to collateral demands and procedural complexity. A young innovator can raise seed funding from an American angel investor faster than they can open a business account at home.

India is full of people moving quickly—and systems moving slowly.

This is not because the systems are malicious; they are simply old. They were built for a simpler India—one where opportunities were few, ambitions were modest, information was limited, and speed did not matter. But India is no longer that country. A young, connected, ambitious population is running on the roads of a bygone era.

And this mismatch creates friction—quiet but constant. The dreams accelerate. The systems lag. The people push harder. The institutions strain. Energy increases. Output does not. It is like watching a rocket with tremendous fuel strapped to a launchpad that was never designed to release it.

Empathy demands we acknowledge the effort. Honesty demands we acknowledge the limitation.

India today has extraordinary momentum—but insufficient bandwidth. Until the systems catch up with the people, ambition will keep outrunning capability. And the gap will widen, quietly shaping the destiny of a country that wants to sprint but must first learn to build legs strong enough to carry its speed.

5.2 — When Scale Meets Fragile Architecture

India's greatest strength—its scale—is also its most unforgiving test. Few nations carry the weight of a billion aspirations. Fewer still attempt to transform themselves while balancing the hopes, demands, fears, and frustrations of such a vast population. And almost none try to do this with an institutional architecture never designed to handle this magnitude.

What works beautifully for ten million collapses at one hundred million. What works at one hundred million disintegrates at one billion.

Yet India continues to stretch systems beyond their original limits—expecting fragile foundations to support skyscrapers of ambition.

Take public services. A welfare mechanism designed for a small, post-independence nation now attempts to serve a population larger than entire continents. Hospitals overflow, schools struggle, local administrations drown under unsustainable caseloads. The machinery keeps moving, but always at the edge of breakdown.

Or look at the talent pipeline. At small scale, India produces brilliance effortlessly. At scale, it produces brilliance unevenly—pockets of excellence surrounded by oceans of underpreparedness. A world-class IIT exists beside a school without basic teachers; a genius coder emerges from a region where thousands lack internet access. Scale magnifies brilliance, but it also magnifies disparity.

Digital governance tells the same story. India digitized faster than any nation in history—but scale stresses it in ways few countries can even imagine. Millions of people connect simultaneously to systems that were never built for such load, resulting in slowdowns, crashes, backlogs, and bottlenecks. What looks efficient at a press conference often feels fragile on the ground.

Infrastructure carries this paradox even more sharply. A new expressway opens and is celebrated—until millions begin using it, overwhelming its design. Metro systems buckle under population pressure. Airports operate at twice the intended passenger flow.

Supply chains that perform predictably elsewhere must stretch impossibly across India's sheer breadth.

This is not failure. This is math.

A billion introduces complexities that no standard architecture can absorb. Everything—traffic, logistics, public service delivery, education, healthcare, governance—scales not linearly, but exponentially. And every crack in the system multiplies under pressure.

The paradox, then, is almost poetic:

India's ambition is gigantic because its population is gigantic. But its systems break for the same reason.

This is why frustration is so common, even among the most capable Indians. They are not frustrated at their effort—they are frustrated at the architecture. They push harder, but the system doesn't respond at the same speed. They innovate, but approvals lag. They dream big, but execution capacity remains small. The human engine accelerates; the institutional gearbox stays stuck in a previous era.

And slowly, something happens beneath the surface—something rarely spoken, but widely felt:

Ambition without matching architecture creates friction, Friction converts into frustration, Frustration becomes fatigue.

This fatigue is India's silent tax, paid daily by millions who want to move faster but are tethered to systems that cannot.

Until India builds architecture that matches its scale, its dreams will continue to outrun its reality—not because the dream is unrealistic, but because the foundation was never meant to carry it.

5.3 — The Psychology of Overestimation: The Illusion of Readiness

There is a quiet, almost endearing force that shapes India's self-perception—a belief that the country is more prepared than it truly is. It is not arrogance; it is optimism. It is not ignorance; it is aspiration. It is the psychology of a nation that sees its own potential so vividly that it sometimes forgets to measure its readiness with the same intensity.

This illusion is fed from many directions. Political narratives amplify success stories and compress timelines. Patriotic sentiment turns achievements into symbols of national destiny. A few global headlines—about moon landings, unicorn startups, GDP rankings—create the impression that India has already arrived. And temporary successes, though important, can create a mirage of sustained capability.

In such a climate, it becomes easy to believe that India is already on par with global leaders—that the country is simply waiting for the world to acknowledge it. But beneath this inspiring surface lie capability gaps that demand attention, not denial.

Technology depth remains uneven. India consumes advanced technology far more than it creates. For every world-class product or innovation, there are countless sectors still functioning on outdated methods. The digital sheen often hides analog realities.

Institutional maturity is still developing. Processes fluctuate across states, departments, and sectors. Predictability, consistency, and long-term planning—hallmarks of mature institutions—are uneven. Systems can deliver brilliantly in moments but struggle to deliver reliably over years.

Execution consistency remains India's hardest challenge. The country is capable of extraordinary achievements when focused, but sustaining that focus across time, layers, and complexity is another story. The gap between announcement and implementation has narrowed, but not closed.

Talent retention is an unresolved paradox. India produces some of the brightest minds in the world, yet many of them either leave or fail to find suitable environments to thrive at home. A world-class pipeline leaks quietly at every stage—not because of lack of talent, but because of lack of matching architecture.

Research ecosystems are still in their adolescence. India has islands of excellence, but not a continental research culture. Funding, freedom, infrastructure, collaboration, and incentives—these pillars are growing, but remain vulnerable to bureaucratic gravity.

And state capacity—perhaps the most understated variable—struggles under enormous weight. Public systems carry more responsibility than they were designed for, leaving them underpowered for the ambitions placed upon them.

To speak of these gaps is not to diminish India. It is to understand it. No rising nation escapes the psychology of overestimation. It is the natural enthusiasm of a country discovering itself after decades of constraint. India is in that moment—a teenager with adult dreams but adolescent infrastructure, sensing its future without fully possessing the tools to seize it.

This chapter does not judge the illusion. It gently places a mirror before it. Because readiness is not a feeling; it is an architecture. And until India sees its true position on the global ladder, it cannot climb confidently into the future that awaits it.

5.4 — The Cost of the Gap: Lost Decades, Missed Windows

Every nation has ambition. But only a few nations learn the discipline of matching ambition with capability. When ambition grows faster than capability, the distance between vision and reality becomes a silent battlefield—one where countries lose not wars, but decades.

This is the true cost of the Ambition–Capability Gap.

It does not appear dramatically. There is no sudden collapse, no loud failure, no crisis broadcast on television. Instead, the cost appears quietly, almost politely, in the form of missed windows—opportunities that come once every few decades, stay briefly, and then close without warning.

India has already lived through some of these windows. In the manufacturing century, the window passed. In the semiconductor century, the window narrowed. Now, in the compute century, the window is wider than ever—but also more unforgiving.

Because the next decade is unlike the ones before it. AI, cloud, chips, automation, data, and digital infrastructure are converging at a pace humanity has never experienced. Nations that build architecture now will define the next fifty years. Nations that improvise or delay will spend those decades catching up—always running, never arriving.

And this is where India stands today: a rising nation with the desire to lead but without the architecture aligned to that desire.

The ambition is enormous. The capability is growing. But the gap between them is widening at exactly the moment when the world is restructuring itself.

This gap is not operational—it is existential. It is not inefficiency—it is destiny. It is not a shortage of effort—it is a mismatch of design.

The danger is subtle: when systems cannot keep up with national ambition, a country enters a cycle of perpetual acceleration without meaningful elevation. It sprints harder, louder, faster—yet covers the same distance. The optimism remains, but progress slips into the illusion of progress. This leads to exhaustion at the human level, misalignment at the institutional level, and stagnation at the national level.

India is not at risk of decline. It is at risk of delay.

And delay, in this decade, is another word for loss. Loss of strategic position. Loss of technological depth. Loss of global leverage. Loss of future possibilities that may never return.

This chapter ends with the truth India must confront:

If India continues sprinting on outdated foundations, it will waste the energy of a billion people and still miss its moment. If India redesigns its architecture, it can convert ambition into ascent.

The next part of the book begins exactly at this fork—where India must choose between carrying its old foundation into the future or building a new one capable of supporting the destiny it seeks.

The window is open. The question is not whether India can rise. The question is whether India can rise in time.

Chapter 6 — Internal Chaos as a Strategic Tax

Fragmentation, noise, and institutional fatigue

The Country That Trips Over Its Own Feet

Imagine a nation preparing to take a giant leap—a country standing tall, chest out, full of potential, ready to rise in the age of compute. The stage is set, the world is watching, the opportunity is real. India takes one confident step forward—and immediately trips over its own feet.

Not because the world pushed it. Not because the path was blocked. But because the country's own shoelaces were tied together.

One lace is political drama—manufactured daily like a factory product. Another is bureaucratic delay—a ritual older than the Republic itself. A third is corruption quietly siphoning the power out of every reform. Then comes the Centre–state turf war, where national priorities are sacrificed at the altar of petty ego. Add incompetent ministers who treat their portfolio like a photo-op, not a responsibility. And regulatory overreach—rules written faster than they can be understood and slower than they can be reformed.

India tries to run, but each step is a negotiation with its own internal chaos.

The scene is almost cinematic. A country with world-class talent. A country with global aspirations. A country with unmatched demographic energy. Yet a country that spends half its time untangling problems it created for itself.

A startup founder builds a breakthrough idea—only to be buried under approvals. A brilliant policymaker drafts reform—only for it to be stalled by political insecurity. A scientist attempts innovation—only to find procurement rules belong to another century. A state government launches a vision—only for the Centre to counter it out of spite, or vice-versa. A civil servant wants to deliver—but is trapped between outdated processes and corrupt intermediaries.

This is not misfortune. This is architecture.

India's internal chaos is not an accident of circumstance; it is a strategic tax—a predictable, measurable cost the nation pays for its own disorder. Every country has friction. India has friction plus noise, noise plus drama, drama plus institutional fatigue.

While other nations lose battles because of external threats, India loses years because of internal clutter.

And here lies the uncomfortable truth: India's biggest obstacle is not China, not Pakistan, not the U.S., not global competition. India's biggest obstacle is India.

Its ambition is global. Its execution engine is local. Its energy is modern. Its systems are medieval. Its opportunities are vast. Its coordination is broken.

This chapter begins by acknowledging a reality most leaders avoid: India is not losing because it lacks capability. It is losing because it keeps tripping over the knots tied by its own political class, its own bureaucrats, its own regulators, and its own complacent culture of institutional neglect.

Internal chaos is not a governance problem. It is a strategic threat. And unless India confronts it without excuses, it will continue stumbling—even when the world is offering it a clear runway to rise.

6.1 — Fragmentation: A Nation Pulling in a Thousand Directions

If India were a machine, it would be a magnificent engine—powerful, complex, full of potential—but with each component operating according to its own rhythm. Pistons firing in different directions, gears misaligned, wires crossing signals, and a dozen drivers fighting over the steering wheel. The engine doesn't break; it simply refuses to accelerate.

This is India's fragmentation: a nation not divided by ideology, but by misalignment.

Every ministry has its own agenda. Every department guards its turf like a kingdom. Every state government treats national priorities as political bargaining chips. And every political actor—regardless of party—seems more invested in spectacle than in synchrony.

Consider the way major reforms unfold. A visionary idea is proposed; newspapers celebrate. But then ministries argue over jurisdiction, departments block each other's files, states reject the reform because their rival party introduced it, and corrupt intermediaries look for ways to monetize the bottlenecks. What began as a national initiative becomes a circus of competing incentives.

A minister appears on television promising transformation—yet cannot transform even their own department. Another delivers grand speeches about innovation—while innovation inside their ministry is constrained by ego and incompetence. Some treat governance like theatre: loud announcements, zero follow-through. They are managers of headlines, not builders of systems.

Departments often work like rival companies rather than parts of the same government. They hoard information. They fight for control. They sabotage each other to gain political favor. Policies are drafted without coordination, executed without clarity, reviewed without honesty.

And states? Some genuinely collaborate; others treat cooperation as surrender. If the Centre proposes a policy, certain states oppose it by default. If the state proposes something innovative, the Centre sometimes blocks it out of insecurity. The political colour of a government matters more than the merit of an idea.

In such an environment, alignment becomes a luxury, not a norm.

Corruption deepens the fracture. Every misaligned system creates opportunity for someone to profit from chaos. When a file moves slowly, someone earns. When coordination breaks down, someone gains leverage. When ambition stalls, someone gets to broker the delay. In India, inefficiency is not just tolerated—it is monetized.

And so the nation moves, but diagonally, inefficiently, wastefully—like a river trying to find its way through a maze built by its own caretakers.

This is no longer an internal governance flaw. It is a strategic tax—a heavy one.

Fragmentation consumes India's time, energy, focus, and opportunity. It weakens its ability to respond to crises, slows its capacity for development, and limits its competitiveness in a world where alignment is the foundation of power.

Every day India spends fighting itself is a day lost in the global race.

The tragedy is not that India lacks capability. The tragedy is that its capability is scattered across a thousand directions, each pulling away from the centre.

Until India learns to move as one engine, its rise will remain uneven—a giant pulled forward by its people but held back by its own fragmented architecture.

6.2 — Noise: The Nation That Mistakes Confusion for Progress

If fragmentation slows India down, noise blinds it completely. Noise is the national soundtrack—constant, exhausting, omnipresent. It fills television studios where grown adults shout over each other like schoolboys fighting for the last bench. It floods social media through propaganda armies, viral misinformation, manufactured outrage, and competitive victimhood. It spills into public discourse—shifting, spinning, distorting—until no one remembers what the real issue was.

India is a nation that confuses movement with progress, volume with clarity, noise with governance.

Every evening, another shouting match masquerades as national analysis. Every morning, another hashtag war erupts between online tribes. Every week, a new scandal replaces the previous one—before the dust of truth can even settle.

This isn't accidental. Noise is useful.

Politicians rely on it. It allows them to perform instead of govern. They substitute headline management for system management. Their speeches are sharp; their files are empty. They deliver commentary instead of results.

Policymakers perform reforms theatrically. A press conference is the reform. A slogan is the reform. A logo is the reform. Policies are launched with fanfare, but the execution engine underneath them is weak, confused, or simply uninterested.

Bureaucrats—many brilliant, many dedicated, but too many exhausted—learn to survive by waiting. In India, a problem ignored long enough becomes someone else's file. Inertia becomes strategy. Silence becomes safety. Chaos becomes camouflage.

Administrations rely on a powerful ally: public memory loss. They know that if they create enough noise, delay enough papers, shift enough blame, manufacture enough distraction—the people will move on long before accountability arrives. It is a governance style built not on delivery, but on distraction.

And while the nation argues on screens, the real work remains undone.

Research doesn't receive steady funding. Planning is done in short bursts of political panic. Execution teams lack continuity because governments prefer reshuffling to reforming. Institution-building gets sidelined because institutions cannot win elections.

Noise corrodes the one thing India needs most in the compute century: focus.

In the age of architecture, nations rise through discipline, long-term vision, alignment, coordination, and uninterrupted concentration. They cannot rise by shouting. They cannot innovate through outrage. They cannot build systems through slogans.

But India's political ecosystem treats noise as oxygen. The louder the narrative, the more successful the actor feels. And in this intoxication of drama, the nation loses clarity. It loses direction. It loses precious time.

The saddest irony is this: India has the talent to become a global leader, but not the silence required to think like one.

Until India learns to quiet the noise—to replace spectacle with substance, distraction with design—its ambition will remain clouded by its own confusion, and its path to the future will remain blurred by narratives that produce heat but no light.

6.3 — Institutional Fatigue: Systems That Are Tired Before the Race Has Begun

Every rising nation stands on the shoulders of its institutions. But India stands on institutions that are already tired—overburdened, under-resourced, politicized, stretched thin, and drained of stamina long before the real race of the compute century has even begun.

Walk into any Indian court and you will see the fatigue laid bare. Courtrooms overflowing, files stacked like geological layers of national dysfunction, judges handling workloads that would break entire systems elsewhere. Justice moves slowly not because judges lack intelligence, but because the architecture of justice is collapsing under the weight of unresolved backlog. A case may take ten years to move forward—but political drama moves forward in ten minutes.

Police forces still operate with 19th-century tools and 20th-century training while being expected to solve 21st-century problems. Overworked, understaffed, frequently under political pressure, and rarely protected by institutional autonomy, they function in survival mode. They deliver miracles occasionally—but are punished for systemic flaws they did not create.

Regulators—whether in finance, technology, education, environment, media, or markets—often exist in name but not in spirit. Some are captured by political masters; others by corporate influence; many by internal fear of backlash. Regulatory appointments frequently prioritize loyalty over competence, connections over capability. The result? Institutions meant to safeguard national interest become extensions of political interest.

Scientific bodies and research institutions suffer an even crueler fate. They are expected to deliver breakthroughs, but are denied autonomy, punished for dissent, suffocated by red tape, and operated through committees that innovate at the speed of tectonic plates. A nation dreaming of quantum leaps often treats its scientists like clerks filling forms.

Civil servants, perhaps the most revealing case of all, live in a strange contradiction. Many are brilliant, hardworking, and idealistic. But the system traps them between ambition and mediocrity. Promotions depend on seniority, not impact. Transfers depend on politics, not performance. Innovation is risky.

Compliance is safe. The architecture rewards survival, not imagination.

And then there is political interference—the slow poison that drains institutional stamina. Every corrupt appointment weakens the architecture. Every political reshuffle disrupts continuity. Every favour-driven transfer erodes morale. Every minister who treats their role like a personal trophy rather than a national responsibility damages an institution more deeply than budget cuts ever could.

India's institutions are not collapsing. Collapse is dramatic. Collapse is visible. Collapse demands immediate response.

India's institutions are exhausted. And exhaustion is far more dangerous—because it is quiet. It accumulates. It becomes normal.

When courts tire, justice slows. When police tire, safety slips. When regulators tire, markets distort. When scientists tire, innovation dies. When civil servants tire, governance stalls. When institutions tire, nations stall.

And when institutions collapse, nations decline.

India is not declining—but it is clearly, visibly, painfully exhausted. It wants to run, but its systems are limping. It wants to build, but its institutions need rest, repair, and redesign. A fatigued state cannot carry an ambitious nation indefinitely.

Before India can leap into the future, it must first restore the stamina of the very institutions meant to carry its ambitions. Otherwise, the race will begin—and India will find that its legs are already giving way.

6.4 — The Strategic Cost of Chaos: How Nations Lose Without Being Defeated

Nations don't collapse only when an enemy attacks. More often, nations decline when their own systems quietly sabotage them. India's struggle today is not an external war—it is an internal erosion. A slow leak of national energy through fragmentation, noise, incompetence, corruption, and the political addiction to short-term theatrics. It is the kind of decline that does not appear on breaking-news screens but shows up in delayed execution, missed opportunities, and a pattern of always being *almost ready*.

Internal chaos is not a governance flaw—it is a strategic national weakness.

Because while India debates, the world builds. While India indulges in noise, others deepen capability. While India fights over turf, others integrate systems. While India's leaders chase headlines, others chase architecture.

This is the real battlefield of the 21st century. And India is losing—not because someone is defeating it, but because it is defeating itself.

Time is the first casualty: Years are spent resolving crises created by India's own political class. Every new government spends its first years undoing the previous one's decisions, and its last years preparing for elections instead of governance. Continuity, the backbone of long-term capability, evaporates in this cycle of perpetual self-interruption.

Energy is the second casualty: A billion-strong nation cannot afford to waste mental, administrative, and emotional stamina on avoidable chaos. Yet India's institutions spend more time managing political drama, ministerial whims, and bureaucratic friction than building systems for the future.

Efficiency is the third casualty: A country cannot accelerate when its governance processes remain stuck in the past, manipulated by corrupt actors who profit from slowness. Every unnecessary approval, every avoidable delay, every corrupt shortcut weakens the foundation on which national ambition stands.

Credibility is the fourth casualty: Global investors, researchers, innovators, diplomats—they all watch not India's speeches, but India's systems. And systems corroded by chaos send a clear message: potential is high, but reliability is low. India doesn't lose deals because others are better; it loses deals because its own architecture is unpredictable.

Opportunity is the final, and perhaps most painful, casualty: The compute century is opening a once-in-a-lifetime window for nations that are disciplined, aligned, and fast. But India risks missing this window because its internal machinery has been hijacked by self-serving politicians, bureaucratic inertia, and a culture that tolerates dysfunction as normal. The enemy is not outside. The enemy is the tax India pays for refusing to confront its own chaos.

And that tax is becoming too large.

This section ends with the quiet warning India needs most: If India cannot control its internal chaos, no external strategy—compute, foreign policy, economics, or alliances—will save it. A nation cannot rise when its own systems pull it down faster than the world can lift it.

India is not losing because it lacks potential. India is losing because it refuses to discipline the disorder within. And unless this changes, the chaos will consume the decade India cannot afford to lose.

Chapter 7 — The Illusion of Strength

The difference between political narrative and executional reality

The Nation Mistaking Applause for Achievement

Picture this: a stadium overflowing with people, lights dancing across the night sky, drums beating like a nation on the rise. A political leader strides onto the stage, greeted by a roar that could shake the earth. Slogans dominate the air, flags wave like victorious armies, and television anchors breathlessly declare it "a historic moment."

For a few hours, India feels invincible.

Scroll forward a few hours and you will find another celebration—a viral social-media trend in full swing. A patriotic song, a fiery speech, a dramatic headline, a flashy government campaign—millions like, share, applaud, and amplify. National pride floods timelines. For a moment, the nation convinces itself that emotion equals progress.

Then you shift the frame.

Away from the stadium, away from the hashtags, away from the artificial electricity of mass sentiment—and you enter a quiet room where the real indicators of national capability sit untouched. Unreformed institutions. Underfunded research labs. Courts drowning in backlog. Bureaucracies stuck in outdated processes.

Ministries with more announcements than outcomes. Infrastructure plans stalled in executional mud. Talent pipelines leaking innovation at every stage.

No cameras here. No applause here. No trending hashtags here. Just India's silent reality—waiting to be acknowledged.

This is the contrast the chapter begins with: the noise of political strength versus the silence of systemic weakness.

India has become a master of performance—mass rallies, spectacular events, marketing-heavy schemes, patriotic spectacles, and a constant stream of narratives that feel like progress even when they deliver very little. A nation that measures success by stadium attendance, television ratings, view counts, election rallies, and public emotion inevitably mistakes applause for achievement.

And that confusion is dangerous.

A country cannot rise because the crowd cheered. A country rises when systems work.

This chapter steps behind the curtains of India's political theatre to examine the deeper truth: India has learned to perform strength far better than it has learned to build it. And unless that illusion breaks, the decade India needs most will slip quietly through its fingers—applauded all the way to loss.

7.1 — Narrative as Governance: How India Sells Strength Instead of Building It

Some nations govern through institutions. Some govern through systems. But modern India increasingly governs through narratives—stories crafted with precision, marketed with confidence, and consumed with enthusiasm. It is governance as theatre, where the script often matters more than the structure beneath it.

In this world, visibility triumphs over viability.

Policies are announced with fireworks before a single line of execution is planned. Schemes are launched with glossy brochures and patriotic slogans long before they acquire budgets or operational clarity. Ministers step in front of cameras to introduce grand ideas that are still at the "thought bubble" stage, dressing half-conceived initiatives as national breakthroughs.

This is not accidental; it is architecture—a deliberate shift from building strength to selling strength.

Look closely and you will see the patterns.

A minister declares a scheme "revolutionary," only for experts to find that the guidelines aren't ready, the funds aren't allocated, and the administrative machinery hasn't been briefed. But the photo-op has been secured, the headline published, and the applause harvested—so the system convinces itself that something meaningful has happened.

Media outlets breathe life into these theatrics. They celebrate foundation stones with more passion than finished projects. They broadcast ribbon-cuttings as if the infrastructure behind them already functions flawlessly. They amplify announcements as if they were achievements, and achievements as if they were miracles.

The deeper tragedy is that bureaucratic machinery learns to adapt to this environment.

Reports are written not to reflect truth but to fit narrative expectations. Success metrics are redesigned to match political speeches. Real challenges are softened, hidden, or reframed because honesty is risky and illusions are rewarded. Officers who quietly deliver results remain invisible; those who manage political narratives climb faster.

In this ecosystem, strength becomes a story—not a system.

A new highway is announced before land acquisition is complete. A mega digital platform is launched without stress testing. A reform is declared "historic" before implementation has touched even 5% of the country. A national campaign is marketed aggressively while the very institution meant to run it remains understaffed and technologically outdated.

India has built an industry around performing power.

Everything is staged: the branding, the slogans, the drama of rollout, the emotional appeal wrapped around political visibility. And because the narrative is so loud, it often overshadows the quiet truth—systems haven't improved at the same pace as stories.

The illusion becomes addictive. And addiction becomes policy.

Over time, the nation begins to believe its own marketing. The government mistakes applause for approval. Citizens mistake announcements for progress. Institutions mistake compliance for competence. And slowly, quietly, the architecture underneath decays—because everyone assumes it is stronger than it actually is.

This section reveals the uncomfortable truth: India has perfected the art of looking strong while remaining structurally fragile.

A country cannot rise on stories alone. Narratives can inspire, but they cannot substitute for operational depth, institutional maturity, or executional integrity. India must confront this gap—between what it says and what it is—before the illusion turns into strategic self-harm.

7.2 — Execution: Where India's Grand Stories Collapse

If political storytelling is India's favorite sport, execution is its most persistent weakness. The distance between announcement and achievement in India is not measured in kilometers or budgets—it is measured in years, delays, red tape, and quiet institutional exhaustion.

Walk through any Indian city and you will see the evidence. A flyover remains half-built long after its inauguration went viral. A digital platform meant to transform governance crashes the day it launches. A reform celebrated as "historic" disappears into bureaucratic dust with no follow-through. A mega project announced with grand rhetoric turns into a political orphan once the cameras move on.

This is where India's grand stories collapse—at the point of execution.

The first fault line is the administrative machinery, which is expected to convert political imagination into operational reality while running on outdated processes, insufficient manpower, and conflicting directives. It is like asking a tired athlete to run a marathon after spending years carrying other people's baggage. The machinery tries—often heroically—but it cannot overcome its structural fatigue.

Corruption further distorts the original intent. A well-designed reform becomes a profiteering opportunity. A public project becomes a nexus of contractors, middlemen, and officials. A noble policy becomes a negotiation. Money moves faster than execution. Intent evaporates long before impact appears.

Accountability, the backbone of execution, dissolves quietly between ministries and departments.

When a project fails, everyone is responsible, which means no one is responsible. One ministry blames another. Another blames the state government. The state blames the centre. The centre blames "unforeseen circumstances." And the public is left staring at a crater where a project was once promised.

Political leadership rarely stays long enough in a department to own consequences. Ministers rotate portfolios like musical chairs. Each new minister announces a fresh vision without completing the previous one. Short tenures incentivize announcements, not results. After all, why fix a long-term problem when a short-term narrative delivers instant political returns?

India's storytelling speed is breathtaking—policies announced overnight, campaigns unveiled with spectacle, slogans printed before strategy is finalized. But India's execution speed is slow, inconsistent, and vulnerable to collapse under its own weight.

This contrast exposes the illusion of strength. A narrative moves at the speed of sentiment. Execution moves at the speed of systems. And systems—India's weakest link—are still calibrated for a different era.

In the compute century, where nations rise on the reliability of their execution engines, India faces a harsh truth: its ambitions are 21st century, but its execution architecture is 20th century with 19th-century bottlenecks.

India will not fail because it lacks ideas. It will fail because it cannot convert those ideas into outcomes.

Until execution becomes a national priority—not a bureaucratic afterthought—the illusion of strength will continue to shine brightly on television screens while crumbling quietly on the ground.

7.3 — The Psychology of National Self-Deception

Nations do not fall into illusions by accident. They fall because illusions are comforting. Because the truth is complicated, and fantasy is convenient. India's belief that it is stronger than it actually is does not arise from malice or arrogance—it arises from a deeply human psychological need: the desire to feel powerful, even when the systems beneath are fragile.

Nationalism, in its healthy form, is a binding force. But when mixed with political marketing, social-media validation, and emotional hunger, it becomes a cocoon that shields the country from uncomfortable truths. Inside this cocoon, India constructs a psychological bubble where sentiment replaces strategy.

People begin to confuse hope with readiness. A successful cricket match becomes a symbol of national capability. A viral patriotic video becomes evidence of global influence. A trending hashtag becomes proof of unity. Hope is beautiful—but when mistaken for readiness, it blinds a nation to the hard work still undone.

Politicians, thriving in an ecosystem where applause brings power, confuse applause with mandate. They see cheering crowds as proof of strong governance, rather than emotional reaction. They mistake rallies for reform, popularity for performance, noise for legitimacy. In this bubble, accountability becomes optional because the narrative already feels victorious.

Bureaucrats, trained in hierarchical obedience, confuse compliance with progress. If the file is signed, the job is done. If the report is submitted, the problem is solved. If the minister is satisfied, the reform is "successful." The system rewards those who maintain the illusion, not those who expose the gaps.

Institutions themselves, overburdened and fatigued, confuse activity with outcomes. Meetings are held. Committees are formed. Recommendations are discussed. Events are organized. Websites are updated. Speeches are delivered. But the core indicators—execution speed, capability depth, systemic reliability—remain unchanged. Institutions keep moving, but often in circles, mistaking motion for momentum.

This ecosystem of self-deception is not sustained by ignorance; it is sustained by protecting egos. Admitting gaps means admitting weakness. Admitting weakness means confronting responsibility. And responsibility is heavy—especially in a nation where political backlash, media trolling, and bureaucratic hierarchy punish honesty more than incompetence.

Thus, illusions survive because they offer a psychological shortcut: It is easier to feel strong than to become strong. It is easier to perform progress than to build progress. It is easier to defend the narrative than to fix the system.

The tragedy is subtle: India's self-deception is not rooted in lack of capability—it is rooted in lack of introspection. The country has the intelligence, talent, and potential to rise. But the collective psyche often chooses flattery over truth, comfort over clarity, applause over architecture.

And so, the illusion persists—bright, loud, emotionally satisfying. But beneath that glow lies a quieter reality, waiting patiently for the nation to mature enough to face it.

7.4 — The Strategic Danger of Illusions: Nations That Believe They Are Strong Stop Improving

Illusions are not harmless. They are the most dangerous form of national weakness because they hide themselves behind pride. A country that knows it is weak will attempt to strengthen itself. A country that believes it is strong will stop improving. And this is how nations lose—not through defeat, but through complacency.

When illusions become national doctrine, hunger fades. Reforms slow. Structural gaps remain untouched. Capability deficits are rationalized away. Geopolitical threats appear smaller than they are. And windows of opportunity quietly close.

India stands at this threshold today. The illusion of strength—amplified by political marketing, patriotic sentiment, selective global praise, and the emotional comfort of victory narratives—has created a dangerous sense of premature triumphalism.

This illusion makes India underestimate global competitors. Countries with smaller populations, quieter politics, and fewer resources are building far more disciplined systems. They invest steadily in education, research, institutions, and compute architecture while India debates controversies on primetime television. Illusions whisper, *"We are already ahead."* Reality replies, *"You are not even in the real race yet."*

This illusion makes India overestimate its readiness for compute sovereignty. Chips depend on global supply chains India does not yet control. Cloud depends on providers India does not own. AI depends on talent India struggles to retain. Yet the illusion persistently claims, *"We are prepared."* Prepared nations don't need slogans—they have systems. India has slogans.

This illusion makes India misjudge its geopolitical vulnerabilities. Believing it has leverage, India walks the tightrope between great powers without recognizing how fragile its architecture is. Narratives say India is a global decider. Systems reveal India is still a global dependent. Illusions turn strategic caution into strategic arrogance.

This illusion makes India mistake political stability for national strength. A government lasting ten years does not mean the country became stronger—it only means the government became better at controlling narratives. Strength is not measured by election cycles but by execution cycles:

- How many institutions improved?
- How many systems modernized?
- How many policies survived political transitions?
- How much capability was built independent of political leadership?

Illusions block these questions. And where questions die, progress dies with them.

The greatest cost of illusions is lost time. Nations do not get unlimited opportunities. The compute century offers India a narrow window—one that will not wait for political dramas to settle or for institutions to recover their stamina. While India applauds itself at rallies and trends hashtags on social media, other nations quietly build the architecture of the future.

Illusions offer comfort. Reality demands courage.

India must choose.

A quiet warning closes this chapter:

The world does not reward nations for believing they are strong. It rewards nations that become strong.

And becoming strong requires something India has avoided for decades: Looking in the mirror without flinching.

Chapter 8 — The Talent Paradox

A world-class mind pipeline... leaking at every stage

The Country That Creates Genius and Then Watches It Leave

Walk into any Indian classroom and you will see brilliance waiting to erupt. A child solving equations faster than the teacher can write them. A teenager dismantling a physics problem with the elegance of a seasoned researcher. A young girl writing code on a borrowed laptop because her family cannot afford a new one. A boy from a small town staying awake till midnight, preparing for an exam that will determine his future—not because he fears failure, but because he believes in possibility.

Step into a coaching centre at dawn. You will find students—half asleep, half alive—cramming concepts their textbooks refuse to teach properly. In every corner of this country, brilliance flickers like a thousand unsheltered lamps: fragile, luminous, and astonishing.

India does not produce talent in pockets—it produces talent in floods.

And yet, something tragic happens.

By the time these young minds reach adulthood, the country begins to lose them. Not to enemies, not to disasters—but to the world. One by one, the brightest leave through airport terminals, scholarship letters, job offers, or silent resignation.

The young scientist goes to a foreign university because Indian labs lack funding. The AI engineer joins a global company because domestic firms don't invest in research. The innovator chooses another country because Indian bureaucracy suffocates invention. The thinker buries their brilliance in a job they never wanted because the system offers no other path.

A country capable of creating genius appears incapable of holding it.

This is India's most painful paradox: the nation is rich in minds but poor in architecture. The raw material is extraordinary, but the container is broken. The intelligence is world-class, but the ecosystem is outdated. The hunger is limitless, but the opportunities are insufficient. Talent grows in India—but careers grow elsewhere.

In this haunting contrast lies the emotional core of the chapter.

The problem is not that India's children dream big. The problem is that India's systems remain too small to sustain their dreams.

The country that can produce mathematical prodigies, engineering wizards, and scientific pioneers somehow lacks the institutions, the research culture, the leadership depth, and the governance muscle to keep them anchored.

This chapter begins with a simple, disturbing truth: India does not suffer from a talent shortage. India suffers from a talent exodus and a talent wastage crisis—created by its own systems.

And the cost is not individual—it is national.

8.1 — The First Leak: Education That Rewards Memory, Not Mastery

India's talent pipeline begins at a place that should have been its strongest foundation—its schools. Instead, it begins with a quiet betrayal. The classroom, which should ignite imagination, curiosity, and mastery, often becomes a factory floor where young minds are trained to reproduce information rather than understand it.

Here, intelligence is abundant. But the system forces it into cages.

From the first day of schooling, children learn that marks matter more than mastery. They discover that questions are dangerous, that curiosity slows syllabus completion, and that creativity is a liability in a world obsessed with standardized answers. A student who wants to understand *why* is pushed aside in favour of the student who can memorize *what*. Mastery takes time; memory takes pressure. India chooses pressure.

This is the first leak in the talent pipeline—a schooling ecosystem that values compliance over competence.

Look closely at any classroom: A girl who could become a brilliant scientist is taught to memorize definitions she could have discovered on her own. A boy who could reinvent mathematics is told to stop asking questions that "aren't in the syllabus." A child who could innovate is assigned the task of filling notebooks to please an examiner who will never meet them.

The tragedy is not lack of talent. The tragedy is the suppression of talent in the name of uniformity.

Teachers, many of them sincere and capable, are trapped in a machinery that denies them freedom. They cannot innovate because the system demands predictable outputs. They cannot experiment because their careers depend on compliance. They cannot nurture genius because they are too busy finishing outdated syllabi that have not kept pace with the world.

Boards and ministries release reforms with glossy presentations, but reform in India is often cosmetic—more visible than viable. Policies change, slogans change, circulars multiply, but the classroom remains frozen in time. Learning outcomes remain weak. Pedagogy remains archaic. Students remain exhausted. And the talent pipeline continues to leak before its potential can take form.

The coaching industry grows in this vacuum—not because students love it, but because schools fail them. Coaching centres become the real classrooms, and schools become administrative checkpoints. Education becomes a survival economy where students learn to endure rather than to excel.

What is lost in this chaos? Genius. Original thought. Experimentation. Confidence. Joy.

India's children do not fail the system. The system fails the children.

And yet, despite all this, India continues to produce extraordinary talent—mathematicians, coders, designers, thinkers, researchers—people who shine globally not because the system nurtured them, but because they survived it. They rise through self-learning, internet-driven exposure, peer networks, resilience, and sheer personal ambition.

India produces brilliance *in spite of* its schooling model, not because of it.

This section ends with a painful truth: India's education system is designed to create followers, not creators. It rewards memory, not mastery. It protects the syllabus, not the student. And in doing so, it causes the first and most damaging leak in the nation's talent pipeline.

8.2 — The Second Leak: Higher Education That Cannot Hold Its Best Minds

If India's schools injure talent, its universities often finish the job. This is the second leak in the pipeline—one that drains not only skill but hope.

Walk across the campuses of India's universities and you will feel two parallel realities. On one side: brilliance, ambition, hunger, possibility. Students debating ideas under trees, coding in dim hostels, building prototypes with borrowed tools, dreaming of research careers that can change the world.

On the other side: institutions that have aged faster than the nation they were meant to serve.

Labs running on equipment older than the students using them. Classrooms with broken projectors and outdated textbooks. Professors forced to manage administrative work instead of mentoring. Vacant faculty positions because good academics refuse to fight the system. Research centres surviving on trickle funding that arrives too late to matter.

This is not lack of intelligence; it is lack of architecture.

India competes with MIT, Stanford, Tsinghua, Cambridge, ETH Zurich, and Tokyo University for its brightest minds. But those institutions are competing globally for talent. Indian universities, by contrast, are competing domestically—for funding, for autonomy, for survival. They cannot match the infrastructure, research ecosystems, academic culture, or intellectual freedom that top global institutions offer. And the best students know it.

The painful truth is this:

Students do not leave India because they want to. They leave because the system gives them no choice.

A brilliant engineering student enters a university excited for innovation—only to find labs running on obsolete equipment and teachers forced to teach outdated syllabi because curriculum committees take a decade to change anything. She dreams of research, but the campus buys sports banners before research tools. Eventually, she writes the GRE and leaves.

A physics prodigy applies to PhD programs in India. He finds that many professors are overworked, under-supported, or politically appointed. He realizes he will spend more time filling forms than running experiments. He leaves for a foreign lab where research is valued, funded, and celebrated.

A young AI researcher wants to stay in India, but cannot find a university with enough compute, enough mentorship, enough direction. Global AI labs offer GPUs, grants, and guidance. Indian labs offer bureaucracy, paperwork, and budget approvals that take months. She leaves.

This is not brain drain by desire—it is brain drain by design.

And behind every lost researcher is a lost industry, a lost patent, a lost startup, a lost innovation, a lost national capability. India trains thousands of brilliant minds every year, but most of them end up building the future for other nations. The country pays the cost of producing talent—but the returns go abroad.

Even those who stay face suffocation. Political appointments turn universities into ideological battlegrounds. Autonomy is threatened. Promotions depend on loyalty, not academic merit. Bureaucratic processes strangle creativity. Administrative committees become more powerful than research councils.

How long can excellence survive in such soil?

The irony is almost poetic. India wants to become a knowledge economy but starves its knowledge centres. It wants innovation but punishes deviation. It wants world-class universities but refuses to build world-class conditions.

This section ends with an uncomfortable reflection: India does not have a shortage of world-class brains. It has a shortage of world-class places for them to grow. And until that changes, the second leak will continue—quietly draining the future, one brilliant mind at a time.

8.3 — The Third Leak: Industry That Consumes Skill But Doesn't Build It

After surviving the schooling bottleneck and navigating the maze of higher education, India's brightest minds enter the workforce—only to encounter the third leak in the pipeline: an industry that consumes skill but rarely builds it.

This is where talent meets the real world—and often disappears into it.

For decades, India's corporate ecosystem has relied on mass hiring without meaningful skill-building. Engineers are recruited by the thousands, trained for a few weeks on scripts rather than substance, and then deployed into roles that neither challenge them nor nourish their potential. The industry optimizes for headcount, not mastery. For billable hours, not innovation. For scalability, not depth.

The largest chunk of India's talent pipeline flows into IT services—a sector that brought foreign exchange, stability, and jobs, but also quietly created an underemployment economy. Brilliant engineers who could have built products end up maintaining legacy systems. Coders with creativity settle into repetitive tasks. Problem-solvers become PowerPoint generators. The mind sharpens with challenge, but dulls with routine—and much of India's workforce is trapped in routine.

Startups, which once promised to break this pattern, often fall into another trap: talent burning without talent mentoring. Many young companies chase hypergrowth without building leadership depth. They expect employees to perform like experts without giving them the ecosystem to become one. The pressure is intense, but the guidance is thin. People learn to survive, not to innovate.

Managers in India are frequently chosen not for leadership, but for loyalty, or for their ability to produce short-term results. Leadership pipelines are weak. Mentorship cultures are fragile. Many supervisors are professionals who climbed because they stayed long enough, not because they understand people, vision, or talent development.

Employees quickly learn the unwritten rule of corporate India: *Do more with less, but don't expect more in return.*

Innovation takes a back seat because companies are risk-averse. Creativity is limited because processes dominate. Career ladders are shallow because organisations are hierarchical. And excellence often goes unnoticed because survival consumes everyone's time.

In this ecosystem, India wastes genius quietly.

A mathematician becomes a data-entry cog because no one saw her potential. An AI engineer works on dashboards instead of algorithms. A designer polishes templates instead of shaping products. A researcher becomes a project coordinator. A problem-solver becomes a process-follower.

Underemployment is not just an economic problem—it is a national tragedy.

India's collective intelligence is being used to keep systems running, not to build new systems. To support global innovation, not to lead it. To execute instructions, not to design architecture.

The corporate world praises "talent" in speeches but treats it as "resource" in practice. The difference is subtle but devastating. Resources are consumed. Talent must be cultivated.

And yet, there is empathy in this critique. Many organisations want to innovate but are trapped in a cost-driven economy. Many leaders care but lack time. Many employees want mentorship but find managers who themselves were never mentored.

India's industry is not malicious—it is misaligned.

It inherited a model optimized for efficiency, not invention; for service, not sovereignty; for execution, not exploration.

This section ends on a reflective note: India does not lack talent. It lacks industries that know what to do with talent.

Until corporate India learns not just to consume skill but to build it, the third leak will continue draining national potential into low-value work—leaving the country with dreams far larger than the systems meant to realise them.

8.4 — The Final Leak: Brain Drain, Emotional Drain, and the National Cost

The last leak in India's talent pipeline is the most painful—not because it is surprising, but because it has become predictable. Every year, the country loses thousands of its finest minds. Some board flights to foreign universities, some accept offers from global companies, some shift careers in frustration, some quietly surrender their dreams, and some remain in India physically but leave mentally—disengaged, uninspired, exhausted. This is not just brain drain; it is emotional drain, institutional drain, civilizational drain. India is losing not just skilled workers, but entire futures.

Consider the researchers who could have built national capability. Every scientist India loses represents an industry India forfeits. The young physicist who might have strengthened India's space program now helps another nation advance. The chemist who could have developed new materials now works in a foreign lab. The AI researcher who could have anchored India's compute evolution now builds models for a global corporation. Research is not a hobby—it is the foundation of sovereignty. When India loses researchers, it loses control of its own long-term destiny.

The innovators who could have anchored new industries face a similar fate. India's startup ecosystem is vibrant, but its deep-tech ecosystem remains fragile. Innovators need patient capital, regulatory stability, and research infrastructure—three conditions India struggles to provide consistently. And so the brilliant engineer goes to Silicon Valley, the hardware innovator to Taiwan or Germany, the biotech pioneer to Boston, and the compute architect to the U.S. or China. India pays to educate them, but others pay to empower them.

The leaders who could have strengthened institutions are also drained away. A quiet tragedy runs underneath: India's best administrative minds rarely enter public institutions. Those who do join the civil services often find themselves transferred frequently, constrained by politics, drowned in outdated processes, punished for initiative, and rewarded for maintaining the status quo. It is no surprise that many choose corporate roles, global institutions, or foreign governments instead—places where leadership is cultivated, not constrained. India loses institution-builders not because they lack patriotism, but because the architecture does not allow them to lead.

The thinkers who could have shaped policy suffer a similar fate. A nation's direction is determined not only by politicians but by thinkers, analysts, researchers, and philosophers who challenge old assumptions and design new frameworks. India produces such minds in abundance, but too often they become UPSC aspirants trapped in memorization hell, underpaid college lecturers with no research support, consultants solving problems for other countries, or voices drowned out by political noise. India does not lack insight; it lacks platforms that respect insight.

And then there is the internal brain drain—the brilliance wasted at home. Not all talent leaves the country; much of it is diverted into roles that fail to use even a fraction of its capability. The brilliant mathematics teacher ends up running a coaching factory. The creative engineer becomes a corporate execution machine. The visionary student becomes a bureaucratic clerk. The passionate researcher becomes a private tutor. The potential innovator becomes a safe job-seeker. This internal brain drain is as damaging as external brain drain, but far less acknowledged.

The national cost of this leakage is staggering. Every nation rises on the shoulders of its talent, but India's shoulders are tired from carrying ambition on weak architecture. The cost of losing talent is not measured in GDP; it is measured in industries never created, technologies never built, institutions never strengthened, ideas never expressed, breakthroughs never realized, and decades never reclaimed. While India loses its talent, other countries silently accumulate it—and convert it into power.

This section ends with the quiet truth the nation must finally confront: India does not lack talent. India lacks the architecture to hold talent. And until this architecture is rebuilt—system by system, institution by institution—the pipeline will continue to leak brilliance into the world, while the nation applauds itself for producing it.

Chapter 9 — India's Architectural Deficit

Why institutions, not governments, decide a nation's fate

The House That Keeps Changing Tenants but Never Repairs Its Foundation

Imagine a grand old house standing proudly in the middle of a busy neighborhood. Every five years, the tenants change. Some arrive with charisma, some with confidence, some with loud promises, some with quiet determination. Each new group repaints the walls, rearranges the furniture, hangs new banners, and throws an inauguration ceremony that draws half the street.

From the outside, it looks vibrant—a house constantly reinventing itself. But step inside the basement, and you will see the truth. The foundation is cracked. The beams are weakened. The wiring is from another era. The drainage overflows. Termites quietly eat away at the pillars. And everyone pretends not to notice.

This is India.

A nation obsessed with changing the tenants—elections, parties, leaders, slogans—while ignoring the far more critical task of repairing the foundation: its institutions.

It is a deeply cinematic irony. The political class campaigns as if governance is theatre. Citizens vote as if leadership is magic. Media celebrates as if announcements are achievements.

But beneath the noise lies the silent architecture on which nations actually rise: the courts, regulatory bodies, universities, research institutes, civil services, enforcement agencies, data systems, and administrative frameworks. These are India's beams, pillars, and underground supports—old, overburdened, undernourished, and rarely rebuilt.

Changing governments without fixing institutions is like repainting a collapsing house. It looks new for a moment. It feels hopeful. But the cracks remain beneath the surface, widening with every storm.

India keeps repainting its walls with slogans, schemes, visions, and narratives. But the foundation—the architecture that determines national capability—has not been modernized to match the ambition of a rising superpower.

Leaders come and go, but the cracks stay. Policies shift, but the structure doesn't. Narratives evolve, but systems don't.

This chapter begins with a sobering realization: India is not failing because of who lives in the house. India is struggling because the house itself is not structurally sound.

Until the nation stops arguing over tenants and starts rebuilding the foundation, it will continue to wobble under the weight of its own aspirations—loud at the top, weak at the bottom.

9.1 — The Myth of Government as the Engine of Progress

India is a country that loves the idea of a strong leader. Every election cycle is framed as a battle for salvation—*this time, this leader will fix everything. This time, this party will transform the nation. This time, the promises will finally match the outcomes.*

But progress has never been the product of personalities. Progress is the product of institutions.

And this is where India repeatedly miscalculates its own destiny.

We mistake elections for transformation. We mistake speeches for strategy. We mistake charisma for competence. We mistake political continuity for national capability.

In doing so, we create a myth—the myth that governments drive progress alone, and that the right prime minister, chief minister, or cabinet composition is enough to fix the nation's structural weaknesses.

It is a comforting illusion, but a dangerous one.

Governments change fast. Institutions change slowly.

This is the core truth India refuses to confront.

A government may change every five years. A minister may change every eighteen months. A political slogan may change every season.

But institutions—the machinery that actually runs a country—move at a far slower pace. Courts take years to evolve. Regulators take decades to mature. Universities require generations to transform. Civil services depend on culture, not elections. Research architectures need stable funding, not dramatic announcements.

Political leadership may create momentum. But only institutions can convert momentum into durable capability.

India often behaves as if the opposite were true.

Politicians claim credit for outcomes they never executed.

A new airport opens, and the minister cuts the ribbon. But the planners, engineers, bureaucrats, regulators, architects, and committees who spent years making it possible remain invisible.

A digital platform is launched. Politicians bask in applause. But the developers, data scientists, consultants, and administrators who built and maintain the system—many overstretched and underpaid—are forgotten.

A social scheme succeeds. The minister takes credit. But the frontline workers, field officers, district administrations, and auditing teams are the real executors.

India has created a theatre where the actors claim the glory and the stagehands carry the burden.

India repeatedly misidentifies "leadership" as "institutional capacity."

A prime minister may have vision. A cabinet minister may have energy. A chief minister may have ambition. A secretary may have competence.

But if the system underneath them is weak—if files take months to move, if coordination is broken, if regulators are compromised, if universities stagnate, if research funding is symbolic, if civil servants are transferred for political convenience, if data systems are incomplete or unreliable—then no leader, no matter how strong, can deliver consistent progress.

Strong leaders without strong institutions create temporary achievements, not lasting capability.

This is why India experiences bursts of progress but rarely sustained, compounding progress over decades.

The illusion: a strong PM or party can substitute for strong systems.

It is an illusion born from emotion, amplified by rhetoric, and reinforced by a political culture that thrives on personalization of power.

But nations do not rise because of single leaders. They rise because their systems rise.

You can replace a leader in a strong country and nothing collapses. You can change a party in a mature democracy and everything keeps working. But in India, when leadership changes, entire systems wobble—because they were never institutionalized in the first place.

This section exposes a truth India must accept before it can grow:

Governments can inspire, but only institutions can build. Governments can promise, but only institutions can deliver. India will not become a great power by strengthening leaders. India will become a great power by strengthening the architecture that survives beyond them.

9.2 — India's Institutional Weak Bones: Designed for Survival, Not Sovereignty

Every nation has a skeleton—an underlying architecture of institutions that carries its weight, absorbs its shocks, and anchors its future. India's ambition today is undeniably 21st century, but its institutional bones remain from another era—built for survival, not sovereignty; for maintenance, not mastery.

To understand India's architectural deficit, one must begin with an uncomfortable truth: India's institutions were never designed to create a superpower. They were designed to prevent collapse. And the country still operates within that defensive blueprint.

The Indian administrative system, forged during colonial rule and refined during early nation-building, has never been fundamentally redesigned. It was built to control a population, not empower it; to maintain order, not accelerate progress. Files move through layers of hierarchy like relics from a bureaucratic museum. Decision-making is slow, risk-averse, and documentation-heavy. Innovation is rare because punishment is certain and reward is uncertain. Administrative culture values stability more than speed. This structure can keep the country functioning, but it cannot make the country formidable.

India does not lack regulators; it lacks regulators with autonomy. From environment to education, from finance to telecom, from media to technology, many regulatory bodies operate under the shadow of political influence. Appointments are often based on loyalty rather than expertise. Mandates shift with elections. Investigations stall when they threaten political interests. Policy cycles reverse every few years due to ideological swings. Regulators are supposed to be the spine of a modern economy, but India's regulators are often forced to bend.

Universities, which should serve as the strategic command centres of national capability, are starved of research funding, trapped in archaic bureaucratic systems, governed by political appointees lacking academic depth, suffocated by outdated curricula, and unable to retain top faculty. A nation dreaming of AI, semiconductors, space, and biotechnology cannot rise on institutions designed for yesterday's world. Innovation needs autonomy, not approvals; funding, not forms; leadership, not loyalty.

India's judiciary, carrying immense moral legitimacy, is operationally exhausted. Case backlogs exceed human imagination. Legal processes move at geological speed. Infrastructure is outdated. Vacancies remain unfilled for years. Complex economic or technological disputes struggle through a 19th-century procedural lens. A slow judiciary weakens investment confidence, national security enforcement, and civil rights. It drains national energy in silence.

Agencies are stretched beyond their mandates, burdened with responsibilities they cannot master. Enforcement bodies handle economic crimes, political controversies, administrative disputes, and even social tensions. Regulatory agencies perform governance tasks. Administrative offices run welfare schemes without adequate manpower. Data bodies manage technology transitions without technical expertise. When every agency does everything, no agency does anything well.

India's ministries operate like separate kingdoms. Coordination is episodic, not structural. Policies overlap, implementation contradicts, data is siloed, and turf wars between departments slow execution more than resource constraints. A nation cannot solve problems—climate, urbanization, AI regulation, semiconductor strategy, national security, healthcare—through isolated ministries when these challenges demand integrated architecture. This fragmentation is not a flaw of individuals; it is the design of the machinery itself.

India wants to be a global manufacturing hub, an AI leader, a semiconductor power, a renewable energy pioneer, a geopolitical balancer, and a $5–10 trillion economy. But ambition must rest on architecture. Today, India's ambitions have outgrown its institutions. The country wants to sprint, but its bones crack under the pressure. It wants to leap, but the spine is too fragile to support the take-off. It wants sovereignty in the compute century, but its institutional infrastructure is not yet fit for sovereignty.

This section ends with a simple, brutal truth: India's institutions were built to survive yesterday. They must be rebuilt to win tomorrow.

9.3 — Political Interference: How Governments Hijack the Architecture They Should Strengthen

If institutions are the bones of a nation, political interference is the slow poison that weakens them from within. It is subtle at times, theatrical at others, but always corrosive. Every government—past and present—promises to strengthen institutions. Yet almost every government ends up bending them, shaping them, or hollowing them to serve short-term political incentives rather than long-term national interest. This is not ideology; it is habit. A habit that has calcified into a governance culture.

India's institutions should be led by the most capable minds in the country. Instead, too many appointments are driven by political allegiance, caste equations, regional bargaining, or ideological alignment. Critical posts—from universities to regulatory bodies, from commissions to councils—are often filled not with experts but with loyalists. A regulator appointed for loyalty cannot regulate those who appointed him. A university vice-chancellor chosen for political comfort cannot protect academic freedom. A committee head selected for ideological alignment cannot produce independent recommendations. Talent loses. Institutions lose. The nation loses.

Transfers, which should be routine administrative tools, have become weapons of control. India's administrative culture is haunted by a quiet threat: one wrong move and you will be transferred. Honest officers are punished, competent officers are sidelined, corrupt officers flourish through negotiation, and everyone learns to protect themselves rather than the public interest. The message is clear: do not disturb the system, or the system will disturb you. Institutional courage evaporates, execution collapses, and innovation dies in its cradle.

Promotions, too, often reward obedience over excellence. Institutions rot when mediocrity rises and merit descends. In India, promotions in many public bodies depend on loyalty—to the minister, the party, the faction, or the ideological corridor of power. Brilliant officers who challenge inefficiency are branded as troublemakers. Those who maintain silence are rewarded. Those who serve political interests progress faster than those who serve national interests. Administration becomes theatre, not governance.

Policy reversals compound the damage. One of India's most chronic institutional diseases is the policy U-turn every election cycle. A long-term project approved by one government is stalled, rebranded, or reversed by the next—not because it was flawed, but because credit must not go to the previous political leadership.

Economic reforms lose continuity, education strategies remain incomplete, health systems fluctuate, infrastructure projects stagnate, and digital frameworks break mid-way. No country can build sovereignty on foundations that shift every five years.

Research and regulation, which demand autonomy, are suffocated under political shadow. Research institutions cannot survive without independence. Regulators cannot function without autonomy. Universities cannot innovate when they fear political retaliation. Yet political interference infiltrates grant approvals, academic appointments, research agendas, regulatory enforcement, and think-tank leadership. Science bends to suit political optics. Regulation bends to suit political narratives. Institutions bend because standing straight is dangerous. This is how nations lose their intellectual backbone.

Centralization of power further chokes long-term capacity with short-term control. Decision-making, administrative authority, policy control, narrative management, and budget allocation are increasingly concentrated at the top. Ministries wait for directions, states wait for approvals, institutions wait for permission. Centralization may deliver speed for leaders, but it creates paralysis for the nation. A centralized architecture cannot scale, cannot adapt, cannot empower, and cannot innovate.

Ministers come and go, but the damage remains. A minister may stay in a department for one or two years, sometimes less. But the institutional wounds they inflict—through bad appointments, reckless decisions, political interference, or short-term gimmicks—can haunt a system for decades. Leadership in India is temporary, but institutional wounds are permanent. A corrupt appointment remains long after the minister is gone. A weakened regulator remains long after the government has changed. A distorted policy ecosystem remains long after the ribbon-cutting ceremony. A demoralized bureaucracy remains long after the political drama fades. In the battle between political ego and institutional integrity, the nation pays the bill.

India's institutions are not weak by destiny. They are weakened by design. Political interference has turned guardians into servants, thinkers into operators, regulators into spectators, and institutions into political instruments. The tragedy is not that politicians interfere—it is that the architecture allows them to.

This section ends with a truth India must confront with maturity: a nation cannot rise when every government reshapes institutions to suit itself. Sovereignty requires strong architecture, not strong men.

9.4 — The Institutional Deficit as Strategic Deficit: Why India Still Cannot Execute at Scale

At some point, every rising nation confronts a moment of truth: ambition alone cannot build the future. Dreams are not strategies. Speeches are not systems. Narratives are not architecture. And political will—however strong—cannot substitute for institutional capacity. India has reached that moment.

The country's most persistent challenge is not political instability, economic volatility, or geopolitical pressure. It is something far deeper, far older, and far more structural: an institutional deficit that has quietly transformed into a strategic deficit. India's inability to execute at scale is not a mystery. It is an outcome—predictable, measurable, inevitable—of weak institutional architecture.

India plans fast but executes slowly. Policies are introduced with fanfare, websites crash on day one, tenders stall, approvals pile up, coordination breaks down, and deadlines stretch from months to years. Projects meant to transform regions lose momentum halfway because institutions cannot sustain speed. Execution does not fail at the top; it fails in the middle—where systems are supposed to take over. This is not a failure of talent. It is a failure of architecture.

India's challenges—AI governance, semiconductor strategy, climate adaptation, data protection, manufacturing scale—cannot be solved by ministries operating as isolated islands. They require horizontal architecture: shared data, integrated execution, cross-sector alignment, unified planning. Yet ministries behave like separate kingdoms. What one approves, another delays. What one regulates, another disrupts. What one mandates, another contradicts. Coordination is episodic, architecture is missing, and outcomes collapse.

The administrative system itself is designed to absorb pressure rather than deliver performance. It was built to manage crises, contain disorder, maintain continuity, and avoid collapse. It was never designed to achieve high-speed execution, global competitiveness, or technological leadership. Chaos is not a glitch—it is a feature baked into the machinery. But in the compute century, chaos becomes a strategic tax the nation cannot afford.

India shines in islands of excellence—a world-class metro system here, an efficient passport office there, a successful digital platform, a model district, a visionary IAS officer. But brilliance is never replicated. Success does not scale. Institutional learning is absent. Best practices die with leadership changes. A nation rises when excellence becomes a system, not an exception.

This weakness becomes most dangerous in the century of architecture—chips, cloud, data, algorithms, and supply-chain sovereignty. Nations with strong institutions rise. Nations with weak institutions become dependencies. India's institutional fragility makes it slow to adopt strategic technologies, unable to retain technical talent, incapable of coordinating large-scale innovation, dependent on foreign compute, reactive rather than proactive in AI governance, and perpetually behind in critical research. This is not an academic problem. It is a sovereignty problem.

Emergencies expose the cracks even more starkly. Floods, pandemics, migrant crises, data breaches, and infrastructure collapses all reveal the same truth: India's administrative system struggles under pressure because its architecture was built for survival, not resilience. Crisis coordination is often heroic—but it is never architectural. Countries become great not by surviving crises, but by learning from them. India survives, but rarely transforms.

Global credibility suffers as well. The world does not take a nation seriously because of loud narratives, strong leaders, large rallies, patriotic speeches, or political continuity. The world takes nations seriously when they deliver consistently, reduce uncertainty, strengthen institutions, and demonstrate capacity at scale. Without strong institutions, India's global credibility fluctuates with political cycles—and the world sees the inconsistency.

Charismatic leaders can inspire, but only institutions can execute. Political cycles last five years. Institutional cycles last fifty. A nation that invests only in leaders but not in institutions builds a temporary illusion of strength. A nation that invests in institutions—whether or not leaders are popular—builds enduring power. India still confuses the two. But real sovereignty emerges not from political stability, but from institutional integrity.

India's future will not be decided by who wins the next election. It will be decided by whether its institutions can be rebuilt for the century of compute. Without architecture, ambition collapses. Without institutions, India remains a narrative—not a power. This is not a political statement. It is a structural law of nationhood. And India is running out of time to choose which it wants to be.

Closing Reflection — Part II

The Mirror and the Map

Part I showed you a world reordered by compute—a global map no longer drawn by armies, GDP charts, or population statistics, but by architecture: chips, cloud, algorithms, coordination, and capability. We saw how the U.S., China, and even Russia now operate through competing operating systems of power. We saw ladders of dependency, hierarchies of sovereignty, and a world where nations rise or fall based on their alignment with technology, talent, and infrastructure.

Part I gave us the map of the 21st century—a landscape where power is structural, silent, and deeply interconnected.

Part II turned that map around and held up a mirror to India.

It revealed a nation rich in ambition but constrained by outdated architecture. A nation bursting with talent but hemorrhaging capability. A nation energized by narrative but exhausted by execution. A nation with world-class dreams—but weak institutional bones.

We saw the Ambition–Capability Gap widening with every year. We saw internal chaos functioning like a strategic tax. We saw illusions of strength replacing the discipline required to build real strength. We saw a talent pipeline leaking brilliance at every stage. And we saw how weak institutions—more than politics, more than geopolitics—remain the primary bottleneck of national destiny.

Together, Parts I and II construct a stark truth:

The world is accelerating, and India is still negotiating with its own architecture. The world is building systems, and India is debating narratives. The world is choosing long-term strategy, and India is trapped in short-term theatre.

And yet—India still has time.

Because history does not demand perfection; it demands direction. Nations rise not by fixing everything at once, but by choosing what to fix first.

That brings us to Part III.

Now the book steps onto the tightrope that will define India's geopolitical reality in the compute century—a rope stretched between two giants:

The United States: integration that empowers, and dependence that weakens. China: competition without confrontation, opportunity without imitation.

And below this tightrope lies the cautionary shadow of a wounded Russia—a reminder that sovereignty through isolation is sovereignty without support.

Part III shifts the lens from India's internal architecture to its external environment, from introspection to strategy, from criticism to calculation.

Because the truth is simple: a nation with internal deficits must navigate external pressures with far greater intelligence. India cannot afford missteps—not in an age where compute defines power, and alliances define survival.

Part III will explore the U.S. dilemma: friendship that empowers but also binds. The China window: rivalry that cannot be escaped, and opportunity that cannot be ignored. The Russian lesson: the price of standing alone in a world built on interdependence. And multialignment as architecture—not ideology—a strategy for sovereignty in a world of competing systems.

With Part III, the book steps out of the Indian home and into the global arena—where India must learn to balance, negotiate, integrate, and compete on a tightrope only a few nations can walk.

The map is ready. The mirror is clear. Now comes the tightrope.

Part III — The Tighthrope

Between The U.S. And China

"A nation's rise is not shaped by the friends it chooses, but by the architecture it builds while choosing them."

Overview

Part III steps onto India's most delicate geopolitical balancing act: navigating the world's two dominant architectures—the American system of integration and the Chinese system of insulation—without losing sovereignty or momentum. This section examines the strategic dilemma of partnering with the U.S., competing with China, and learning from Russia's painful isolation. Here geopolitics is not described through ideology or diplomacy, but through infrastructure, supply chains, compute access, talent flows, and narrative ecosystems. India is positioned not as a passive observer, but as a nation walking a tightrope suspended between opportunity and vulnerability. In a century defined by architecture, not alliances, India must craft a multialignment strategy built on capability, clarity, and courage.

Chapter 10 — The U.S. Dilemma

Integration vs Dependence. Trust vs Vulnerability

The Partner That Can Empower You... or Eclipse You

Picture a long table in South Block late at night—papers scattered, screens glowing, a handful of policymakers leaning over a document titled *Strategic Cloud Framework (U.S.–India).* No one says it aloud, but every mind in the room carries the same tension: this agreement could turbocharge India's digital future—or bind it irrevocably to an architecture built elsewhere.

Across the city, in a glass tower in Gurugram, a tech CEO raises a toast with investors from Silicon Valley. The smiles are real, the capital is welcome, the access is thrilling. Yet beneath the champagne bubbles lies a silent truth: the innovation story being celebrated is powered by cloud credits gifted from abroad, algorithms licensed from abroad, and hardware manufactured abroad. Growth—yes. Sovereignty—not quite.

In a quieter corner of Delhi, an ambassador prepares talking points for the next strategic dialogue with Washington. The language is warm, diplomatic, polished. But between the lines sits geopolitical arithmetic: India needs America's technology, capital, intelligence networks, and market access. America, in turn, needs

India's scale, geography, and counterweight potential. Interests align—but only for as long as they align.

And somewhere far from the corridors of power, in a small coaching centre in Kota, a brilliant teenager imagines walking into MIT. In his mind, the U.S. is not a country—it is a portal. A gateway to labs that work, professors who mentor, institutions that empower, and a life unconstrained by India's architectural fatigue. For millions of young Indians, America has become the second homeland of their ambition.

This is the U.S. dilemma in one sweeping frame: the United States is the partner that can accelerate India's rise—or quietly eclipse it.

Not ally. Not adversary. A gravitational field.

A nation so deeply embedded in the world's compute, cloud, semiconductor, financial, and cultural architecture that proximity to it feels like power—but dependence on it feels like vulnerability. India stands on a bridge built by America, knowing fully well that the bridge also casts the largest shadow.

The question that haunts Delhi is simple but strategic, whispered more often than it is spoken: *Can India rise with the U.S. without becoming shaped by the U.S.?*

This chapter begins with that tension—quiet, dramatic, unavoidable.

10.1 — Integration: The Power of Standing Close to the Sun

If global power were measured by proximity to innovation, India already stands near the brightest orbit—the United States. And there is no denying it: America has become India's most transformative catalyst. Alignment with the U.S. unlocks doors that no other nation can offer at this scale. It provides access to frontier technology, chip ecosystems, the world's largest cloud infrastructure, capital markets and venture networks that turn ideas into industries, universities that sharpen intellects and research systems that create future Nobel laureates, and global legitimacy—because being on America's side recalibrates how the world views you.

This alignment is visible everywhere. A Bangalore startup boasts of its "US-based investors" as if it were a badge of destiny. A Hyderabad biotech lab runs simulations on American cloud credits that Indian infrastructure cannot yet support. IT giants in Noida and Pune rely on U.S. software stacks, patents, certifications, and markets. Even strategic sectors—defense procurement, satellite systems, cybersecurity frameworks—depend on American cooperation to move beyond outdated capabilities.

India's integration with the U.S. is not merely diplomatic. It is architectural. Cloud is mostly American. AI models are mostly American. Chip design is mostly American. Venture capital pipelines are dominantly American. Narrative machinery—from news to culture to research—is deeply American.

This integration gives India speed—astonishing, unprecedented speed. It allows India to leapfrog slow, bureaucratic pathways and tap into hyper-efficient ecosystems built over decades. It offers a shortcut to the future, a direct route into the world's most advanced scientific, technological, and economic networks.

But speed borrowed is not speed owned.

Standing close to the sun gives warmth—but also casts shadows. For every startup that scales because of American backing, there is a missing Indian investor who could not match the capital. For every cloud platform that accelerates national services, there is an Indian data centre ecosystem pushed two steps behind. For every researcher who thrives in an American lab, there is an Indian university starved of capacity. For every dependency eased by U.S. integration, a new dependency quietly emerges.

This is the paradox at the heart of India's strategic relationship with the U.S.: America is the most beneficial partner India can have—and also the partner most capable of overshadowing India's own architecture-building ambitions. Integration gives India wings. But reliance can clip them.

India must therefore walk a tight line—drawing power from the American system without becoming absorbed by it. Using U.S. partnerships to accelerate capability, not substitute it. Welcoming integration without surrendering direction.

Because no nation, however well-intentioned its ally, builds another nation's sovereignty for free.

10.2 — Dependence: The Shadow Beneath the Alliance

Integration with the United States gives India extraordinary advantages. But woven into that acceleration is a quieter, more delicate truth—dependence. Not the old dependence of colonial memory or military imbalance, but a new, architectural dependence that lives inside code, hardware, contracts, and invisible infrastructure.

India's digital public goods may win applause, but the foundational layers beneath them are overwhelmingly American. Government portals run on U.S.-owned clouds. Critical databases depend on foreign servers. AI initiatives train on models developed in Silicon Valley. Financial platforms rest on American-authored cybersecurity protocols. Even entire startup ecosystems hinge on venture capital decisions made in glass towers in California.

This is not ideological vulnerability. This is structural vulnerability.

A single export control in Washington can stop a semiconductor shipment that fuels Indian manufacturing. A single regulatory change can limit India's ability to access advanced AI chips. A single sanctions framework can freeze cross-border financial flows. A single policy update from a cloud giant can alter the economics of India's digital ecosystem. A single narrative push from American media or think tanks can shift global perception of India overnight. In each case, the lever is not in Delhi's hands.

History offers enough warnings. Nations once embraced as partners suddenly found themselves blocked from critical technology—Japan in the 1980s, Turkey in the 2010s, even close NATO allies who discovered that American friendship has clear transactional boundaries. Technology bans, export restrictions, SWIFT cutoffs, and defense supply suspensions have all been used before—not out of hostility, but out of strategic calculation.

This is not a critique of the United States. It is an acknowledgment of how power behaves.

India's dependence is not military; India is not a client state. The Indian Army does not require U.S. permission to act. India's sovereignty is not about borders or boots. It is about the backbone of modern power—compute, chips, cloud, algorithms, and financial architecture. And if the U.S. ever pulls a critical lever—even unintentionally—entire sectors in India could freeze.

Manufacturing lines could stall for lack of chips. Digital services could slow if cloud agreements shift. AI development could halt if compute access narrows. Startups could collapse if capital dries up. Research pipelines could shrink if visas tighten or collaborations pause.

The shadow beneath the alliance is not hostility. It is asymmetry.

America has built the rails on which global modernity runs. India rides those rails brilliantly—but does not own them. And the uncomfortable truth is that nations do not weaken others out of malice; they simply prioritize their own interests. What benefits India today may be rebalanced tomorrow.

Respect for the U.S. does not require blindness. Partnership does not eliminate vulnerability. Goodwill does not guarantee insulation.

In the compute century, dependence is not dramatic—it is silent. It does not look like conflict—it looks like pause. And pause, in a world moving at algorithmic speed, is defeat.

10.3 — Trust: The Temptation of the American Promise

There is a reason India wants to trust the United States—and it is not merely strategy. It is sentiment. It is memory. It is aspiration. When Indians look at America, they do not just see a superpower; they see possibility. A country where merit rises faster than caste. A country where bureaucracy steps aside for innovation. A country where institutions bend less under political weight. A country where the future feels like a hallway lit from every direction.

Trust, therefore, does not emerge from treaties. It emerges from experience.

Generations of Indian students have walked through the doors of American universities, discovering labs that function, textbooks that evolve, professors who challenge, and ecosystems that reward excellence rather than compliance. They return home—or choose not to—with stories that become national mythology: *"There, I could breathe." "There, I was finally seen." "There, the system was not against me."*

The Indian diaspora—its CEOs, doctors, professors, entrepreneurs—shapes this trust further. When the world sees Indians leading Google, Microsoft, IBM, and dozens of global firms, it reinforces the notion that America is not merely a partner—it is an amplifier. A place where Indian talent finds a second home, often more nurturing than the first.

Culturally, too, India has absorbed the American rhythm: the optimism, the entrepreneurial impulse, the language of freedom, the appeal of scale, the aspiration to become global. Hollywood, Silicon Valley, Ivy League campuses, tech conferences, bestselling books—these soft power streams create comfort, familiarity, and emotional trust that rarely exists with any other major power.

Add to that the strategic logic: a shared discomfort with China's rise, a shared desire for an open Indo-Pacific, a shared belief in democratic frameworks (however imperfect), and decades of quiet cooperation in defense, science, and intelligence. All of this makes trusting the U.S. feel natural—almost inevitable.

But nations do not move by emotion; they move by interest. And interests, unlike friendships, do not stay constant.

This is the uncomfortable truth beneath the comfort of the American promise: the United States has no permanent friends—only permanent priorities. India may be a partner today, a counterweight tomorrow, a competitor the day after, and a negotiation chip in some future bargain. This is not betrayal; it is geopolitics functioning exactly as it should.

India's occasional over-romanticization of its U.S. relationship blinds it to the deeper pattern. Washington collaborates generously—but always for reasons aligned to its own architecture of power. If those reasons change, the warmth of partnership can cool swiftly. Export controls, tech restrictions, visa shocks, and military recalibrations have struck even its closest allies.

Which is why trust must be balanced with sobriety.

India can admire the American ecosystem. India can benefit from American alignment. But India cannot outsource its sovereignty to American goodwill.

Soft power can build affection. Shared values can build comfort. But only aligned interests can build durable trust.

And interests, like power, shift with time.

10.4 — Vulnerability: The Cost of Leaning Too Hard on One Pillar

In the end, the real question for India is not whether it should partner with the United States. That answer is obvious—America is indispensable for India's rise. The real question is more delicate, more strategic, and far more consequential: *How much dependence is tolerable before sovereignty begins to erode?*

Because the danger of leaning too heavily on America is not dramatic confrontation—it is quiet vulnerability. It is the slow shifting of strategic weight from Bharat to Washington without anyone noticing the tilt.

Architectural dependencies do not announce themselves with headlines. They accumulate silently.

When India's AI ecosystem depends on American models, its worldview becomes shaped by choices made in California boardrooms. When India's public infrastructure depends on American cloud, the nation's digital heartbeat is synced with contracts written under U.S. jurisdiction. When India's semiconductor ambitions depend on American equipment, every technological leap requires permission—explicit or invisible—from Washington. When India's startup economy depends on American capital, domestic innovation becomes vulnerable to foreign sentiment cycles. And when India's narratives depend on American media, think tanks, and cultural ecosystems, perception becomes a product imported instead of produced.

This is the quiet danger: dependence does not feel like dependence when everything is working. The alarm rings only when the tap is turned off.

A sanctions ripple. A visa recalibration. A supply chain choke. An export control shift. A geopolitical disagreement.

A single incident can expose the thin scaffolding beneath India's confidence.

The compute century has created a new form of sovereignty—one determined not by armies or borders, but by architecture ownership. If a nation does not own the deeper layers of its digital, technological, and narrative stack, it may hold elections, flags, and parliaments—but its power remains capped by someone else's operating system.

This is where India's vulnerability becomes strategic.

Overdependence on the U.S. risks algorithmic lock-in, where Indian systems must adapt to foreign updates; compute dependence, where AI breakthroughs hinge on access to American GPUs; chip fragility, where manufacturing ambitions collapse without U.S.-approved equipment; innovation stagnation, where domestic ecosystems grow complacent under foreign cushioning; narrative capture, where global perception becomes hostage to non-Indian platforms; and policy constraints, where foreign architecture limits domestic decision-making.

None of this implies hostility from the U.S. It simply acknowledges that power asymmetry creates structural risk—even between friends.

The United States will always be a partner worth having. But no nation in history has risen by outsourcing its architecture.

India's challenge, therefore, is not to choose between America and autonomy. It is to integrate without being absorbed. To benefit without becoming dependent. To partner without surrendering leverage.

This is the tension that will define India's next decade—the delicate balance between acceleration and sovereignty, between leaning and standing, between the glow of integration and the shadow of vulnerability.

And it is here, on this thin tightrope, that India must now learn to walk.

Chapter 11 — The China Window

Competition Without Confrontation; Growth Without Mimicry

The Giant Next Door That India Wants to Beat... Without Fighting

Picture a dimly lit conference room in Delhi, where a group of policymakers huddle over a massive screen displaying China's infrastructure map. High-speed rail lines cut across the country like nerves in a perfectly engineered organism. Megafactories hum at industrial tempos India has not yet learned to conduct. A digital dragon stretches across the skyline—Alibaba, Tencent, Huawei, BYD—each a reminder that China plays a different game, at a different speed, with different rules. They do not speak with hostility. They speak with calculation, with curiosity, with a hint of envy they do not dare admit aloud.

Across the city, an Indian CEO sits with his leadership team reviewing the latest shipment delays. The PowerPoint slide stares back like a quiet accusation: *"Dependence on China: 72% of supply components."* The room falls silent. Everyone knows the contradiction—India wants to beat China, but its factories breathe through Chinese supply chains. Compete, yes. Confront, no. It is a rivalry powered not by anger, but by necessity.

Meanwhile, in a coworking space in Bangalore, a group of young founders dissect a Chinese startup case study as if it were sacred scripture. They admire the speed, the scale, the aggression, the clarity. They copy the app design, the growth hacks, the distribution playbook—until someone murmurs, *"But their execution environment is not ours."* Still, the fascination remains. China is the threat India fears and the template India keeps borrowing from.

And in the quiet corners of the Indian intelligence establishment, analysts study China's governance system—the relentless coordination, the five-year plans executed like military operations, the iron discipline of institutions. They acknowledge the paradox: China's strengths come from architectures India cannot adopt. And its weaknesses come from rigidities India does not wish to inherit.

This is the China dilemma—India's most complex equation. A rival in markets. A competitor in manufacturing. A benchmark in infrastructure. A paradox in governance.

India does not want war with China—not military, not ideological, not systemic. India wants something more subtle: to outrun China without provoking it, to build independence without confrontation, to claim the century without inheriting China's methods or China's mistakes.

As India stands on the tightrope between aspiration and architecture, China is not merely the giant next door. It is the mirror India looks into—sometimes with admiration, sometimes with fear, always with the awareness that the reflection is sharper than the reality at home.

This chapter begins at that intersection of tension and truth: India cannot ignore China. India cannot imitate China. And India cannot rise without outgrowing China.

11.1 — The China Benchmark: The Rise India Cannot Ignore

For two decades, China has been the silent measuring scale against which India's ambitions keep colliding. Not because India chose China as its benchmark, but because China's sheer velocity forced the world—and India—to rethink what scale, discipline, and execution can look like when a nation aligns its machinery toward a single direction.

China did not just grow; it multiplied. China did not just industrialize; it reorganized itself around ambition. China did not just build infrastructure; it built at a speed that made textbooks obsolete.

Step into any Indian policy meeting today and you will feel the shadow of China in the room. Not as fear. Not as envy. But as an unavoidable reference point—an uncomfortable reminder of what coordinated national intent can achieve when its institutional spine is engineered for performance.

China's manufacturing muscle alone is a benchmark India cannot ignore. Where India debates industrial strategy, China deploys it. Where India discusses ease of doing business, China executes it. Where India negotiates with states, ministries, and departments for consensus, China moves with a clarity Indian governance has never experienced.

Its supply chain dominance is not accidental. It is architectural. Industrial zones are built like ecosystems, not real estate. Ports are designed around throughput, not ceremony. Regulatory frameworks are aligned to outcomes, not opinions. Incentives are crafted with precision, not political calculation. China built an industrial civilization while India was still arguing about which committee should study industrial reforms.

And then comes the part India rarely likes to acknowledge: institutional clarity. China's institutions—whatever one thinks of their political character—move with frightening coordination. Ministries talk to each other. Agencies execute together. Plans cascade like choreography. The national direction, once set, does not wobble every election cycle.

India, in contrast, remains a federation of competing ambitions—states arguing with the Centre, ministries operating in silos, bureaucrats pulled in seven directions, policies rewritten because a political calculation changed at midnight.

Where China built coherence, India built commentary. Where China built factories, India built paperwork. Where China built long-term strategy, India built five-year election cycles.

Even in compute—a domain India dreams of dominating—China has already built what India is still debating: semiconductor independence, domestic cloud giants, AI labs with global scale, supercomputing corridors, and a research ecosystem that functions on national priority rather than bureaucratic mood.

China's lesson is uncomfortable: nations rise when their institutions move faster than their citizens—not the other way around.

This section is not about praising China. It is about facing the truth India avoids. China represents the benchmark India must overcome because China has mastered the art India still struggles to learn—national alignment. Not ideology. Not uniformity. Alignment.

China shows what execution looks like when systems work. India shows what execution looks like when systems argue.

And this is why China remains India's unavoidable reference point—not as a model to copy, but as a challenge to surpass.

11.2 — The Trap of Imitation: Why India Cannot Copy China

Every few months, somewhere in India's political or business circles, someone leans back in a conference room chair and sighs: *"If only we had China's discipline, China's speed, China's efficiency..."* It is the fantasy of a shortcut—the belief that India can import China's execution model the way it imports its electronics. But fantasies collapse when they collide with architecture.

India cannot copy China for the simplest reason: India is not China. Not in governance. Not in social structure. Not in political culture. Not in institutional design. Not in national temperament.

Where China is a tightly-strung orchestra, India is a million musicians improvising simultaneously—and occasionally arguing over which song to play.

Yet the temptation to imitate persists. Politicians admire China's expressways, but forget the governance machinery that acquired land in months, not decades. Industrialists admire China's megafactories, but ignore the labor codes and centralized coordination that make them possible. Bureaucrats admire China's "policy-to-execution" velocity, but overlook the system that aligns ministries under a singular national direction. Even think tanks romanticize China's five-year planning precision, while conveniently skipping the part about institutional discipline India has never cultivated.

India tries to isolate China's outcomes from China's architecture—as if speed, scale, and efficiency grow independently of the soil they emerge from. This is where the imitation trap becomes dangerous.

India is a riotous democracy—noisy, diverse, argumentative, structurally allergic to enforced uniformity. What China achieves through centralization, India must achieve through coordination. What China executes through command, India must execute through consensus. What China designs top-down, India must negotiate bottom-up.

Trying to import China's methods into India is like trying to install a jet engine in an auto-rickshaw: impressive idea, catastrophic execution.

The more India tries to mimic China superficially—copying industrial parks, creating "special zones," issuing grand announcements—the more it discovers a bitter truth: China's success came from architecture, not aesthetics. From system design, not slogans. From institutional discipline, not political drama. From alignment, not imitation.

And in India, alignment is a luxury. State governments contradict central priorities. Ministries sabotage each other for credit. Political incentives change every election cycle. Courts intervene where execution collapses. Bureaucracy drags what politics rushes. Public opinion reshapes every decision in real time.

Trying to copy China inside India's governance environment is not only unrealistic—it is destabilizing. India's strength lies in its democratic texture, its open society, its messy but resilient pluralism. These may slow execution, but they also prevent the rigidity that often turns efficiency into fragility.

The India–China comparison must therefore evolve beyond imitation. China is not a manual for India. China is a reality check—a reminder that outcomes cannot be photocopied without inheriting the system that created them.

Imitation is the shortcut India cannot afford. And China is the template India cannot follow.

11.3 — Competition Without Confrontation: India's Strategic Balance

India's equation with China is not built on affection or hostility—it is built on gravity. Two civilizational giants rising side by side, sharing borders, markets, ambitions, vulnerabilities, and a history that oscillates between rivalry and restraint. China is the competitor India must engage with, but not the adversary India can afford to provoke.

This is where India's strategy must become subtle, almost surgical: compete fiercely, confront rarely, stabilize always.

The world expects India to counter China, but India's real goal is deeper—to escape China's gravitational pull in supply chains, technology, trade flows, and regional influence. India wants to rise in the same era, but not in the same orbit. That requires a new kind of competition—one waged not through confrontation, but through architecture.

The first battleground is manufacturing. China's factories power the world; India's factories aspire to power at least itself. But India cannot match China by copying its methods. It must rebuild its manufacturing base through trusted global partnerships—Japan, South Korea, Taiwan, the U.S., the EU—bringing technology, capital, and ecosystems that collectively dilute China's dominance. This is not an anti-China move. It is an India-first recalibration.

Electronics is the next frontier. Every smartphone assembled in India still has China inside it—components, chips, motherboards, displays. To compete, India must architect alternative electronics corridors stretching from Vietnam to Taiwan to Europe, turning itself into the final assembly node of a new, diversified supply chain.

Semiconductors follow naturally. India will not beat China or Taiwan in chip manufacturing overnight. But India can become the world's most reliable secondary hub by specializing in packaging, design, and critical materials. A partnership-driven ecosystem—not a China-style megafactory sprint—is India's realistic strategy.

Green tech, too, is a race India cannot lose. Solar panels, batteries, EV components—China dominates all of them. India must reclaim this space by building joint ventures with nations that fear overdependence on China as much as India does. If India becomes the trusted alternative, competition becomes inevitable.

And then, the crown jewel: AI. Here, confrontation with China is unnecessary—and unwise. Instead, India can strengthen its own AI ecosystem through open-source models, sovereign compute corridors, and partnerships with democratic tech alliances. Competing on values, not scale.

Across all these sectors, the principle remains the same: outcompete China without provoking it, rise beside China without shadowing it, stabilize the region while strengthening the nation.

India doesn't need to defeat China. India needs to prevent China from determining India's trajectory.

This is the essence of strategic maturity—understanding that geopolitical victories do not always come from confrontation, but from capability. India's quiet competition—through diversified supply chains, strategic alliances, institutional strengthening, and technological sovereignty—is more powerful than any dramatic public rivalry.

And when India finally builds an architecture strong enough to stand independently, the gravitational pull weakens. That is when India stops orbiting China—and begins defining its own path in the century.

11.4 — Growth Without Mimicry: The India Model Must Be Original

Every rising nation faces a moment when imitation becomes tempting. For India, China's rise has often been that temptation—a ready-made blueprint of speed, scale, and state power. But the truth India must finally confront is this: no nation has ever risen by using another nation's operating system. China became China by refusing to mimic the West. India will become India by refusing to mimic China.

India's growth cannot come from borrowing China's architecture. India's growth must come from converting its own strengths into structural advantages.

Where China has uniformity, India has diversity—a complexity that is painful at times, but also fertile. Where China has centralized command, India has democratic dynamism—chaotic yet creative. Where China has surveillance-driven stability, India has freedom-driven innovation—messy but resilient.

India's strengths are not weaker versions of China's strengths. They are entirely different levers: democracy—imperfect, noisy, but globally trusted; demographic diversity—not a burden, but a marketplace of ideas, cultures, and skills; the services engine—flexible, adaptive, globally integrated; diaspora leverage—a silent superpower that gives India influence inside the world's most powerful institutions; English fluency—a bridge language that accelerates global integration; narrative power—a uniquely Indian ability to persuade, inspire, negotiate, and build soft alliances; cultural capital—an asset China cannot replicate.

If India strengthens its institutions, these advantages become architecture. If India fails to strengthen them, these advantages become illusions.

India must design an economic model that aligns with its own nature—not China's. A model where manufacturing is rebuilt through global partnerships, not authoritarian coordination. A model where innovation grows through freedom, not fear. A model where institutions serve as stabilizers, not obstacles. A model where the state enables ecosystems, not controls them. A model where diversity becomes a competitive advantage, not a governance headache. A model where India's cultural, economic, and democratic assets combine into a 21st-century development philosophy.

This is India's opportunity—to show the world that there is more than one way to rise. China demonstrated what alignment and acceleration can achieve in a controlled system. India can demonstrate what ambition and architecture can achieve in a free one.

China shows what is possible at scale. India must show what is possible with freedom.

That is the India model the world is waiting to see—original, confident, modern, democratic, and deeply capable. And as India steps into the next chapter of this book, that model becomes not just desirable, but necessary.

Chapter 12 — The Russian Lesson

Why India Cannot Afford the Price of Sovereignty Through Isolation

The Superpower That Ran Out of Networks

Imagine standing in Red Square on a winter morning. The Kremlin walls glow under a pale sun, St. Basil's Cathedral rises like a painting from another century, and the vast Russian landscape stretches beyond imagination—eleven time zones of raw power, natural resources, military might, and a history carved into geopolitical stone.

By every metric of the 20th century, Russia still looks like a superpower. Nuclear arsenal second to none. A battle-tested military. Oil and gas reserves that fuel continents. Cultural depth, scientific legacy, space achievements. A nation too large to be intimidated, too proud to be ignored.

And yet—beneath this grandeur—there is a quiet hollowness. A superpower with no access to advanced semiconductors. A military machine unable to replace critical components. Factories paralyzed because global supply chains stopped at its borders. Banks disconnected from the world's financial nervous system. Researchers leaving because their labs have fallen decades behind. A country that once reached for the stars now struggles to build a modern microchip.

This is not the collapse of a nation. This is the collapse of an architecture.

Russia did not fall because its geography shrank. It fell because its networks disappeared. No matter how many missiles it possessed, it could not manufacture the chips inside them. No matter how many scientists it trained, it could not retain them without global collaboration. No matter how much land it controlled, it could not rebuild supply chains alone. No matter how fiercely it asserted sovereignty, isolation stripped sovereignty away.

In the compute century, power does not come from land size, population, or even military muscle. It comes from being plugged into the world's invisible engines—chips, cloud, capital, talent, research, standards, and shared innovation.

Russia had walls. But the world had networks. And networks won.

This is the haunting lesson India must absorb: a nation can be mighty and still be fragile. A country can be sovereign and still be isolated. A superpower can run out of networks long before it runs out of weapons.

This chapter begins with the echo of Russia's miscalculation—a warning carved across the Eurasian landscape: In an interconnected world, isolation is not strength. It is suffocation.

12.1 — The Failure of Fortress Sovereignty

For decades, Russia imagined sovereignty as a fortress—massive, insulated, impenetrable. A sovereignty built on self-reliance, suspicion, and the belief that true power comes from standing alone. This worldview was shaped by history: invasions, betrayals, ideological battles, and a Cold War that taught Moscow to equate interdependence with vulnerability.

And so Russia invested in the wrong kinds of independence. It built energy sovereignty but ignored semiconductor dependence. It built military sovereignty but neglected technological ecosystems. It built geographic sovereignty but allowed its innovation networks to decay. It built propaganda sovereignty but failed to build computational capability. It built political centralization but weakened institutional collaboration.

Russia prepared for a 20th-century threat while the world moved into a 21st-century architecture. Its governance structure treated globalization as infiltration, integration as compromise, and technological interdependence as a Trojan horse. Institutions were trained to close doors instead of open them, to resist partnerships instead of cultivate them, to pursue autarky instead of architecture.

This model worked as long as power meant territory and deterrence. But then the century changed. Technology replaced ideology as the axis of power. Compute replaced land as the engine of influence. Supply chains replaced borders as the lines of control. Networks replaced armies as the primary levers of national capability.

Russia misread the moment. It assumed sovereignty was a matter of distance—from the West, from global markets, from interdependence. But sovereignty today is a matter of connectivity—to talent, to standards, to infrastructure, to global innovation flows.

By insulating itself, Russia became more vulnerable. By distrusting global systems, it weakened its own. By resisting technological interdependence, it suffocated its economy. By choosing isolation over integration, it mistook walls for strength.

The world did not need to attack Russia to weaken it. Russia weakened itself by standing alone in a century that rewards those who stand connected.

This is a lesson India cannot afford to overlook. India has its own soil of suspicion—politicians who confuse integration with dependence, bureaucrats who equate global standards with Western intrusion, ideological groups who mistake self-reliance for self-isolation. If India follows Russia's path—rejecting global networks while failing to build equally powerful alternatives—it will inherit the same fragility buried under illusions of strength.

Fortress sovereignty does not work in a world where power travels through cables, servers, standards, and supply chains. A castle is impressive until the world moves to airplanes. An army is imposing until the battlefield moves to algorithms.

Russia built fortresses. The world built networks. Networks won.

12.2 — Sanctions and the Architecture Shock: When a Nation Loses the Tools of Modern Power

When sanctions hit Russia, the world expected political tremors, diplomatic outrage, currency turbulence. What no one fully anticipated—not even Russia—was the architectural shock that followed. Overnight, a nation that looked self-reliant discovered that self-reliance in the wrong domains is an illusion.

The first blow landed in the semiconductor sector. Suddenly, Moscow could not import advanced chips—the tiny slivers of silicon that power missiles, aircraft, telecom networks, medical equipment, industrial automation, and even the tractors plowing Russian soil. Factories that once hummed with Soviet confidence were reduced to scavenging the global black market for outdated processors. Missiles were found carrying components pulled from washing machines. Drones were repaired with consumer-grade electronics.

A superpower does not collapse in theory. It collapses in supply chains.

Next came the manufacturing paralysis. Critical industries—automotive, aviation, heavy machinery—crumbled under the weight of missing parts, broken supply routes, and a lack of substitutes. Russia had steel, oil, gas, minerals. But it did not have what the 21st century requires most: precision components built through distributed global ecosystems. A nation that once built space stations could not produce modern airbags.

Then came the silent exodus. Russia's brightest scientists, engineers, and technologists—already frustrated by aging infrastructure—found themselves trapped in a country suddenly cut off from global research networks. Laboratories lacked equipment, universities lacked funding, institutions lacked purpose. And so talent flowed outward in waves, draining the country of the one resource it could not replace: intellect.

Meanwhile, financial isolation detonated beneath the economy. Removing Russia from SWIFT was not merely a banking penalty—it was a severing of the arteries connecting its economic body to global circulation. Transactions froze. Supply chains seized. Capital evaporated. Even countries sympathetic to Russia could not transact freely. The world did not need weapons to weaken Russia; it simply unplugged it from the grid.

And the harshest irony emerged: interdependence—something Russia had long feared—returned as a weapon, but now aimed against it.

The nation that rejected global integration became the nation most vulnerable to global disconnection. Not because it lacked military strength. Not because it lacked natural resources. Not because it lacked national will. But because it lacked architecture—computational, industrial, financial, and technological architecture woven into global systems.

Russia discovered too late that modern power does not live in territory or treaties. It lives in networks. And when those networks disappear, power dissolves with them.

This is the cautionary tale India must internalize: a country can survive political sanctions. It cannot survive architectural isolation in a century where chips, cloud, capital, and talent are more decisive than tanks.

Russia did not fall because the world attacked it. Russia fell because the world unplugged it—and it had built no alternative plug of its own.

12.3 — The Indian Contradiction: High Ambition, Low Connectivity Risk

India dreams of global leadership—of becoming the world's third-largest economy, a technological powerhouse, a civilizational voice, a geopolitical anchor in Asia. Yet walk through India's political discourse, bureaucratic corridors, and ideological conversations, and you will hear an echo from another century: *"Self-reliance means standing alone." "Foreign integration is dependency." "Global standards dilute national identity."*

These are not merely outdated notions. They are dangerous.

Russia has already shown the world what happens when a nation confuses sovereignty with isolation. And yet, India occasionally tiptoes toward the same trap—not out of malice, but out of misplaced pride, political posturing, and administrative inertia.

Politicians love the phrase *Atmanirbhar Bharat* but sometimes interpret it as *Bharat without the world.* They announce local manufacturing while quietly importing every crucial component. They talk of innovation ecosystems while starving universities, underfunding labs, and dragging reform through ideological mud. They speak of technological sovereignty while relying on foreign chips, foreign cloud, foreign algorithms, and foreign patents.

Bureaucrats compound the problem. Some resist global standards because they threaten existing hierarchies. Some oppose foreign collaborations out of insecurity, not strategy. Some reject world-class regulatory frameworks because adopting them requires effort, transparency, and competence—three things many institutions struggle to maintain.

Then comes the ideological ecosystem—voices that mistake openness for weakness, international alignment for surrender, global partnerships for dependency. They forget the simple truth: no nation becomes strong by closing windows. Strength comes from opening them intelligently.

India's contradiction is painful yet clear: ambition at global scale, connectivity at provincial scale.

India wants to become a semiconductor hub—while rejecting the international partnerships needed to build fabs. It wants to dominate global supply chains—while clinging to bureaucratic restrictions that repel investors. It wants AI sovereignty—while underfunding domestic compute and relying on foreign models. It wants world-class research—while refusing the global integration that feeds world-class research.

This is not sovereignty. This is self-sabotage dressed as nationalism.

Sovereignty in the compute century does not mean isolation. It means strategic entanglement—building so many diversified, resilient connections that no single partner can control you, and no single shock can break you.

Russia disconnected itself and paid the price. China connected selectively and gained strategic leverage. The U.S. connected globally and became the operating system of the world.

India must not withdraw in the name of pride. It must integrate in the name of power.

India's path to sovereignty runs through partnerships with democratic tech alliances, global supply chains, international universities, open scientific networks, cross-border capital, and global standards.

The question is not whether India should connect. The question is whether India is connecting fast enough.

Because in the compute century, isolation is not independence. Isolation is irrelevance.

12.4 — The True Lesson: Build Strength Through Networks, Not Walls

In every century, there comes a moment when the old definition of sovereignty collapses. The 20th century equated sovereignty with armies and borders. The 21st century rewrote the rules—so quietly that Russia never noticed the shift. But India must.

Real sovereignty today is not the ability to stand alone. Real sovereignty is the ability to stand connected without being controlled.

The nations that thrive now are not the ones that build walls; they are the ones that build networks—vast webs of technological partnerships, diversified supply chains, collaborative research ecosystems, and institutional bridges that turn interdependence into power.

India's path to autonomy does not lie in withdrawal. It lies in strategic integration—choosing partnerships that strengthen capability, not dilute control.

To build sovereignty, India must diversify supply chains so no single disruption cripples the economy; build semiconductor corridors with friendly nations; join global AI alliances while developing domestic compute capacity; tap into international research networks; strengthen institutions so foreign collaboration does not become foreign capture; expand the diaspora's influence in science, technology, and geopolitics; invest in domestic innovation while integrating global best practices; and build economic partnerships that increase leverage in negotiations, not dependence.

This is not dependence. This is design.

A nation becomes vulnerable when it relies on one dominant partner. A nation becomes sovereign when it relies on many—none of whom can dictate its destiny.

The paradox of the compute century is simple: you stay independent by staying connected. You stay sovereign by staying integrated. You stay powerful by staying plugged in.

India must understand this deeply—not as a policy line, but as a national philosophy.

Because the alternatives are clear. Russia tried to build walls. The walls collapsed inward. China built tightly controlled networks. The networks became armor. The United States built open global networks. The networks became dominance.

For India, the choice is not ideological. It is architectural.

Isolation is no longer a symbol of pride. Isolation is no longer a path to autonomy. Isolation is no longer survivable.

In a century where power flows not through borders but through chips, clouds, capital, and narratives, standing alone is not sovereignty—it is strategic suicide.

The true lesson of Russia is not about sanctions. It is about architecture.

A nation survives because of the bridges it builds— and collapses because of the bridges it refuses to cross.

Chapter 13 — Multialignment in the Compute Century

Foreign Policy as Architecture, Not Ideology

The Map That No Longer Matches the Territory

Picture a war room in India's foreign ministry—not the dramatic kind from old spy thrillers, but a modern command centre humming with quiet urgency. On one wall hang faded geopolitical maps, relics from a world that believed power was a question of borders, flags, alliances, and ideological camps. Lines dividing East and West. Circles marking "allies" and "adversaries." Arrows pointing toward strategic chokepoints.

But no one in the room is looking at those maps.

Instead, a small group of diplomats stands around a set of glowing digital screens displaying something far more revealing: a global semiconductor supply chain that runs through Taiwan, Japan, the Netherlands, and California; a cloud infrastructure heatmap dominated by three U.S. corporations; a flowchart of India's electronics imports, almost all of which pass through China; and an AI capability matrix showing how compute access now shapes national destiny.

On another screen, a junior officer zooms into undersea cable routes—each line representing the fragile arteries through which

India's digital economy breathes. A senior diplomat taps the map lightly and murmurs: *"If one of these lines snaps, half our foreign policy collapses."*

This is not the language of ideology. This is not the vocabulary of old diplomacy. This is the architecture of power talking.

Foreign policy has undergone a quiet revolution—so quiet that many politicians have not yet noticed. The world no longer aligns around who shares your values or who signs your treaties. It aligns around who controls your chips, your compute, your cloud, your supply chains, your narratives, your energy grids, your data routes.

The traditional map—alliances drawn in red and blue—has become irrelevant. It shows territory, but not power. It shows borders, but not influence. It shows nations, but not the architectures that bind or break them.

In this war room, no one is asking whether a country is "friend" or "foe." They're asking: Can they supply us chips? Can they give us compute? Do they own the cloud we rely on? Are they a chokepoint or a bridge? Are they a risk or resilience?

This is foreign policy in the compute century—quietly transformed, quietly ruthless.

And this is India's new strategic reality: to rise, it must navigate a world where alignment is no longer ideological but architectural. Where diplomacy is defined not by slogans, but by systems. Where partnership is measured in bandwidth, supply continuity, and access—not in speeches, summits, or sentiment.

The map of the past hangs on the wall. But the map that decides India's future is glowing on a screen. And it looks nothing like the one we grew up studying.

13.1 — The End of Old Alliances: Why Ideology No Longer Defines Friends

For most of the 20th century, the world looked like a chessboard. You were either with the United States or with the Soviet Union. You belonged to NATO or the Warsaw Pact. You were a capitalist democracy or a socialist republic. Alliances were drawn in thick ideological lines, and foreign policy was a moral theatre disguised as strategy.

That world is gone.

It did not collapse with a war. It dissolved quietly—replaced by a world governed not by ideology, but by architecture.

Today, nations do not choose partners because they share political systems or cultural histories. They choose partners based on something far more practical, far more urgent: who can give us chips, who can give us compute, who can give us cloud, who can secure our supply chains, who can co-develop technologies, who can guarantee market access, who can enhance our resilience.

If ideology mattered, Vietnam would not partner with the U.S. If ideology mattered, India and Israel would never have become strategic allies. If ideology mattered, Gulf nations would not invest in India's tech infrastructure. If ideology mattered, Japan and South Korea would not rely on each other economically while disagreeing historically.

The old world aligned around values. The new world aligns around capability.

This is why old diplomatic categories—"friend," "foe," "bloc," "camp," "axis"—feel childishly outdated. A country might buy your weapons but vote against you at the UN. A nation might criticize your politics but depend on your chips. A partner might sanction you rhetorically but integrate your supply chains privately.

The alliances of the compute century are messy, multi-layered, transactional, fluid. They shift not with ideology, but with upgrades.

India, however, carries the emotional inheritance of the Non-Aligned Movement—a Cold War posture designed for a world that no longer exists. Non-alignment was meaningful when power blocs were rigid and technology flowed slowly. But in a world of undersea cables, semiconductor bottlenecks, and AI monopolies, *non-alignment* sounds like a refusal to choose—but also a refusal to build.

India does not need non-alignment. India needs multialignment.

A foreign policy where one country provides defense tech, another provides semiconductor equipment, a third provides compute access, a fourth co-develops AI, and a fifth anchors supply chain resilience.

Partners chosen not for ideology, but for interoperability. Not for sentiment, but for strategic complementarity. Not for rhetoric, but for architecture.

This shift demands a new diplomatic instinct: agility over loyalty, capability over comfort, architecture over alliances.

India cannot afford old emotional frameworks—admiration for one superpower, suspicion of another, nostalgia for past movements. In the compute century, foreign policy is not a political poem; it is an engineering diagram.

And that diagram must place India at the center—connected, leveraged, resilient, and unbound by old loyalties.

The era of ideology is over. The era of architecture has begun.

13.2 — Architecture Diplomacy: Aligning with Many, Depending on None

Foreign policy, for most nations, is still spoken in the old language of alliances—flags, handshakes, declarations, and carefully crafted communiqués. But India cannot afford that nostalgia. The compute century has rewritten the rulebook. Today, a nation's foreign policy is not a map of friends and enemies; it is a blueprint of interdependencies. A nation does not need allies; it needs pillars that support its technological sovereignty.

This is the birth of a new paradigm: *Architecture Diplomacy.*

India must build a web of relationships where every partnership strengthens a different layer of the national architecture—semiconductors, compute, cloud, energy, manufacturing, security, innovation, research, and markets. Not because these nations share ideology, but because they each carry a capability India cannot afford to ignore.

The U.S. offers the world's deepest compute stack—chips, cloud, AI labs, venture capital, scientific networks, and defense technology. India does not need to worship America, but it must integrate where value flows—silicon, software, and science.

Japan brings precision manufacturing, semiconductor equipment, and engineering discipline—everything India lacks in its industrial DNA. Japan is a capability anchor, not a geopolitical trophy.

Taiwan represents the world's most sacred chokepoint—advanced chip manufacturing. India does not need Taiwan's politics; it needs Taiwan's process—the discipline of atomic-level engineering.

The European Union provides regulatory frameworks, green tech, data protections, advanced research clusters, and clean energy leadership. India does not need Europe's ideology; it needs Europe's institutional maturity.

Israel contributes cyber capabilities, defense innovation, agricultural technology, and startup culture forged under pressure. India does not need Israel's geopolitical worldview; it needs Israel's practical intelligence.

Southeast Asia offers supply chain diversification and strategic positioning. India's manufacturing ambitions cannot rely solely on its domestic ecosystem; ASEAN partners provide the complementary links.

Africa represents future markets, demographic partners, mineral corridors, and diplomatic alignment in global forums. India's rise cannot occur without Africa rising alongside it.

The Gulf brings energy security, sovereign capital, diaspora roots, and infrastructure partnerships. India does not need their governance model; it needs their financial and logistical ecosystems.

This is the architecture map of a rising nation—not dependent, not isolated, not loyal, not adversarial—simply strategically aligned.

India's power must come from diversification, not devotion. A diversified architecture protects India from geopolitical shocks, sanctions, supply chain disruptions, technology lock-ins, and algorithmic dependence. It creates a nation that cannot be cornered because its weight is distributed across multiple pillars.

The principle is simple: no single partner should become the oxygen line. No single adversary should become the bottleneck.

Where old diplomacy asked, *Whom do you stand with?* Architecture diplomacy asks, *What can we build together?*

Where old alliances demanded loyalty, the new architecture demands interoperability. And where old foreign policy worried about ideology, the new paradigm worries about resilience.

India does not need to choose a side. India needs to choose an architecture.

A structure supported by many, captured by none.

13.3 — The Compute Century Bargain: What India Must Offer and Demand

For decades, India approached foreign policy like a cultural exchange—warmth, symbolism, speeches, and shared photographs. But the compute century has no patience for ornamental diplomacy. It operates on a harder, colder logic: capability for capability. The nations that rise are those that negotiate technological leverage, not sentimental alignment.

India must walk into every room with a clear sense of what it offers and what it must demand—a transaction, not a tribute.

What India Offers the World

First, the world needs India more than it admits:

- **Scale**: 1.4 billion people becoming consumers, creators, innovators, and experimenters on a planetary scale. No global technology, supply chain, or digital architecture can ignore India's market gravity.
- **Talent**: A mind pipeline unmatched in depth—engineers, scientists, coders, researchers, data architects, managers—trained in adversity and capable of solving high-complexity problems under tight constraints.
- **Democracy**: The world's largest democratic environment—messy but magnetic—offering legitimacy, stability, and global trust that authoritarian competitors cannot replicate.
- **Logistics and Geography**: A location that touches every major maritime corridor, offering Asia-to-Africa and Indo-Pacific linkages that supply chains desperately need to rebalance.
- **Narrative Influence**: Indian diaspora reach, media credibility, cultural penetration, and intellectual presence give India a unique ability to shape global discourse—something China cannot buy and America cannot monopolize.

India is not a junior partner. India is a strategic amplifier.

What India Must Demand in Return

And for this amplification, India must negotiate—not request—five non-negotiables:

1. **Technology Transfer** — Not "access," not "deployment"—but co-ownership. India must insist on learning, absorbing, modifying, and building upon technologies it adopts. No more black-box solutions.
2. **Joint IP Creation** — Partnerships must result in shared intellectual property. If India contributes talent, scale, data, or infrastructure, it must own a part of the patents—not merely license them.
3. **Supply Chain Relocation** — India must demand physical anchoring of global value chains—semiconductors, electronics, battery systems, pharma, sensors, critical minerals processing—on Indian soil.
4. **Compute Access and Infrastructure Sovereignty** — India cannot be a digital colony. Cloud, compute, AI models, and semiconductor ecosystems must come with strategic autonomy layers—data residency, local control, encryption independence, and diversified architecture.
5. **Research Co-Development** — Every major partnership must include joint labs, cross-country research clusters, and integrated innovation ecosystems—where India does not merely execute but defines.

This is the compute century bargain: if the world wants India's scale, talent, and legitimacy, India must receive sovereignty-shaping capabilities in return.

The Core Insight

Multialignment is not a dance—it is a negotiation model.

India must stop playing the polite guest. India must enter the room as the future host.

Foreign policy now has an economic thesis, a technological thesis, a data thesis, and a semiconductor thesis. And India must set the price of partnership, not passively accept it.

The compute century rewards nations that bargain with clarity—and punishes those that bargain with emotions.

India's rise will not come from symbolism. It will come from systematic, capability-linked, architecture-driven negotiation.

13.4 — The Future: Power Comes from Networks, Not Camps

The Philosophical Punchline

For most of modern history, global power was arranged like seating in a classroom—two or three big groups, everyone else standing behind one of them. Nations joined camps, adopted ideologies, pledged loyalty, and lived within the boundaries of someone else's worldview. But the compute century has quietly broken all such structures. Power no longer radiates from capitals—it flows through networks.

A semiconductor treaty here, an AI alliance there, a green-tech corridor elsewhere—each forming its own gravitational field. Defense agreements operate in one orbit; data governance in another. Innovation clusters rise and fall without waiting for geopolitical consensus. And suddenly, the global order resembles not a map, but an overlay of intersecting ecosystems, each demanding capability, interoperability, and strategic clarity.

In this landscape, India cannot behave like a Cold War state choosing a camp; it must behave like a platform nation integrating multiple architectures at once.

India may work with the U.S. on defense and compute ecosystems. With Japan and Taiwan on semiconductors. With Europe on green tech and regulation. With Southeast Asia on supply chains. With Africa on markets and talent mobility. With the Middle East on energy transitions and capital flows.

There is no contradiction—only configuration.

This is the new doctrine: in a network-polar world, power comes not from who you stand behind, but from how many systems you belong to.

India's rise will depend on its ability to plug into diverse capability pools without losing its autonomy. Its strength will emerge not from isolation or allegiance, but from intelligent interdependence—choosing partnerships that enhance sovereignty rather than dilute it.

And the final insight is quietly revolutionary:

India's destiny will not be written by choosing sides, but by choosing systems. The nations that understand this will shape the century. The ones that cling to ideological camps will be left behind as architecture rewrites geopolitics.

India stands at the threshold of this shift—not as a follower, but as a potential architect.

Calm, confident, networked power is the only path forward.

Closing Reflection — Part III

Walking the Tightrope in a World Without Handrails

Part III brought us face to face with the new geometry of power—a world where strength no longer flows from ideology, military alignment, or diplomatic loyalty, but from the architectures a nation chooses to inhabit. Between the gravitational pull of the United States, the scale of China, and the cautionary tale of Russia's isolation, India is learning a truth most nations discover too late: great powers are not inherited; they are constructed.

We saw the U.S. offering acceleration—but also dependence. China offering a benchmark—but not a blueprint India can copy. Russia offering a warning—the price of sovereignty without networks.

Together, these lessons form the tightrope India walks each day. Not because India is weak, but because India is unfinished. Not because ambition is absent, but because the architecture required to stand independently in the compute century is still incomplete.

Part III closed with a fundamental recognition: India cannot rise by choosing camps. It must rise by choosing systems. By building connections that enhance sovereignty rather than erode it. By engaging with multiple networks without being captured by any single one. By redesigning foreign policy as architecture-first, ideology-last.

And now, with clarity drawn from the outside world, we turn inward—toward the most decisive section of this book.

Part IV — The India Equation: A Formula For 2035

Here, India's fate is distilled into a practical doctrine. Everything learned—about compute, architecture, geopolitics, talent, chaos, and alignment—converges into a single actionable formula:

National Power = Capability × Stability × Integration.

Not slogans. Not political messaging. A mathematically clean, strategically brutal, operationally testable doctrine for India's next decade.

Part IV is where diagnosis ends and architecture begins. Where ambition meets execution. Where India's tightrope becomes India's runway.

Now we move forward—to define the equation that will decide 2035.

Part IV — The India Equation

A Formula For 2035

"Nations do not rise through hope or heritage. They rise when capability meets stability and connects to the right networks."

Overview

Part IV distills the entire narrative of this book into a single doctrine: **National Power = Capability × Stability × Integration.** This section transforms the insights of Parts I, II, and III into a practical operating system for India's ascent. We move from diagnosis to design—laying out the pillars India must strengthen, the chaos it must resolve, and the networks it must embed into to secure sovereignty in the compute century. Each chapter becomes a blueprint: capability through compute and talent; stability through social and institutional equilibrium; integration through strategic multialignment. This is not theory—it is India's survival architecture for the decade that will define its next hundred years.

Here, India confronts the formula that will decide whether 2035 becomes its breakthrough—or its breaking point.

Chapter 14 — The Core Doctrine

National Power = Capability × Stability × Integration

The Equation Hidden in Plain Sight

New Delhi, late evening. A storm gathers outside, scattering dust across Rajpath, but inside the high-security conference room the air is still—thick not with silence, but with competing truths. Around a long polished table sit the familiar faces of India's national deliberations: a finance minister defending GDP projections like a courtroom argument, a general outlining troop readiness with disciplined confidence, an economist presenting decade-long growth curves, a technology advisor racing through slides on AI adoption, a diplomat mapping alignments across continents, and a chief secretary lamenting state-level bottlenecks.

Everyone talks. Everyone argues. Everyone believes their domain is the domain. GDP must rise. Defense budgets must expand. Trade deals must intensify. Startups must scale. Manufacturing must accelerate. It is the familiar orchestra of Indian ambition—loud, passionate, ceaseless. Yet beneath the noise lies the quiet flaw: every conversation happens in isolation. The ministers chase growth. The generals chase strength. The diplomats chase partnerships. The technocrats chase innovation. The bureaucrats chase survival. Each speaks their own language, pushing their own metric, their own agenda. And still, not one person in the room sees the invisible architecture binding all their efforts together.

If a camera were to slowly zoom out from this spirited meeting—rising above the table, above the ministries, above the city itself—one truth would become clear: India's rise is not determined by any single pillar. It is determined by the equation that multiplies them. National Power equals Capability multiplied by Stability multiplied by Integration. A doctrine hidden in plain sight. A formula no one says aloud, yet every failure India experiences traces back to one missing variable.

A nation may have high capability but low stability, and collapse under its own friction. It may have high stability but low capability, and drift into irrelevance. It may possess both capability and stability but lack integration, and find itself vulnerable, dependent, sidelined. And so, in that Delhi meeting room—filled with energy, talent, and intent—the real question remains unasked: are India's variables aligned, or is the equation already breaking?

Outside, thunder cracks across the sky. Inside, the conversation moves on—still loud, still confident, still fragmented. No one realizes that nations do not rise by winning individual debates. They rise when capability, stability, and integration align like gears—each amplifying the other, each multiplying the nation's power. One weak gear, and the entire machine stalls.

The equation was always there. India simply never learned to read it.

14.1 — Why the Old Measures of Power No Longer Work

For most of modern history, nations measured power the way accountants measure balance sheets—through large, visible, comforting numbers. GDP tallies, army headcounts, population charts, square kilometres of land, steel output, foreign reserves. These metrics created the illusion that nations could be weighed like cargo: the bigger the number, the stronger the state. India embraced these yardsticks with confidence, repeating them like mantras—fifth-largest economy, fourth-strongest military, biggest democracy, youngest population, vast geography. On paper, the story sparkled. But the compute century quietly rewrote the physics of power while the world clung to its old equations.

Today, power no longer flows through sheer size; it flows through invisible architectures—semiconductor supply chains, cloud dependencies, algorithmic ecosystems, institutional coherence, research depth, execution capability. The nations that dominate the 21st century are not the biggest, but the most networked, the most technologically sovereign, the most institutionally aligned. A small island like Taiwan wields global influence because it produces the chips the world breathes through. Israel punches above its weight because it builds frontier innovation ecosystems no one else can replicate. South Korea shapes global markets through supply chains, standards, and manufacturing precision. None of these countries owe their power to population or geography—they owe it to capability multiplied by stability multiplied by integration.

Meanwhile, nations with enormous GDPs but fragile technological sovereignty find themselves cornered. Many G20 economies—comfortable in their size—woke up to the startling truth that they do not control the chips inside their machines, the cloud where their data sleeps, the AI models shaping their markets, or the supply chains feeding their industries. Their GDPs glow impressively on charts, but their strategic leverage dims in every negotiation. Their money is large; their autonomy is small.

India, too, has been seduced by these old metrics. GDP growth becomes a festival, military parades a spectacle, population numbers a badge of demographic pride. Yet these metrics hide more than they reveal. A large military cannot compensate for dependence on foreign chips. A booming GDP cannot offset weak institutional capacity. A young population becomes a burden if talent leaks at every stage. A vast geography offers no advantage if supply chains bypass it. The country celebrates its quantity while ignoring its quality, proudly measuring itself with tools that belonged to another era—and another world.

What India has not yet confronted is the uncomfortable truth that the world no longer rewards size; it rewards architecture. Nations rise today because they sit on top of strategic technologies, not mountains. They command supply chains, not slogans. They operate resilient institutions, not emotional narratives. They integrate into multi-layered global networks that amplify their internal strengths and shield their weaknesses.

This is the drama of the compute century: the small can become mighty, and the mighty can become irrelevant—depending on what sits beneath their numbers.

India's tragedy is not that it lacks capability. It is that it measures its rise with yardsticks that no longer matter. The world has moved on to a new equation of power, but India is still solving the wrong problem. And unless it rewrites its metrics, it may never rewrite its destiny.

14.2 — Variable One: Capability — The Engine of Real Power

Capability is the most misunderstood word in India's national vocabulary. Too often it is mistaken for talent, or intent, or ambition—three things India has in abundance. But capability is none of these. Capability is architecture. It is the cold, structural, unforgiving backbone of national power: the compute a nation controls, the chips it can design, the algorithms it can produce, the factories it can operate, the research it can translate into technology, the institutions that can scale execution without collapsing under their own weight. Capability is not what a nation dreams of becoming; it is what a nation can reliably do, repeatedly, at scale, under pressure.

In the compute century, capability begins with semiconductors—the new oxygen of civilization. A country that cannot access or produce advanced chips does not control its own destiny. Chips sit beneath every weapon system, every digital service, every industrial machine, every power grid, every critical infrastructure. They are the base layer of sovereignty. Without semiconductor depth, nations remain customers in a world where only creators hold leverage. India talks about chips with the enthusiasm of a child discussing rockets, but its manufacturing ecosystem remains skeletal. Ambition is loud; capability is quiet, patient, and slow to build—and India has not yet paid the price required to catch up.

Next comes AI and algorithmic independence—the new language of power. Nations that build frontier models shape global narratives, economic flows, defense strategies, industrial productivity, and cultural influence. Generative AI is not a tool; it is infrastructure. Yet India consumes more AI than it creates, relying on foreign models for everything from healthcare analytics to linguistic processing. In the hierarchy of capability, consumers sit at the bottom, shapers in the middle, creators at the top. India remains somewhere in the middle—talented enough to contribute, but not independent enough to lead.

Manufacturing depth is another pillar India glorifies in slogans but struggles with in reality. Without strong supply chains, precision engineering, and process discipline, a nation cannot compete in semiconductors, aerospace, batteries, robotics, green technologies, or advanced electronics. Capability demands factories that produce at scale, consistently, without political drama or bureaucratic drag.

Yet India's manufacturing ecosystem still fights internal battles: land delays, power inconsistency, regulatory confusion, corruption in procurement, and a culture that glorifies *jugaad* while the world demands reliability.

Talent is the one resource India proudly exports, but capability is not built by exporting talent—it is built by retaining it. Every leak in the pipeline—students suffocated by outdated education models, researchers blocked by funding deserts, engineers trapped in repetitive service-sector jobs—reduces national power. Capability requires talent embedded in institutions that empower it, not dispersed across the world solving other nations' problems.

Execution ability is the next, often invisible, pillar. Nations succeed not because they announce big ideas, but because they convert those ideas into outcomes systematically. For this, India's institutions are too fragmented, too politicized, too fatigued. Ministries operate in silos, states sabotage each other's priorities, bureaucracies prioritize procedure over progress, and reforms die in the trenches long before they reach the street. Capability collapses without execution.

Research ecosystems complete the picture. A nation rises when its universities, labs, startups, and industries operate in a single continuous innovation loop. India's loop is broken into disconnected islands—brilliant researchers with no industry partners, startups building products without scientific depth, ministries funding research without understanding the frontier. Capability requires integration; India offers fragmentation.

The brutal truth is this: India has infinite potential but limited capability. Potential is emotion. Capability is physics.

Capability is the only variable that can accelerate India's rise exponentially—because capability compounds. One breakthrough strengthens five industries. One strong institution unlocks ten reforms. One retained genius influences a generation. Capability is not additive; it is multiplicative.

Until India stops mistaking ambition for capability, it will continue building castles in the air—beautiful, inspiring, but structurally unsupported. And in the compute century, unsupported structures collapse faster than ever.

14.3 — Variable Two: Stability — The Multiplier the World Underestimates

If capability is the engine of national power, stability is the multiplier that determines whether that engine ever leaves the ground. Nations do not rise simply because they have talent, technology, or institutions. They rise because those assets operate inside a predictable, coherent, and calm environment where progress compounds instead of constantly resetting. Stability is not glamorous—it does not cut ribbons, trend on social media, or make speeches go viral. Yet in the long run, stability decides whether capability becomes power or collapses into noise.

Stability begins with social harmony, the most undervalued form of national capital. A society fractured along religious, linguistic, caste, or ideological lines wastes its cognitive energy on internal battles rather than national acceleration. When communities distrust each other, innovation slows, investment hesitates, and institutions bend under political pressure. Harmony is not the absence of disagreement; it is the presence of a shared commitment to progress over polarization. In India, this commitment routinely loses to theatrics—fueled by political incentives that reward division over development.

Political maturity follows, a quality nations rarely appreciate until they lack it. Political maturity means governments that think beyond elections, opposition that constructs rather than obstructs, and parties that refuse to burn institutions for short-term gains.

India's political landscape, however, often resembles a marketplace of outrage. Ministers fight on television instead of in boardrooms, parties treat policymaking as combat, and national priorities are rewritten every five years to suit new slogans. Capability suffocates in such volatility.

Economic predictability is another silent pillar. Investors, entrepreneurs, researchers, and global collaborators do not demand perfection; they demand consistency. They need to know that tax regimes will not flip overnight, that reforms will not be reversed arbitrarily, that contracts will be honoured regardless of who wins elections. Yet India's economic environment often oscillates between enthusiasm and uncertainty. Sudden bans, unpredictable regulations, bureaucratic overreach, and politically motivated interventions create fear disguised as caution. Even capability cannot survive long in soil that keeps shifting.

Regulatory consistency is the compass of national strategy. Regulations are meant to create clarity, not confusion. But India's system often delivers the opposite—rules that contradict each other, departments that overlap like competing kingdoms, approvals that depend more on relationships than merit. Regulations change faster than institutions can adjust, leading to paralysis on the ground. Entrepreneurs waste years deciphering what the government wants—because the government itself often does not know. In such an environment, capability becomes costlier to build, harder to scale, and easier to abandon.

Institutional continuity is another cornerstone. Strong nations preserve their institutions across political cycles, shielding regulators, universities, courts, scientific bodies, and civil services from ideological capture. India, however, treats institutions like personal property—reshaping, re-staffing, and weaponizing them at the convenience of whichever group sits in power. Every political cycle becomes a reset; every reset becomes a delay; and every delay becomes a drag on the nation's trajectory. Capability requires decades of uninterrupted growth, yet India often struggles to maintain stability for even five years at a stretch.

And finally, there is internal chaos—the everyday turbulence India has normalized. Bureaucratic delays treated as tradition. Corruption disguised as culture. Policy U-turns justified as flexibility. Social-media tribalism distracting the public from real national challenges. A political class more committed to optics than outcomes. A media environment addicted to adrenaline rather than analysis. Each fracture acts like sand poured into a machine—grain by grain, slowing every moving part until the engine stalls.

This is the hidden tax India pays daily: chaos consumes capability faster than capability can compensate for chaos.

Stability is the multiplier India rarely acknowledges because it is not visible, not glamorous, not ideological. But it is essential. Without stability, the best talent leaves, the best investors hesitate, the best institutions tire, and the best plans fail long before execution. Stability is what allows nations to think beyond the moment, beyond the crisis, beyond the noise.

The compute century does not reward nations that shout the loudest. It rewards nations that hold steady while others lose balance.

And until India learns to silence its own chaos, its capability—no matter how impressive—will remain forever discounted.

14.4 — Variable Three: Integration — The New Source of Sovereignty

For most of the 20th century, integration was treated as a matter of ideology—aligned with the West, aligned with the Soviets, aligned with the Non-Aligned Movement, aligned with some imagined moral middle path. But in the compute century, integration is no longer ideological. It is architectural. It is the quiet, structural process of embedding a nation into the world's most strategic networks—supply chains, semiconductor pathways, cloud ecosystems, research corridors, financial rails, and trade webs that determine how fast a country grows and how well it survives shocks. Integration is not a diplomatic choice; it is a technological requirement.

Supply chain alignment is the first artery of modern power. Nations that sit inside global supply chains do not merely receive economic benefits; they inherit stability, bargaining leverage, and resilience. When factories plug into global manufacturing loops, when ports anchor global logistics, when industries are woven into regional production ecosystems, national destiny becomes linked to shared prosperity rather than isolated struggle. India's problem is not ambition—it has plenty—but internal chaos, regulatory unpredictability, and infrastructural gaps that keep pushing it to the margins. Nations outside supply chains do not shape the future; they wait for it.

Compute partnerships are the new diplomatic agreements of the century. Cloud collaboration, AI model access, shared compute clusters, sovereign cloud frameworks, quantum alliances—these are not optional friendships; they are lifelines. A nation cut off from compute today is like a nation cut off from oil in 1973: powerless, breathless, dependent. Integration ensures India does not remain a customer at the mercy of global tech empires but becomes a co-author of platforms that define humanity's next leap.

Semiconductor access is the new passport to sovereignty. No nation builds every chip it needs; even the most advanced economies rely on cross-border ecosystems. But nations must be integrated enough to ensure priority access, shared production, diversified sourcing, and strategic reserves. Semiconductors are not a product; they are a geopolitical stabilizer. The countries closest to the semiconductor web—politically, economically, diplomatically—will possess leverage disproportionate to their size. India cannot reach its 2035 ambitions if it stays at the periphery.

Cloud interoperability follows naturally—the ability of India's public and private systems to operate securely across global providers without being locked into any single one. Independence does not mean isolation; it means flexibility. The nations that thrive will be those whose digital infrastructures can move, adapt, negotiate, and shift without breaking. India must craft its own sovereign cloud while maintaining deep interoperability with global platforms—a delicate equilibrium, but a necessary one.

Research corridors are the invisible highways of innovation. Nations that link their universities, labs, startups, and industries into global research networks multiply their intellectual capital. Breakthroughs come not from isolation but from collisions—Indian mathematicians collaborating with American physicists, Indian AI researchers working with Japanese hardware labs, Indian biotech startups partnering with European regulatory bodies. Integration accelerates discovery; isolation delays it by decades.

Export networks and diplomatic agility complete the picture. Nations with diverse export routes survive economic shocks with grace. Nations with agile diplomacy navigate conflicts without becoming collateral damage. Integration means India can sell to many, buy from many, negotiate with many, and depend on none. It means India can withstand U.S.–China tensions, supply chain disruptions, financial instability, and geopolitical crises—because it is anchored in multiple networks rather than trapped in a single orbit.

Here lies the philosophical truth: sovereignty no longer comes from standing alone. It comes from standing at many intersections simultaneously. Integration is not dependence. Dependence is leaning on one pillar. Integration is balancing across many pillars so no single one can break you.

The nations that integrate intelligently accelerate. The nations that integrate blindly become dependent. The nations that avoid integration altogether collapse into irrelevance.

For India, the challenge is not whether to integrate—but how. How to join the world's most strategic networks without surrendering autonomy. How to build deep partnerships without becoming a client state. How to embed in the global architecture while building its own parallel backbone.

Done well, integration becomes India's shield and engine. Done poorly, it becomes India's new cage.

And that is why, in the equation of national power, integration is not an accessory. It is the third force that transforms capability and stability from potential into power.

14.5 — The Equation in Action: Why Multiplication, Not Addition

Every nation believes its strengths will save it. Every government clings to the idea that one strong pillar—military force, economic growth, political stability, population size—can compensate for its weaknesses. But the compute century has exposed this myth brutally. Power today is not additive; it is multiplicative. A nation is only as strong as its weakest structural variable. And when one variable collapses, the entire equation collapses with it.

This is why Capability × Stability × Integration is not just a doctrine—it is a diagnostic lens, a forecasting tool, a survival mechanism. Multiplication forces honesty. It does not allow a country to hide behind one oversized strength while ignoring foundational weaknesses. It holds a mirror without mercy.

Consider the first failure mode: high capability multiplied by low stability equals collapse. A country may have factories, compute, research depth, and military power—but if its institutions fracture, its politics polarize, its society burns, or its leadership becomes erratic, capability becomes irrelevant. History is full of nations that fell not because they lacked strength, but because they lacked stability. The Soviet Union had nuclear weapons, scientific brilliance, and global influence—but it imploded from internal cracks. Iran has immense talent and intellectual depth—but instability and ideological rigidity suffocate its potential. Even today, several resource-rich nations sit in economic stagnation because their societies remain divided and their institutions compromised.

Then comes the inverse: high stability multiplied by low capability equals stagnation. Nations like this do not collapse; they simply stop rising. Their societies are orderly, their politics predictable, their institutions functioning—but their engines have no horsepower. Much of Europe falls into this category today. Stable, comfortable, civilized—yet unable to compete in semiconductors, AI, energy independence, or industrial growth. They rely on American security, Asian manufacturing, Middle Eastern energy, and global talent. Stability keeps them afloat, but lack of capability keeps them from leading. They are spectators in a century that demands builders.

And then there is the quiet third failure mode: capability and stability without integration equals vulnerability. This is Russia's story. A nation with scientific pedigree, military depth, cultural coherence, and enormous natural resources—but cut off from global networks. A country that believed sovereignty meant self-reliance, not realizing that in the compute century, isolation decays capability faster than incompetence. When sanctions hit, Russia discovered how much of its power was illusion: no chips, no supply chains, no financial rails, no innovation partners, no semiconductor access. Capability without integration is sand without cement—impressive until touched.

Contrast these failures with the nations that mastered the equation. China's rise is the result of extraordinary capability scaled through stability and reinforced by selective integration. A disciplined state, predictable institutions, world-class execution machinery, and relentless focus on manufacturing and semiconductors created capability. Social and political control created stability. Strategic ties with global supply chains created integration. China multiplied its variables—and the result was historic acceleration.

America's persistent dominance comes from a different formula: its capability is unmatched, its institutional stability—despite political noise—remains structurally strong, and its integration with global networks is unparalleled. The U.S. does not just join networks; it builds and owns them—cloud, chips, AI, academic corridors, financial rails, cultural ecosystems. Even when one variable weakens, the other two remain strong enough to sustain global leadership. America is not the most stable, nor the most disciplined—but it remains the most integrated and most capable. The equation holds.

And then there is India—the paradox. A nation with immense potential, uneven capability, fragile stability, and selective integration. India grows fast but executes slowly. Innovates brilliantly but inconsistently. Attracts talent but also loses it. Speaks like a rising power but thinks like a developing one. Its equation swings between moments of brilliance and moments of breakdown. One variable strengthens; another collapses. India has never multiplied its strengths; it has merely added them—and addition cannot build a superpower.

This is the philosophical punchline of the doctrine: multiplication does not forgive weakness. It exposes it.

If India strengthens all three variables simultaneously capability, stability, and integration—then 2035 becomes not just a milestone, but a launch window, a rare convergence of demographic, technological, and geopolitical momentum. But if even one variable remains weak, then 2035 becomes the year India misses the last train—a decade remembered not for what it achieved, but for what it almost achieved.

Nations rise by mastering equations. And India's equation is now on the table.

Chapter 15 — The Building Blocks of Modern Sovereignty

Capability: Compute, Talent, and Industry

The Nation That Aspires to Run a Marathon With Weak Muscles

Imagine India standing at the starting line of the greatest marathon in human history—the global race for AI supremacy, semiconductor independence, manufacturing competitiveness, scientific breakthroughs, and institutional excellence. The stadium is enormous, the crowd restless, the stakes colossal. On the track beside India stand the world's most prepared athletes: nations with deep compute infrastructure, disciplined manufacturing ecosystems, elite research institutions, and talent pipelines that retain their finest minds instead of exporting them. They have trained for decades in silence, building muscle fiber by fiber, system by system.

India, meanwhile, arrives with extraordinary enthusiasm—heart swelling with ambition, lungs full of hope, and the loudest cheering squad in the world. The spirit is undeniable. The intent is sincere. The potential breathtaking. But when the warm-up begins, a quiet discomfort fills the air. The nation stretches, flexes, tests its limbs—and discovers what it had refused to acknowledge for years. Its muscles are not ready.

The compute muscle is thin, overworked, and dependent on borrowed strength. The talent muscle is powerful at birth but weakens through neglect, outdated training, and continuous leakage. The industrial muscle is enthusiastic but inconsistent—capable of brilliance on some days and basic errors on others. The research muscle, once promising, has grown stiff under layers of bureaucracy, underfunding, and political interference. And yet, India still believes it can outrun competitors who have trained harder, smarter, and longer.

It is a painful scene: a nation that wants to sprint in a century that demands marathon discipline; a nation with grand ambition but an inadequate training regimen; a nation convinced that passion can compensate for preparation. India has the heart of a champion but the infrastructure of an amateur athlete still learning how to breathe correctly.

The starter's pistol has not yet fired, but the world is already moving. AI revolutions gain momentum. Semiconductor chains reorganize. Manufacturing standards rise. Research ecosystems deepen. Nations upgrade their capability muscle groups every quarter, every year, every decade. Meanwhile, India keeps jogging in place—awkwardly, proudly, loudly—telling itself the race is long, the competition beatable, the future inevitable.

But marathons do not honor sentiment; they honor strength. They reward endurance, not excuses. They elevate discipline, not declarations. The truth is uncomfortable but unavoidable: India wants the medal before it has built the muscle. It wants sovereignty without capability, influence without infrastructure, leadership without preparation. The spirit is inspiring—but spirit alone does not win the marathon of nations.

And so the hook lands with quiet force: before India imagines victory, it must rebuild its body. Before it dreams of 2035, it must strengthen every muscle that carries the weight of capability. The world will not slow down. India must speed up—and train like it has never trained before.

15.1 — Compute: The First Pillar of Sovereignty

In the 20th century, nations fought over oil. In the 21st, they fight over compute—the silent, invisible fuel powering every system that defines modern civilization. Compute is no longer a technical asset; it is the first pillar of sovereignty. It determines whether a nation merely participates in the global economy or shapes it. It decides whether a military can defend its borders or becomes dependent on foreign algorithms. It governs whether industries can innovate or are forced to import intelligence. Compute is not the future—it is the foundation.

To grasp its gravity, imagine turning off India's compute supply overnight. Hospitals collapse as diagnostic AI freezes. Banks halt transactions. Flights stall mid-systems. Logistics grids drift into chaos. Research labs go silent. Military command networks lose real-time analytics. Factories stop optimizing. Even WhatsApp forwards—the unofficial national communication network—go quiet. The country does not slow down; it stops.

This is why domestic compute capacity is no longer optional. Nations that rely on external hyperscalers for the majority of their critical workloads surrender a piece of their sovereignty every day. Not because foreign companies are malicious, but because the infrastructure that powers national life is not under national control. India talks proudly of digital public goods, of UPI as a revolutionary model, of Aadhaar as a transformational platform—but even these systems ultimately sit atop compute layers India does not fully own. Sovereignty cannot exist atop borrowed machinery.

Cloud without sovereignty is dependence. Cloud is not just storage and servers; it is the backbone of national intelligence. Whoever controls your cloud pathways controls your digital nervous system. Today, the majority of India's commercial cloud workloads run on American platforms. Government workloads are slowly shifting to "sovereign cloud" models, but the transition is incomplete, underfunded, and politically fragile. Data localization without compute localization is a half-measure—a nation insisting its valuables stay inside the house while the keys to the house remain with someone else.

At the heart of compute sovereignty lie semiconductors. Chips are not components; they are the architecture of power. Without advanced semiconductors, no nation can build smart weapons, secure communication networks, competitive industries, autonomous systems, advanced robotics, or frontier AI. Every missile, every drone, every data center, every electric vehicle, every piece of modern medical equipment—every one of them runs on chips India does not produce, cannot produce, and will not produce at scale for years unless it accelerates faster than ever before. A country without semiconductor access is a country negotiating its sovereignty at the mercy of others.

AI capability follows naturally—and the compute that fuels it. Nations love to speak of AI as innovation, but in truth, AI is infrastructure. It requires not just algorithms but massive compute clusters, GPU farms, high-bandwidth data systems, low-latency networks, and long-term investment in model training. Without domestic compute, a country becomes an AI consumer—dependent on foreign models that shape its markets, its narratives, its governance, its risks. India's AI ambitions will remain PowerPoint presentations until its compute architecture catches up.

The diagnosis is uncomfortable but unavoidable: India's compute ecosystem is fragmented, imported, underfunded, and strategically exposed. Fragmented, because ministries, states, industries, and defense bodies operate compute infrastructure with no unified strategy. Imported, because nearly every layer of hardware, GPU, cloud stack, or chip architecture is foreign. Underfunded, because India spends less on compute infrastructure than what private companies in the U.S. spend in a single quarter. Exposed, because geopolitical pressure, sanctions, export controls, or corporate policies can disrupt entire sectors overnight.

India cannot become a global power while renting the machinery of modern power. Compute is not a product; it is a multiplier. It does not add strength; it unlocks it. It does not follow sovereignty; it precedes it. A nation rises when it controls the energy source of its era. Coal powered empires. Oil powered superpowers. Compute will power civilizations.

And India—ambitious, talented, spirited India—is standing at the gates of a compute century with a toolbox borrowed from others. If India wants to shape 2035 instead of chasing it, the first step is brutally simple: build compute, own compute, protect compute. Because without compute, capability is illusion. And with compute, capability becomes inevitable.

15.2 — Talent: The Pipeline That Leaks at Every Stage

If compute is the machinery of capability, talent is the organism that animates it. Nations do not rise on infrastructure alone—they rise on the people who imagine, build, maintain, reform, and reinvent that infrastructure. Scientists, engineers, mathematicians, coders, researchers, administrators, policy designers, managers, entrepreneurs, and thinkers form the neural network of national capability. But India's neural network, brilliant as it is at the level of the individual, begins to break at the level of the system. Talent is India's greatest gift—and its most underestimated tragedy.

The pipeline begins in early schooling, where creativity and curiosity should ignite but too often suffocate. Children enter classrooms brimming with imagination, only to be handed outdated textbooks, rigid syllabi, and an exam culture that measures memory over mastery. A system designed for the industrial age still governs a nation aspiring to lead the digital age. Teachers who want to innovate are constrained by bureaucracy, curriculum boards that move slower than technology cycles, and an obsession with marks that crushes exploration. India produces brilliant young minds not because of its schooling system, but in spite of it.

Those who survive the first leak enter universities, where the second leak widens. India's higher education system has pockets of excellence but a landscape of mediocrity. Universities that should be incubators of breakthrough research become exam factories. Labs lack funding. Professorships are plagued by shortages, outdated pedagogy, and political appointments. Bureaucratic procedures suffocate academic freedom; committees replace creativity; hierarchy overshadows merit. Many students still dream of contributing to India's progress, but the system quietly signals that their best chance lies elsewhere.

The third leak occurs when talent enters industry. India's corporate ecosystem, especially in IT and services, is structured around consumption, not creation. Fresh engineers are absorbed into repetitive workflows, low-complexity outsourcing, template-driven tasks, and managerial pyramids where loyalty outranks leadership. The brightest minds write someone else's code, maintain someone else's product, execute someone else's strategy. Startups, though vibrant, often burn talent through chaos, poor mentorship, and unrealistic growth expectations. Manufacturing units, constrained by cost pressures and outdated machinery, rarely offer environments where engineering brilliance can flourish. The result is a slow-burning frustration—a sense of genius underutilized, effort undervalued, creativity unrecognized.

Then comes the bureaucracy, the fourth leak. India's administrative system, while filled with intelligent individuals, is architecturally hostile to talent. Promotions reward compliance over innovation. Transfers punish originality. Files move slower than ideas. Ministries operate in parallel universes that seldom converge. Young officers enter with optimism and leave with exhaustion. Researchers hoping to influence policy encounter paperwork thicker than their proposals. Scientists in government labs navigate politics more than physics. The system does not merely waste talent—it absorbs it into a cycle of fatigue.

And finally, the most painful leak of all: the global absorption of Indian talent. The world recognises what India fails to retain. Foreign universities eagerly welcome Indian students for their discipline and brilliance. Global corporations recruit Indian engineers to build world-class products. Research labs abroad offer autonomy Indian institutions struggle to provide. Nations from the U.S. to Australia to Germany design immigration pathways specifically to capture Indian minds. Every year, India exports more capability than it can ever import back. Talent does not migrate because it lacks patriotism; it migrates because it lacks ecosystems.

This is the silent tragedy of the Indian rise narrative: India creates more genius per square kilometre than almost any nation on Earth, but it converts only a fraction into national power. A nation cannot become powerful on borrowed muscles. A civilization cannot outsource its imagination. A rising power cannot depend on talent trained at home and harvested abroad.

The global race for capability is not a fight between nations—it is a fight between ecosystems. And India's ecosystem leaks at every stage: childhood, adolescence, university, early career, mid-career, and institutional leadership. The brightest minds leave, and those who stay spend half their lives navigating friction instead of producing breakthroughs.

Talent is not India's weakness; it is India's squandered strength. Capability will not rise until talent stops escaping. And talent will not stay until systems learn to breathe with the minds they hold.

If India wants to claim 2035, it must fix the leaks—every single one of them. Because no nation becomes a superpower by gifting its genius to the world.

15.3 — Industry: From Jugaad to Precision

For years, India has comforted itself with a powerful myth—that it is a manufacturing giant in waiting, a nation destined to become the world's factory simply because it has youth, ambition, and a legendary culture of *jugaad*. But the global industrial landscape has no sentimental attachment to slogans. It rewards precision, not improvisation. Discipline, not enthusiasm. Reliability, not rhetoric. And it is here, in the transition from aspiration to architecture, that India's manufacturing story begins to fracture.

Supply chain discipline is the backbone of modern industry. Manufacturing superpowers function like orchestras—every supplier, transporter, warehouse, port, and quality control unit operating in synchronized rhythm. But India's supply chains often resemble traffic jams—chaotic, fragmented, unpredictable. Lead times fluctuate wildly. Vendor quality varies erratically. Coordination between states is inconsistent. One disrupted highway, one bureaucratic delay, one local political issue, and the entire chain collapses. *Jugaad* may rescue a crisis, but it cannot anchor a factory.

Infrastructure compounds the problem. Manufacturing does not thrive on passion; it thrives on power availability, water reliability, high-speed logistics, and urban planning. Despite improvements, India still battles frequent power fluctuations, congested freight corridors, underdeveloped industrial clusters, and ports that struggle with turnaround times. In the compute century, where milliseconds matter, India still negotiates hours. Investors see potential; their CFOs see unpredictability.

Logistics costs further weaken competitiveness. Moving goods across India often costs more than moving them across continents. Poor multimodal integration, overloaded highways, rail bottlenecks, and regulatory stoppages inflate costs. Manufacturing cannot scale if each truckload must overcome geography, bureaucracy, and inefficiency. China moves containers like clockwork; India moves them like court cases—eventually, but after unnecessary drama.

The regulatory environment remains a labyrinth. Rules vary between states, interpretations differ between officers, and approvals depend too often on personal relationships rather than transparent processes. Policies shift with political winds; incentives appear and vanish; labor laws conflict; land acquisition becomes a saga. Factories operate not just with operating manuals but legal survival kits. The world does not invest where clarity is absent—and India still confuses announcements with implementation.

Then comes the painful truth: the shortage of high-quality factories. Not assembly lines—factories. Factories with precision tooling, automation, global-standard quality control, and disciplined process engineering. India has islands of excellence—automotive clusters in Tamil Nadu, pharma hubs in Telangana, electronics pockets in Karnataka and Noida—but lacks wide industrial depth. Too many units operate with outdated machinery, inadequate testing labs, minimal safety protocols, and inconsistent output quality. Global companies cannot integrate Indian factories into their premium supply chains if quality varies batch to batch.

Beneath all this lies a deeper structural flaw: weak innovation-to-industry pathways. India's researchers innovate in silos, startups experiment in isolation, and industries manufacture without scientific feedback loops. Patents rarely become products.

Products rarely scale into industries. Industries rarely invest in frontier research. There is no conveyor belt connecting idea to prototype, prototype to manufacturing, manufacturing to export. Nations that dominate manufacturing—Germany, Japan, South Korea, China—built this conveyor belt deliberately over decades. India still relies on *jugaad*: intellectual improvisation in the absence of structured architecture.

This is where the romance of "Make in India" collapses against the reality of industrial ecosystems. Manufacturing is not a patriotic act; it is a precision discipline. It requires predictability, quality, consistency, scale, and a cultural respect for process. *Jugaad* may be charming; it may solve problems creatively—but the world's factories do not run on creative fixes. They run on calibrated systems.

India must confront the uncomfortable truth: it cannot manufacture like China, Germany, or South Korea by wishing itself into their league. It must transform its habits, its mindsets, its institutions, and its infrastructure. The global supply chain does not reward potential; it rewards performance. It does not reward passion; it rewards precision. It does not reward slogans; it rewards systems.

Until India transitions from *jugaad* to discipline—from improvisation to process, from ambition to architecture—it will remain a spectator in the industrial race it desperately wants to win.

The world is ready to give India a manufacturing role. The question is whether India is ready to give itself the manufacturing ecosystem it deserves.

15.4 — Research & Innovation: The Missing Bridge Between Ideas and Outcomes

India has never lacked intelligent individuals. What it has lacked are intelligent systems—ecosystems capable of taking a brilliant idea, nurturing it, protecting it, funding it, testing it, scaling it, and converting it into national capability. For decades, India's research landscape has resembled a constellation of bright stars—isolated, scattered, shining alone—but never forming a galaxy. And without a galaxy, there is no gravitational force strong enough to build industries, transform economies, or shift global power equations.

The first fracture lies in research funding, chronically low, inconsistent, and bureaucratically suffocated. Proposals navigate endless layers of committees, forms, permissions, audits, and approvals—by the time funding arrives, the idea has aged, the global frontier has moved, and the researcher has lost momentum or motivation. Labs operate with outdated equipment. Projects are evaluated not by scientific merit but by administrative comfort. Young scientists spend more time justifying expenses than generating discoveries. A nation cannot innovate when its brightest minds are trapped in paperwork.

The second fracture is the fragmented innovation ecosystem. India loves talking about startups, incubators, unicorns, and entrepreneurship, but these sit disconnected from research institutions, manufacturing clusters, and long-term industrial strategy. Startups reinvent what research labs have already discovered because there is no bridge connecting them. Universities conduct research that industries never use because there is no pipeline to transfer it. Ministries launch isolated schemes—each impressive on its own, yet meaningless without integration. The ecosystem is vibrant at the edges but hollow at the center.

This fragmentation deepens with the chronic disconnection between academia and industry. In powerful nations, universities and industries operate as a single breathing organism—research informs production, production funds research, and the cycle repeats. In India, universities speak the language of conferences while industries speak the language of quarterly targets. Collaboration is rare, transactional, or superficial. Professors hesitate to enter industry because incentives are misaligned; companies hesitate to fund research because timelines are long and outcomes unpredictable. As a result, India imports technology that its own scientists could have developed—if only the bridge existed.

Intellectual property generation remains another weak link. Not because India lacks ideas, but because it lacks systems that convert ideas into protected patents, commercial products, and global standards. Patents filed are often defensive, not pioneering. Many scientists do not receive support for filing international patents. Startups focus on speed rather than IP strategy. Companies license foreign technology instead of building domestic capability. Nations rise when they own the ideas that shape the world; India, too often, merely rents them.

And beneath all of this lies a corrosive issue: political interference in scientific institutions. Research bodies, laboratories, universities, and councils become tug-of-war zones for ideological influence, bureaucratic control, or administrative reshuffling. Leadership roles are appointed politically rather than scientifically. Institutional autonomy is diluted. Fear replaces intellectual freedom. Vision collapses into compliance. Nations lose decades when their scientific institutions are treated as extensions of political machinery rather than engines of national progress. No breakthrough emerges from an environment where scientists must worry more about alignment with a ministry than alignment with truth.

Together, these fractures reveal a painful structural reality: India produces genius, but it does not produce breakthroughs at scale. Not because the country lacks intelligence, but because the system lacks integration. Capability collapses the moment research collapses. Compute and industry cannot advance without scientific depth. Talent cannot flourish without research pathways. Manufacturing cannot leap without innovation cycles.

This is the missing bridge between ideas and outcomes. Other nations built it slowly, methodically, deliberately. India keeps trying to leap across the gap without building the bridge.

Innovation is not a miracle; it is an ecosystem. Breakthroughs are not accidents; they are engineered. Capability is not wishful thinking; it is architecture.

And until India constructs a research ecosystem that is funded, protected, autonomous, connected, and mission-driven, it will continue exporting brilliance and importing capability—an equation no rising power can sustain.

For India to claim its place in the compute century, it must rebuild the bridge it has ignored for too long. Because nations do not rise by producing smart people. They rise by producing smart systems that convert intelligence into power.

15.5 — Institutional Capacity: The Execution Engine India Never Built

Capability is not only about chips, compute clusters, patents, talent, or industry. Capability is also administrative. It is the quiet, invisible machinery that converts ideas into outcomes, policies into programs, money into infrastructure, and ambition into reality. It is the part of nation-building India rarely talks about because it is not glamorous—but it is the part that determines whether nations rise or remain stuck in a loop of false starts.

India's first fracture lies in ministries that cannot coordinate. Each ministry functions like a sovereign kingdom with its own language, metrics, priorities, and political imperatives. Collaboration is episodic, driven by crisis, or forced by the Prime Minister's Office. Long-term cross-ministerial programs—semiconductors, compute infrastructure, research corridors, green transitions—collapse under the weight of administrative isolation. Departments duplicate work, sabotage timelines, or simply wait for someone else to "own" the outcome. Governance becomes a negotiation, not a mechanism.

Regulators add another layer of weakness. Not because they lack intelligence, but because they lack autonomy, resources, data systems, and political protection. In sectors that demand rigor—finance, telecom, pharmaceuticals, energy, digital infrastructure—India's regulators are often underpowered against the scale they are tasked to supervise. Enforcement wavers. Quality collapses. Global investors hesitate. Domestic firms exploit loopholes. And the regulatory architecture, instead of enabling growth, becomes a bottleneck that slows capability formation.

The civil service, once the backbone of the Indian state, is now trapped between legacy processes and modern demands. Civil services that cannot scale are not a failure of individuals; they are a failure of design. Officers are expected to manage 21st-century complexity with 20th-century tools and 19th-century staffing ratios. They rotate too frequently to build expertise. Innovation is discouraged by risk-averse cultures. Ambitious officers are exhausted; mediocre ones are comfortable. Nations rise when civil services become strategic enablers. India still uses them as administrative firefighters.

Fragmentation deepens when state governments operate in silos, each with its own political agenda, bureaucratic rhythm, and development philosophy. India's federal structure could have been its greatest strategic advantage—a distributed capability engine—but political rivalries convert cooperation into conflict. National programs stall because one state refuses alignment. Industrial corridors die because land acquisition collapses in a single district. Education reforms devolve into political controversies. The nation attempts a coordinated march; the states pull in opposite directions.

Overshadowing all of this is the tyranny of political cycles that reset progress. Five-year cycles for political credit clash with twenty-year cycles required for capability. Ministers come and go; long-term reforms are abandoned midstream; institutions lose continuity. The next government renames schemes, reshuffles leadership, suspends prior frameworks, and rebuilds the same architecture under new branding. This creates an execution environment where progress is not cumulative; it is constantly rebooted.

In the compute century, nations do not gain power through flashy budgets or grand announcements. They gain power through invisible execution systems—hyper-coordinated ministries, autonomous regulators, mission-driven civil services, interoperable data infrastructures, disciplined federal alignment, and institutional continuity across political cycles.

This is the execution engine India never modernized. And without this engine, even the best policies remain theoretical, the best talent remains underutilized, the best technologies remain imported, and the best intentions remain unconverted into capability.

Capability is not built in conferences. Capability is built in systems. Nations rise not because leaders speak with force, but because institutions execute with precision.

Until India builds institutional capacity that is modern, resilient, coordinated, and autonomous, the gap between ambition and achievement will remain brutally wide—no matter how inspiring the national narrative becomes.

15.6 — The Capability Formula: Build, Don't Borrow

In the final analysis, capability is not a procurement strategy. It is not a diplomatic agreement. It is not a budget announcement. Capability is architecture—constructed brick by brick, layer by layer, over decades of disciplined effort. Nations do not buy capability; they build it. And every country that tried to shortcut this truth eventually discovered the same fate: borrowed strength collapses the moment pressure arrives.

Real sovereignty begins with indigenous capacity—the ability to design chips, build cloud infrastructure, manufacture with precision, maintain energy security, and generate intellectual property without waiting for foreign approval. Imported expertise may accelerate momentum, but it cannot substitute for domestic mastery. Nations that buy solutions become markets. Nations that build solutions become powers.

But architecture is not technical alone. Sovereignty requires retained talent—scientists who stay, engineers who innovate domestically, researchers who anchor long-term projects, administrators who operate as capability multipliers. When a country loses its best minds, it loses not just skill but future institutional memory. Talent is not a commodity. It is the engine of national endurance.

Capability also requires resilient manufacturing—supply chains that cannot be blackmailed by geopolitical shocks, factories that meet global standards from day one, logistics that are predictable, and industrial corridors designed for scale, not ceremony. Manufacturing is not a slogan; it is a behaviour. And India must shift from *jugaad* to discipline if it wants factories to become geopolitical assets.

Above all, capability demands domestic compute—the new lifeblood of power. A nation without sovereign compute is like a nation without electricity in the 20th century—forever dependent, forever exposed. To build compute is to build freedom.

And holding all these pillars together is an integrated innovation ecosystem—where universities, research labs, industries, regulators, and investors operate as a continuous pipeline, not isolated islands. Innovation cannot thrive in silos. It thrives in corridors—corridors that India must still design, build, and protect from political volatility.

This is the universal truth hidden behind every successful nation: capability cannot be imported, outsourced, rented, or wished into existence. It must be constructed—slowly, painfully, methodically, through discipline that outlives political cycles and leaders who invest in foundations rather than applause.

And this truth leads to the quiet, prophetic insight that defines India's future: if India builds capability now—seriously, structurally, unapologetically—2035 becomes the year of takeoff, the beginning of a century where India is not just participating in global architecture but shaping it.

But if India delays—if it keeps borrowing strength, outsourcing ambition, importing critical systems, and exporting talent—capability will become the bottleneck that defines the next hundred years.

In the compute century, nations rise through what they build. Not through what they borrow.

Chapter 16 — The Stability Equation

Stability: Social, Economic, and Institutional Equilibrium

The Country Trying to Run With an Earthquake Under Its Feet

Picture India in motion—a billion people leaning forward, the economy pulsing with ambition, startups sprinting toward global markets, and policymakers announcing reform after reform as if momentum alone could bend history. Foreign investors circle with curiosity and optimism; global headlines flirt with the idea of an "Indian decade." On the surface, it looks like acceleration. It feels like ascent. It sounds like progress.

But beneath that charged, upward energy, the ground keeps trembling. Social tensions crack open without warning—one speech, one slogan, one careless spark can throw entire regions off balance. Policies swing from bold to bewildering overnight, the result of political insecurity rather than strategic clarity. Courts, drowning under the backlog of decades, take years to decide matters that shape industries in months. Institutions built to provide continuity wobble under pressure, starved of autonomy and fatigued by constant political turbulence.

Even as the nation tries to run, its internal floor shifts under each step. Noise replaces direction, spectacle replaces substance, and every long-term agenda must first survive a daily battlefield of drama, disruption, and contradiction. Corporates hesitate because regulations feel unpredictable; researchers lose rhythm because funding cycles behave like weather; states bicker with the Centre even when national strategy demands alignment.

It is a country moving fast in spirit but stumbling in structure—each stride powered by ambition, each stumble caused by instability. And in this cinematic opening frame, the unsettling truth becomes impossible to ignore: no nation can accelerate when its foundations behave like an earthquake zone.

India's problem is not lack of intent. It is lack of stability. And stability, in the compute century, is not a luxury—it is the prerequisite for acceleration.

16.1 — Social Stability: The Silent Multiplier Nations Ignore

Every rising nation in history has enjoyed one invisible advantage before it enjoyed anything else: social stability. Not the fragile silence created by fear or surveillance, but the deeper stability that comes from trust—trust between communities, trust in institutions, trust in the future, trust in the idea of the nation itself. It is the multiplier no economist can quantify, no politician openly credits, and no headline will celebrate. Yet it is the force that determines whether a country moves like a coordinated organism or a collection of competing fragments.

India's greatest paradox is that it tries to accelerate without this multiplier. The nation wakes up each morning to a new fault line—identity battles amplified by political greed, communal tensions reheated for electoral gain, social media outrage engineered to polarize, and misinformation designed to exhaust public focus. Every day becomes a contest not of progress but of narratives, as if the country's primary sport were internal friction.

The cost of this instability is rarely acknowledged because it is not measured in numbers—it is measured in lost attention. A polarized population cannot align around common goals. A society addicted to outrage cannot build institutions that require patience. A nation constantly provoked into emotional battles cannot invest its cognitive bandwidth into innovation, research, or long-term statecraft. When political actors weaponize divisions for a few thousand votes, the entire country pays in decades lost. When bureaucrats fail—or refuse—to manage local tensions early, fires spread that take years to calm and billions to repair.

Social instability is not an emotional issue. It is not a cultural concern. It is not a "law-and-order situation." It is a brutal productivity drain.

Every riot delays investment. Every polarizing speech derails reforms. Every outrage cycle distracts administrators from execution. Every identity conflict fractures national cohesion. Every misinformation wave corrodes trust.

This is the unseen tax India pays daily: a nation forced to divide its energy between building the future and surviving itself.

And behind this quiet tragedy lies a simple truth: no country can run fast with a social fabric that tears each time someone pulls a political thread.

Stability is not soft. Stability is strength. Stability is strategy. Stability is sovereignty. And without it, acceleration becomes an illusion.

16.2 — Economic Stability: Predictability as a Strategic Asset

Economic power is not built on ambition, slogans, or even GDP growth. It is built on predictability—the quiet, disciplined rhythm that allows businesses to plan, investors to commit, institutions to scale, and global partners to trust. Nations rise when their economic environment behaves like a stable architecture, not a casino where the rules change depending on who is in power or what headlines dominate the week.

This is where India repeatedly injures itself. The country does not lack growth potential; it lacks continuity. Every time India begins to gain momentum, the ground shifts—policies reversed overnight for political optics, tax structures reinterpreted without warning, regulators suddenly waking up after years of silence, and bureaucratic overreach sending tremors through entire sectors. Investors do not fear risk; they fear arbitrariness. And India, far too often, behaves like a country still deciding whether it wants to reward long-term commitment or short-term compliance.

The pattern is painfully familiar. A reform is announced with fanfare, but implementation is half-hearted. A sector blossoms, only to be throttled by sudden regulation. Businesses scale, but corruption at local levels quietly distorts competition. Fiscal policy becomes a political instrument instead of a national compass. Enforcement is strict where it should not be, and absent where it must be.

The result is not weakness—it is interruption.

Indian entrepreneurs are globally admired for resilience because they spend half their energy navigating unpredictability rather than building innovation. Foreign investors remain cautiously optimistic, not because India lacks opportunity, but because they must constantly calculate political surprises, bureaucratic discretion, and regulatory U-turns. Domestic industries hesitate to make bold long-term bets because the rules of the game rarely stay constant long enough to justify them.

Economic stability is not a luxury; it is a strategic asset. It signals maturity. It builds credibility. It transforms talent into ecosystems and startups into industries. It attracts the kind of capital that stays for decades, not quarters. It allows global supply chains to treat a nation as a dependable node rather than a volatile market.

India is not an unstable economy—it is an economy repeatedly interrupted by its own system. A nation with world-class potential sabotaged by unpredictable governance.

If India wants to play at the top of the global value chain, it must learn the fundamental lesson that every advanced economy mastered long ago: strength is not in growth numbers. Strength is in the ability to sustain them.

16.3 — Institutional Stability: The Backbone That Carries Acceleration

Every nation that has risen—every economy that has matured, every society that has scaled, every technology ecosystem that has taken flight—has done so on one invisible foundation: institutional stability. Courts that deliver justice on time. Regulators that enforce rules consistently. Police forces that protect without bias. Civil services that execute without fear. Universities that nurture talent without political meddling. Oversight bodies that prevent excess before it becomes crisis.

These institutions are the silent backbone that carries acceleration. They create the continuity that long-term progress demands. They ensure that capability—no matter how impressive—has a channel through which it can convert into results. Without them, a nation may sprint for a few years, but it cannot run the distance.

This is where India's cracks become impossible to ignore. Institutions designed decades ago—some even before Independence—are now expected to govern a hyper-digital, hyper-connected, billion-scale nation. But many are exhausted, politicized, under-resourced, or structurally compromised. Courts drown in backlogs that stretch for years, sometimes decades.

Regulators oscillate between silence and overreaction, driven more by political instructions than by independent judgment. Police forces remain trapped in colonial-era frameworks, battling modern crime with outdated tools. Universities suffocate under bureaucracy and political appointments, unable to become true engines of innovation. Civil servants—some brilliant, many sincere—struggle in a system that rewards survival over excellence.

And then comes the most corrosive force of all: political interference. Governments of every stripe have eroded institutional autonomy—stacking key positions with loyalists, using transfers as intimidation, bending regulatory bodies to fit electoral narratives, and weakening oversight to protect allies. Turf battles between ministries, departments, and states further fracture coherence. Administrative fatigue—caused by constant firefighting, poor incentives, and leadership churn—renders even competent systems unable to sustain momentum.

The tragedy is not that India lacks capability. The tragedy is that India lacks stable systems to deploy capability. Brilliant officers burn out. Talented researchers give up. High-quality enforcement collapses under political pressure. Visionary policies die during execution because the machinery beneath is rusted, overstretched, or compromised. And every time an institution weakens, the nation's trajectory dips—quietly, invisibly, but decisively.

Institutional stability is not glamorous. It does not trend on social media. It does not win elections. But it is the backbone of national power. Nations collapse not when leaders fail, but when institutions can no longer carry the weight of ambition.

India aspires to accelerate—but acceleration requires a chassis strong enough to hold speed. Without stable institutions, even the best policies will skid, the best talent will scatter, and the best reforms will stall before they reach the ground.

If India wants to climb the ladder of global power, it must begin by strengthening the very scaffolding that holds the nation upright.

16.4 — Political Stability: Maturity vs. Majoritarianism

Political stability is often misunderstood in India—reduced to the number of seats in Parliament or the longevity of a ruling party. But real political stability is not about dominance; it is about maturity. It is the ability of a political system to produce continuity without suppressing dissent, to deliver consistent policy without dismantling institutional autonomy, and to think beyond electoral cycles without sinking into personality cults.

India today confuses majoritarian control with stability. A government with a strong mandate may create the appearance of order, but if that mandate erodes institutional independence, weakens checks and balances, centralizes authority excessively, or silences criticism, the long-term result is not stability—it is fragility disguised as strength.

The distinction is sharp and unavoidable: political maturity means governments trust institutions; political dominance means governments replace institutions with themselves. In a mature political ecosystem, ideas compete, but institutions remain neutral. In a dominant political ecosystem, dissent is framed as disloyalty, and institutions slowly morph into extensions of the ruling party's will. India experiences this tension daily—media houses aligning with political narratives, investigative agencies becoming tools of leverage, universities shifting their academic priorities based on ideological climates, and state governments weaponizing governance against each other.

And then comes the cycle that kills strategy: election logic. Policies get rewritten every five years. Long-term projects are abandoned midstream. Populist schemes override structural reforms.

Budgets are theatrically adjusted to win votes rather than strengthen systems. Political attention swings like a pendulum—today infrastructure, tomorrow religion, the next day freebies—while the national agenda remains fragmented and reactive.

The result is collapse of strategic continuity. Even strong ideas fail because no institution is allowed to carry them across cycles without interference.

India's political class on all sides bears responsibility for this. Leaders talk of "vision 2047," but behave as if their horizon ends five months before an election. Parties promise reforms but backtrack when reforms threaten vote banks. Bureaucrats oscillate between caution and opportunism, reading political winds instead of national priorities. And the entire system mistakes noise for mandate.

Political stability in the compute century requires three qualities India has not yet mastered. Respect for institutional autonomy—governments must govern, institutions must operate independently. When this boundary collapses, predictability dies. Cross-party continuity on national strategy—nations rise when certain policies outlive governments, whether in industry, research, defense, education, or compute. And a political culture that rewards competence over charisma—elections can choose leaders, but institutions must be allowed to choose experts.

Without these, political dominance becomes a liability, not an asset.

Political stability is not the absence of opposition—it is the presence of coherence. A nation becomes stable when power is distributed wisely, dissent is respected, institutions are independent, and the political class behaves like custodians of long-term national interest rather than performers in a five-year spectacle.

Until India achieves political maturity, its acceleration will remain hostage to cycles, narratives, and personalities—never to strategy.

16.5 — The Stability Equation: Why Chaos Kills Acceleration

Stability is not the absence of conflict—it is the presence of coherence. It is not a passive state of calm; it is an active infrastructure that multiplies capability. Nations do not accelerate because they are loud, energetic, or ambitious. They accelerate because their internal systems stop working against each other and start resonating in alignment.

Chaos, on the other hand, is not random noise—it is a structural tax that India keeps paying willingly.

Chaos turns every reform into a debate. Instead of moving forward, the nation argues about whether to move at all. Whether it is farm policy, education reform, judicial overhaul, digital regulation, or economic modernization, chaos ensures that the conversation always collapses into ideological battles, identity politics, and street-level theatrics. The reform dies before it ever breathes.

Instability slows execution. Even when policies are right, execution falters because administrators are distracted, states are misaligned, ministries feud silently, and political incentives reward optics over outcomes. India becomes a nation of big announcements and slow delivery—because instability erodes the machinery that converts intent into impact.

Polarization reduces national bandwidth. A divided society cannot problem-solve. When energy is spent on proving each other wrong, none is left to build what is right. Communal tensions, partisan outrage, and culture wars drain the cognitive surplus that should be invested in innovation, research, institution-building, and global strategy.

Unpredictability scares capital and talent. Investors do not fear high risk; they fear unclear rules. Talent does not fear competition; it fears chaos. A country that changes regulatory norms overnight, weaponizes enforcement unpredictably, or flips policy after elections signals instability—not ambition.

No institution can innovate when it is fighting for survival. Courts, regulators, universities, police, and civil services today spend more energy managing political pressure, public expectation, and resource scarcity than building capability. Innovation is impossible in institutions trapped in survival mode.

And then comes the philosophical punchline: chaos kills acceleration because chaos kills confidence—confidence in systems, in governance, in rules, in fairness, in the future.

External rivals cannot slow India down as effectively as internal dysfunction can. China may challenge India, the U.S. may overshadow India, global markets may test India—but none of them can sabotage India the way India sabotages itself through instability.

India's biggest enemy is not China. India's biggest competitor is not the U.S. India's biggest barrier is not the global order. India's biggest enemy is its own tolerance for chaos.

Until India confronts that truth, no amount of ambition, capability, or geopolitics will change its destiny. Stability is not optional—it is the multiplier without which acceleration collapses into noise.

This is the cost India must stop paying.

Chapter 17 — The Integration Equation

India's Strategic Lever

The Nation That Grew Every Time It Plugged Into the World

Imagine India standing at a crossroads, holding a thousand-year history in one hand and a billion dreams in the other. It is a nation that has always wanted to rise, always believed it could rise, and on rare occasions, has actually risen—spectacularly, unexpectedly, almost explosively. And every single one of those rises happened for the same reason: India plugged itself into the world.

The sweep across decades tells the story clearly. In the 1990s, India opened its markets, and suddenly a stagnant economy began to breathe. IT services connected to American corporations, and a middle class appeared where hopelessness once lived. Pharma companies integrated with global regulatory systems, and a local industry became a global lifesaver. Space scientists collaborated with foreign agencies and transformed a struggling program into a frontier of global relevance. Indian students landed in foreign universities and returned as catalysts of innovation—or stayed abroad and became India's most powerful soft-power network.

Each time India integrated, it expanded. Each time it isolated, it suffocated.

And yet, even in 2025, India remains conflicted—caught between ambition and insecurity. Politicians sell the fantasy of autarky. Slogans promise self-reliance without the hard work of building capability. Bureaucrats fear foreign collaboration because it exposes domestic inadequacy. National pride often mistakes openness for weakness, forgetting that India's greatest successes were born from connection, not isolation.

India emerges here as a character—brilliant, restless, ambitious—but unsure whether to reach out or retreat. The world is reorganizing into supply-chain spheres, compute alliances, semiconductor coalitions, cloud clusters, and talent corridors. Nations are no longer rising because of ideology; they are rising because they know how to integrate strategically.

The hook lands with quiet force: India's competitive advantage has always come from connection, never from withdrawal. India grows when it plugs in. India stalls when it unplugs.

The question is no longer whether India should integrate. The question is whether India can integrate deeply enough, fast enough, and intelligently enough to seize the 2035 window before it closes.

The rest of the chapter begins from this truth: in a world built on networks, integration is not an option. It is India's most powerful lever.

17.1 — The Architecture of Integration: Power Through Networks, Not Borders

For decades, India imagined global power the old way—through borders, armies, trade agreements, and diplomatic speeches. But in the compute century, the map has quietly changed. Nations no longer rise because of the land they hold or the flags they fly. They rise because of the networks they belong to and the architectures they are plugged into. Power has become infrastructural, not ornamental. And integration—deep, structural, multidimensional integration—is the new currency of national acceleration.

Think of today's global order not as continents and countries, but as stacked architectures—semiconductor routes, cloud grids, research corridors, logistics chains, capital flows, AI ecosystems, and data exchanges. These are not alliances. They are operating systems. And in this world, sovereignty is no longer the ability to stand alone; it is the ability to stand connected without being controlled.

A nation with weak networks is a nation with weak leverage. A nation with strong networks becomes powerful—even if its geography is small. Taiwan is not a military superpower; it is the heart of global chips. Israel is not a resource giant; it is a hub of defense-tech and research clusters. Singapore has no hinterland; it has supply-chain mastery. Japan's economic muscles weakened, but its integration into manufacturing and tech networks keeps it globally relevant. Power has shifted from flags to frameworks, from borders to bandwidth.

Here lies India's blind spot: we still speak the language of territorial sovereignty while the world speaks the language of architectural sovereignty. We debate diplomacy while ignoring supply-chain geometry. We celebrate trade deals but overlook whether we sit at the top, middle, or bottom of the architecture that defines them. We obsess over traditional alliances while the world quietly builds semiconductor pacts, cloud coalitions, quantum corridors, and AI alignment blocs.

Integration is not friendship. It is leverage. Integration is not dependence. It is amplification.

When India plugs into global research networks, its talent multiplies. When India aligns with semiconductor alliances, its manufacturing ambitions gain oxygen. When India integrates into cloud grids with negotiation—not blind adoption—it gains compute sovereignty. When India becomes part of supply-chain clusters, it suddenly matters.

This exposes a quiet but profound shift: the world is now divided between nations inside the architecture and nations outside it. Nations inside accelerate. Nations outside improvise.

India today sits in the middle—powerful enough to influence, weak enough to be influenced, ambitious enough to want more, but architecturally under-integrated to claim it. And integration is not a philosophical aspiration—it is an engineering discipline that nations must practice deliberately.

Borders protect nations. Networks elevate them. Integration is the architecture through which India can convert potential into power.

This is where the real chapter begins.

17.2 — The Integration Dividend: How India Has Always Won Through Openness

If you trace the curve of India's rise over the last three decades, a startling pattern appears—every phase of national acceleration coincided with moments when India opened its windows to the world. Every leap forward happened when India connected, collaborated, borrowed, partnered, and learned. And every slowdown followed attempts to withdraw, shield, isolate, or reinvent the wheel alone.

The story begins in 1991—the year India finally exhaled. When the economy opened, global capital flowed in, multinational corporations arrived, governance modernized, and local businesses shed their license-raj chains. It was not ideology that saved India—it was integration. Without global markets, global investors, and global trust, the Indian middle class would not exist. Openness did not just lift GDP; it lifted people.

Then came the IT revolution—India's first real integration miracle. Bangalore did not rise because of slogans. It rose because American companies needed talent and India had it. Integration with U.S. markets created millions of jobs, globalized India's workforce, and birthed an entirely new industry. India's tech sector grew faster than any domestic reform could have allowed. The country's digital economy was born through global demand, not domestic doctrine.

Pharma followed—a journey from generic manufacturer to global health partner. Indian pharma grew not by hiding behind protectionist walls, but by aligning with Western regulatory standards. Integration with FDA, EMA, WHO, and global medical supply chains transformed a local industry into a world lifesaver—culminating in India's leadership during global health crises.

Space, renewables, startups, and research collaborations tell the same story. ISRO's partnerships with international agencies. Indian startups scaling through foreign capital and global cloud infrastructure. Renewable energy expanding through imported technology and global financing models. Scientific breakthroughs emerging from Indo-U.S., Indo-EU, and Indo-Japan research corridors. India's soft power exploding through its diaspora—the most powerful ambassador network any nation has ever had.

This is the integration dividend: when India opens to the world, the world opens India.

The deeper truth is older still. India's greatness has always come from synthesis, not isolation. Ancient India thrived because it was a trading, learning, exchanging civilization. Knowledge flowed in from Greece, Persia, Southeast Asia, Arabia, Europe, and Africa—and India turned those inputs into intellectual wealth. Modern India behaves no differently: it rises when it connects.

And yet, the irony persists. India often celebrates success without acknowledging the networks that enabled it. People praise IT giants, pharma leaders, space achievements, unicorn startups—but rarely credit the global ecosystems that made these possible. The danger is not a lack of achievement; the danger is misdiagnosing how the achievements happened.

India has never been harmed by openness. India has only been harmed by believing it can rise without it.

This truth, once accepted, becomes India's most strategic advantage: integration is not a necessity; it is a force multiplier waiting to be wielded.

17.3 — The Danger of Selective Isolation: When Politics Disrupts Progress

Integration has always rewarded India—but every time India begins to rise, a familiar force pulls it back: the seductive, self-defeating fantasy of isolation. It appears in new packaging each decade—"self-reliance," "economic nationalism," "protect local industry," "global powers can't be trusted"—but beneath the slogans lies the same structural misunderstanding: a belief that India can achieve global-scale outcomes without global-scale connectivity.

It begins innocently—politicians exploiting emotional rhetoric around national pride, bureaucrats interpreting global exposure as threat rather than opportunity, and special-interest groups lobbying for protectionist bubbles that allow inefficiency to flourish. But the consequences are far from innocent: sectors stagnate, supply chains choke, foreign investors hesitate, and innovation suffocates under the weight of domestic overconfidence.

The anatomy of selective isolation reveals itself with quiet precision. Semiconductor alliances are delayed because they look "foreign." India's political class loves the idea of chip sovereignty—until they realize it requires foreign equipment, foreign technology, foreign fabs, and foreign partnerships. Instead of negotiating smartly, India hesitates under the illusion that sovereignty can be achieved by restricting global participation. Meanwhile, competitors form semiconductor coalitions overnight.

Protectionist policies shield inefficiency rather than build capability. Industries hide behind tariffs, quotas, and sentiment-driven buy-local campaigns. Instead of improving quality, they lobby for insulation. India ends up consuming inferior products at higher prices while global competitors march ahead with technology and discipline.

Bureaucrats block collaborations because they fear being exposed. International academic partnerships, research exchanges, and technology-sharing proposals often die on bureaucratic desks—not because they are flawed, but because institutions fear scrutiny. Insecure systems prefer local mediocrity over global excellence.

Political groups treat foreign investment as ideological contamination. States reject factories for posturing, unions resist modernization, and parties weaponize ownership narratives. Each of these pushes India back into stagnation.

Regulatory nationalism suffocates startups. Instead of creating clear rules, regulators create unpredictable ones. Compliance becomes a maze, capital becomes cautious, and global partnerships retreat. India begins looking like a risky bet—despite its talent, market, and momentum.

This dynamic is not described with anger, but with tired clarity—as if speaking to a nation that keeps making the same mistake, decade after decade.

The deeper insight emerges: India is not against globalization; it is selectively against the parts that require discipline, transparency, or institutional strength. India welcomes global capital but resists global standards. Welcomes foreign tech but resists foreign competition. Welcomes diaspora talent but resists diaspora influence. Welcomes global recognition but resists global accountability.

This selective openness produces a dangerous illusion: India believes it is integrating while actually fragmenting.

Politicians fuel anti-global fantasies to score emotional points. Bureaucrats block global integration to protect their fiefdoms. Crony networks lobby against global entry to preserve monopolies. Ideologues manufacture fear around foreign collaboration to maintain power.

But the harsh truth stands unshaken: no nation has ever achieved sovereignty through isolation in the compute century. The more India resists global frameworks, the more it delays capability. The more it delays capability, the more dependence deepens. And the more dependence deepens, the more vulnerable India becomes.

India cannot afford isolation—not selective, not symbolic, not intellectual. Every time India withdraws, the world moves on without it. And catching up later is always more expensive than integrating now.

Isolation protects egos; integration builds nations.

17.4 — Strategic Integration: Aligning Without Becoming Dependent

Integration is not surrender. Integration is strategy. It is the art of connecting deeply enough to accelerate, yet widely enough to stay autonomous. In a century where power flows through chips, clouds, research corridors, talent networks, and supply-chain geometry, India's rise depends on its ability to align with many—without being captured by any. This section shifts the lens from critique to architecture, offering a clear, disciplined roadmap for how a billion-scale democracy can plug into the world intelligently, not emotionally.

The first step is breaking the false binary that dominates Indian political imagination: "Either we depend on the world or we isolate ourselves." This is not how modern nations think. Silicon Valley integrates with Taiwan. Japan integrates with the U.S. Korea integrates with Europe. Even China—despite its insulation—remains deeply entangled with global manufacturing and capital flows. Sovereignty today comes from structured interdependence, not autarky.

India's strategic path unfolds with clarity.

Diversify Partnerships: Power Through Many Anchors

India cannot afford a one-axis foreign policy—neither U.S.-centric nor China-phobic nor Europe-dependent. True integration means constructing a multi-pillar sovereignty architecture: the U.S. for compute, cloud, and research ecosystems; the EU for regulatory excellence, green tech, and advanced manufacturing; Japan for precision engineering, capital discipline, and technology transfer; Taiwan for semiconductor manufacturing and chip design; Israel for defense-tech, cyber capability, and innovation frameworks; Southeast Asia for supply-chain diversification; Africa for long-term markets and geopolitical influence. Each partner offers a different piece of India's future. Dependence arises only when India leans on one. Sovereignty emerges when India stands on many.

Negotiate, Don't Absorb: Technology Transfer as Policy, Not Dream

India's historical weakness has been buying technology it should have built, renting technology it should co-own. Strategic integration demands joint IP creation, not one-sided imports; co-owned fabs, not foreign-run assembly plants; research partnerships with mandatory knowledge transfer; algorithmic alliances where India shapes—not just consumes—AI models; defense partnerships that create domestic manufacturing ecosystems. This is not nationalism. It is negotiation discipline. Nations rise when they refuse to play the role of permanent customer.

Embed Talent Globally: The Indian Brain as Strategic Capital

No country possesses a global talent diaspora of India's scale—not even China. But India has never used it strategically. Strategic integration means placing Indian researchers inside global R&D centers, embedding Indian managers inside global supply chains, positioning Indian founders inside global innovation corridors, and drawing returning talent into India's domestic capability-building. The world has already accepted Indian minds. India must now deploy them intentionally.

Build Domestic Muscle in Parallel: Integration Must Create Capability, Not Replace It

The mistake many nations make—Russia, Latin America, parts of Africa—is letting integration replace domestic investment. India must integrate while building its own compute clusters, its own semiconductor capacity (even partial), its own research institutions, its own manufacturing precision, its own cloud infrastructure, its own leadership pipelines. Integration is the scaffolding; capability is the building. One cannot stand without the other.

Use Networks as Leverage, Not Crutches

This is the intellectual center of the section. India should treat global networks as accelerators, not anchors; bridges, not cages; amplifiers, not substitutes. Strategic integration means always asking: does this connection increase India's power—or merely outsource it? And adjusting course immediately when the answer drifts toward dependence.

Dependence is when a nation relies on one partner. Integration is when a nation leverages many. Sovereignty is when a nation uses integration to build capability—not import it.

For India, integration is not a vulnerability. It is the lever that transforms a billion-scale nation into a global-scale power.

The chapter shifts toward a quiet crescendo: India cannot isolate its way into the future. But it can integrate its way into leadership—if it learns to align without surrender.

17.5 — Integration as Competitive Advantage: India's Unique Leverage

If capability is India's engine and stability is its chassis, then integration is the open highway—wide, powerful, accelerating everything that sits on top of it. But unlike many nations struggling against geography, culture, or political history, India possesses something rare: an inherent structural advantage in global integration that no other major nation has.

This is not merely necessity. It is leverage. It is India's superpower waiting to be activated.

India's Trust Advantage: The Currency China Cannot Buy and Russia Cannot Borrow

In a world fractured by suspicion, India stands in a uniquely favourable position. Western nations trust Indian democracy. Asian nations trust Indian neutrality. African nations trust Indian partnership. The Middle East trusts Indian labour, talent, and reliability. Unlike China, India's intentions are not feared. Unlike

Russia, India's systems are not distrusted. Unlike the U.S., India is not seen as overbearing. This rare position allows India to integrate into multiple blocs without triggering insecurity. In a century where trust shapes supply chains, this becomes strategic gold.

India's English Fluency: The Bridge Language of Global Networks

India underestimates its linguistic superpower. English is the gateway to global research, capital, diplomacy, education, technology ecosystems, and governance norms. From Silicon Valley to Singapore to London to Sydney, India's linguistic alignment creates seamless integration. China has capital but lacks linguistic access. Japan has precision but lacks linguistic reach. Europe has structure but lacks linguistic uniformity. India flows across all these domains with almost unnatural ease.

India's Diaspora: The World's Most Strategic Unofficial Foreign Policy Arm

No other major nation has such a powerful, globally embedded, economically influential diaspora. CEOs of major tech companies, leading researchers in global labs, top faculty in universities, venture partners in VC ecosystems, innovation leaders in AI, pharma, biotech, and policy influencers across continents. These are not expatriates—they are India's distributed capability grid. Their influence opens doors India cannot open diplomatically or economically. Integration for India is not a policy—it is a lived global footprint.

India's Market Gravity: The Magnet That Pulls Partnerships, Not Pressure

Nations integrate with India because of its demand power: 1.4 billion consumers, the fastest-growing digital economy, a rising middle class, a tech-hungry youth demographic, massive healthcare, education, and mobility markets. India does not need to chase alliances—alliances come seeking India, because few nations offer growth potential at this scale. The market itself becomes negotiating leverage. Integration becomes easier when the world wants a seat at your table.

India's Democratic Identity: The Global Differentiator

In a century where many nations slip into authoritarian patterns, India's democratic identity—though noisy, imperfect, and often chaotic—remains a global differentiator. It gives India legitimacy in Western alliances, comfort in Asian partnerships, flexibility in Middle Eastern engagements, credibility in African development networks. Democracies are more trusted in network-centric global architectures. And India is the largest, youngest, and most strategically located among them. India must weaponize democracy—not merely celebrate it.

India as the Connector Nation: The Architecture No One Else Can Build

India is the only major power that can be friend of the West without being an extension of the West, partner of the East without being subordinate to the East, ally of the Global South without being trapped by it. India can sit in multiple networks simultaneously—in compute with the U.S., in manufacturing with Japan, in energy with the Middle East, in diplomacy with Africa, in supply chains with Southeast Asia, and in cultural influence everywhere. India's uniqueness is not its size—it is its compatibility across systems. No other nation can do this without provoking paranoia. India alone can become the world's integration hub—the place where global networks converge because they find comfort, scale, and stability.

Every nation is searching for stability in a fragmented world. Every nation is searching for talent. Every nation is searching for trusted partners. India can be all three—if it embraces integration as its defining strategy.

Integration is not India's weakness. It is its leverage. Its multiplier. Its global identity.

And if India uses this leverage wisely, its rise will not be contested—it will be welcomed.

17.6 — The Integration Equation: Plug In, Rise Up

Integration is India's velocity. Not a support mechanism, not a diplomatic tactic, not a trade preference—velocity. The force that determines how fast India can climb the global ladder before the 2035 window closes.

Every nation has a growth engine. But engines alone do not decide the journey—roads do. And in the compute century, the roads are not made of asphalt or treaties. They are made of supply chains, data networks, research corridors, semiconductor alliances, AI partnerships, capital flows, and global trust. These are the highways of national acceleration. And India cannot reach the destination of great-power status if it insists on driving on local roads while the rest of the world zooms ahead on connected ones.

The equation is clean, unavoidable, mathematical:

Capability gives power. Stability gives direction. Integration gives velocity.

No matter how much capability India builds—chips, cloud, AI, manufacturing, talent—it needs integration to amplify it. Stability keeps the nation steady, but integration propels it forward.

The contrasts are instructive. A nation with strong capability but weak integration becomes Japan—brilliant yet restrained. A nation with strong integration but weak capability becomes the UAE—fast-moving but reliant. A nation with capability, stability, and integration becomes South Korea—small but globally decisive. A nation with instability but high capability becomes Russia—dangerous yet collapsing. And a nation with capability and ambition but low integration becomes India—potential waiting to be converted.

India has the talent. India has the market. India has the trust of the world. India has the demographic window. India has the entrepreneurial hunger. What India lacks is integration maturity—the ability to sit inside global architectures without losing autonomy, the wisdom to diversify partners without diluting self-interest, and the confidence to negotiate technology, capital, and capability on equal footing.

Integration is not about surrender—it is about scale. Integration is not about dependency—it is about leverage. Integration is not about alignment—it is about architecture.

Without integration, every domestic success remains domestic. With integration, every domestic success becomes global.

India does not rise by isolating itself from the world. India rises by becoming indispensable to it.

If India plugs in wisely now, the world will accelerate with it. If it hesitates, the world will accelerate without it.

The integration equation is not a choice. It is India's path—or India's ceiling.

Chapter 18 — The 2035 Moment

The year India either accelerates or slips into dependency

History Does Not Give Second Chances

Picture a giant clock mounted above the world—not ticking toward midnight like in old geopolitical thrillers, but ticking toward 2035, the year when the architecture of global power will quietly lock into place. Not with an explosion, not with a crisis, not with a war—but with a final click, like a circuit completing. And once that circuit locks, every nation will either be inside the grid... or permanently outside it.

In this cinematic frame, India stands at the edge of a narrow bridge stretched across two centuries. Behind it lies the world of potential—talent, youth, markets, democracy, ambition. Ahead lies the world of architecture—chips, compute, AI ecosystems, supply-chain alliances, research networks, institutional sophistication, political maturity.

India has never had a decade as important as the one between now and 2035. Not even 1991 carried stakes this large. In 1991, failure meant economic crisis. In 2035, failure means strategic irrelevance—a future where India remains big but not powerful, busy but not influential, proud but not sovereign.

Inside a high-level strategic meeting in Delhi, ministers present GDP forecasts. Advisors project demographic advantages.

Economists discuss consumption-led growth. Everyone is excited. Everyone is optimistic. But on one side of the room, a quiet screen displays something far more important: global chip alliances forming, AI monopolies consolidating, compute grids being redrawn, supply-chain blocs tightening, research ecosystems choosing their hubs.

The room is debating yesterday's indicators while the world is reorganizing itself on tomorrow's. And this gap—between what India is celebrating and what the world is building—is the essence of the 2035 moment.

The hook ends with a revelation that feels both exhilarating and frightening:

In 2035, the world will not ask whether India had potential. It will ask whether India built capacity. Whether India stabilized itself. Whether India integrated intelligently.

Nations rise only when capability, stability, and integration align at the right moment in history. India's moment is now. Its window is narrow. And history does not give second chances to nations that arrive unprepared.

2035 is not a year. It is a verdict. A verdict on whether India became a power—or remained a possibility.

18.1 — The Global Clock: A World That Won't Wait for India

The world is moving with a speed and precision that India can no longer ignore. Power is no longer negotiated through summits or speeches—it is engineered through compute, chips, supply chains, and AI ecosystems being built right now, in real time, by nations that fully understand the stakes of the decade. And the part India fails to see clearly is this: the global clock is not synchronized with India's political rhythms, bureaucratic delays, or cultural comfort with procrastination. The world is racing ahead. India is debating whether to start running.

The panoramic sweep across the planet reveals the urgency.

The United States

Washington has already decided the architecture of its next 20 years: AI dominance, semiconductor control, cloud centralization, quantum supremacy, global talent absorption, and narrative control through platforms, media, and academia. The U.S. is locking its alliances—the CHIPS Act, QUAD tech corridors, AI safety coalitions, cloud geography rules, and research networks. By 2030, it expects to cement foundational control not by force, but through infrastructure every nation will depend on. If India does not align early, it aligns late—and late alignment is merely dependence in polite packaging.

China

China's clock is even more aggressive. Beijing has decided to become self-contained by 2030 and strategically indispensable by 2035. While the West debates ethics and regulation, China is mass-producing: fabs, batteries, drones, solar, EVs, robotics, AI applications, logistics nodes, rare-earth choke points. By 2035, China expects to control significant portions of green tech supply chains, AI-driven industrial automation, consumer hardware ecosystems, Belt-and-Road digital infrastructure, and global manufacturing architecture. If India does not build counter-architecture now, it becomes a consumer of Chinese ecosystems—no matter how strong its political rhetoric.

Europe, Japan, South Korea, Taiwan

Europe is consolidating regulatory and AI sovereignty. Japan is rebuilding industrial alliances and semiconductor revival plans. South Korea is expanding memory and chip ecosystems globally. Taiwan is locking in its role as the world's irreplaceable fabrication powerhouse. All of them operate on a 2030–2035 horizon—a global architecture freeze date. After that, everything becomes locked: supply chains, AI corridors, semiconductor alliances, compute grids, R&D clusters.

The Middle East and Southeast Asia

Saudi Arabia, UAE, Singapore, Vietnam, Indonesia—all are transforming themselves into global-capability hubs. They are moving faster than India in AI adoption, cloud infrastructure, logistics modernization, startup funding, and talent attraction. They are small, but nimble. India is big, but slow. And the world now rewards speed more than size.

The Global Window Is Narrow, Not Generational

This is the part India underestimates most. India behaves like it has 50 years. The world knows it has barely 10. By 2035, the verdict will be clear: which nations control chips, which nations control cloud, which nations control AI standards, which nations control supply-chain geography, which nations define the next century of innovation. After that, latecomers don't join—they follow.

India's Misalignment With the Global Clock

India's political class believes it is navigating a long, slow drama. But geopolitics is now a high-frequency game. While the world is building for 2030, India is planning around elections. While the world is consolidating architecture, India is debating identity. While the world is stabilizing its institutions, India is overloading its own with noise. While the world is forming blocs, India is still deciding what it wants to be. The discrepancy is not merely concerning—it is existential.

The world is not waiting for India because the world cannot afford to wait. And India cannot afford to pretend the world will.

The global clock is accelerating. India's clock must match it—or India will live in a future designed by others.

The 2035 moment is not a deadline imposed on India. It is a deadline imposed by reality.

18.2 — India's Internal Timeline: The Architecture That Must Be Built Before the Window Shuts

If the global clock is racing toward 2035, India's internal clock is stuttering—sometimes sprinting, often pausing, frequently looping backwards. The danger is not that India lacks ambition; the danger is that its ambition is not aligned with the timeline the world has already set. India imagines it has decades to prepare. In truth, it has a single decade to overhaul its architecture or accept permanent dependency.

This is not a matter of aspiration. It is a matter of sequence, pace, and precision. The reforms India must undertake are not optional—they are structural imperatives. And the order in which they are built will decide whether India arrives prepared or arrives late.

Compute Infrastructure: The First Non-Negotiable

Without domestic compute, there is no AI sovereignty, no digital sovereignty, no military sovereignty, no industrial sovereignty. India cannot rent cloud from U.S. companies indefinitely and dream of becoming a tech power. Before 2035, India must build national compute clusters, hyperscale sovereign cloud zones, AI training infrastructure, GPU availability pipelines, and domestic data centers tied to domestic energy grids. Right now, India imports its computational oxygen. By 2035, it must produce at least part of its own supply—or forever operate with borrowed lungs.

Semiconductor Capability: Even Partial, But Real

India cannot build a full semiconductor ecosystem by 2035—no nation can do it from scratch in 10 years. But India can secure critical positions in packaging and testing, specialty fabs, mature nodes, chip design, and ecosystem components such as chemicals, materials, and equipment services. Without this, India becomes the world's largest consumer in a domain where consumption brings dependence, not leverage. A country of 1.4 billion cannot rely on Taiwan, Korea, and the U.S. without strategic risk. By 2035, India must anchor itself in the chip value chain—even if only in key segments.

Supply Chain Modernization: The Backbone of Industrial Sovereignty

India cannot become a global manufacturing node with 19th-century logistics and 20th-century bureaucracy. Before 2035, India must build reliable ports and multimodal logistics, modernize customs and inspection systems, repair the broken last-mile ecosystem, simplify compliance, reduce regulatory unpredictability, and enforce contracts cleanly. If this remains unresolved, “Make in India” becomes a slogan tied to political cycles rather than a structural transformation. Global supply chains will choose Vietnam, Indonesia, Mexico, or Eastern Europe. India will fall off the map.

Talent Architecture: Fixing the Leakages Across the Pipeline

Demographics mean nothing if the pipeline leaks at every stage. Before 2035, India must reform schools to move from rote learning to conceptual mastery, universities to attract and retain global-level faculty, research institutions to free them from bureaucratic suffocation, industry to shift from mass hiring to deep capability-building, startups to build technical depth rather than valuation theatrics, and the public sector to upgrade skill levels in governance and regulatory bodies. Without talent architecture, capability collapses. India cannot become a leader in compute while exporting its best minds and under-using its brightest talent.

Institutional Strengthening: The Stability Engine

Before 2035, India must stabilize courts, regulators, civil services, scientific bodies, investigative agencies, and state–centre coordination mechanisms. Even the best capability cannot overcome institutional fragility. Ambitious reforms drown in weak execution. Global investors withdraw at the first sign of unpredictability. Foreign partners hesitate when institutions seem politically captured or operationally inconsistent. If India enters 2035 with unstable institutions, it enters 2035 unprepared.

Political Maturity: Reducing Noise and Increasing Continuity

India cannot afford constant policy U-turns, ideological distractions, election-driven governance, populism overriding structural reforms, or personality-centric politics that reset progress every five years. Before 2035, India must cultivate political maturity—regardless of who is in power. Strength must come from systems, not individuals; from continuity, not chaos.

Strategic Integration: Choosing Where India Must Embed Itself

India must intentionally enter global architectures: QUAD tech corridors, U.S.–Japan semiconductor alliances, EU regulatory cooperation, Indo-Israel defense-tech ecosystems, Indo-Australia supply chain networks, and Africa development corridors. If India does not choose where it belongs, someone else will choose for it. Late entry into global structures results in dependence, not partnership.

The most dangerous assumption India makes is that the window will stay open. It won't. By 2035, the architecture of the century will be finalized.

India must build: compute → chips → industry → institutions → integration—all at once, all in the same decade.

If it succeeds, India joins the architecture. If it fails, India becomes a user of someone else's.

The internal clock is ticking—and unlike elections, extensions will not be granted.

18.3 — The 2035 Decision Point: Build, Borrow, or Break

This is the section where the narrative sharpens—where the abstract timeline becomes a concrete decision India cannot postpone. If

Section 1 established the global window and Section 2 mapped India's internal architecture, Section 3 becomes the moment of truth: what will India choose? Because by 2035, the world will not wait, the markets will not pause, and geopolitics will not negotiate with indecision. India must choose its architecture—deliberately, urgently, intelligently—or live with the consequences that follow.

The First Fork: Build Your Own Architecture

This is the sovereignty path—arduous, expensive, politically inconvenient, institutionally demanding, but ultimately the only route to true national power. If India chooses to build, it means investing billions into compute and chip ecosystems without expecting instant political dividends, upgrading universities and research institutions even if reforms disrupt entrenched interests, strengthening courts and regulators without political interference, aligning states with national missions, creating a talent pipeline that prioritizes mastery over mass certification, and building domestic innovation capacity instead of waiting for foreign technology. This is the hardest path—because it requires maturity, patience, and discipline in a system addicted to shortcuts and announcements. But if India takes it, 2035 becomes the beginning of acceleration—not its end.

The Second Fork: Borrow Capability and Hope for Stability

This is the most tempting path—and the most dangerous. If India chooses to borrow rather than build, the next decade will look deceptively successful: cloud giants providing cheap compute, foreign semiconductor partners offering packaging or assembly deals, global AI companies integrating Indian datasets, international investors pouring capital into India's scale story, foreign universities absorbing Indian talent and returning managerial elites, global supply chains using India as a low-cost link. On the surface, everything will look bright. Underneath, India will be outsourcing sovereignty—dependency disguised as partnership. Borrowed capacity makes India fast, but never strong. Borrowed architecture makes India important, but never indispensable. Borrowed capability gives India headlines, but not leverage. Nations that rise through borrowed strength remain vulnerable to the lender.

The Third Fork: Break Under the Weight of Missed Deadlines

This is the path no one chooses explicitly—yet nations reach it through denial, distraction, ego, and political comfort. If India refuses to decide, refuses to reform, refuses to acknowledge its architectural deficits, by 2035 it will face consequences that no narrative can mask: compute deficits will make AI impossible to scale, chip scarcity will stall manufacturing growth, talent flight will deepen, institutions will collapse under rising demand, industry will hit a productivity ceiling, India's geopolitical leverage will shrink dramatically, economic growth will stagnate into middle-income irreversibility, global networks will bypass India in favor of more predictable partners. History shows: nations do not fall because of enemies. They fall because they miss the pivot points that determine the next century.

The Structural Choice Beneath the Surface

India's decision is not between the U.S., China, or autarky. It is between building capability or importing it, strengthening institutions or bypassing them, creating talent or exporting it, stabilizing governance or politicizing it, integrating strategically or reacting emotionally, becoming an architecture nation or a user nation. 2035 is not a geopolitical year; it is a structural milestone. The world will have chosen its winners. Systems will be locked. Technologies entrenched. Supply chains finalized. Talent pools allocated. Compute hierarchies cemented. India must decide before the cement dries.

The real danger is not that India chooses the wrong path. The real danger is that India refuses to choose at all.

2035 is not about destiny; it is about decision-making. Nations rise through clarity, not hope. Sovereignty is not inherited; it is engineered. India stands before the fork, holding ambition in one hand and uncertainty in the other.

The world has already started running. India must decide whether it will build its engine—or be carried, or be left behind.

18.4 — The Consequence Curve: Nations Don't Collapse Suddenly—They Drift Quietly

This section shifts from analysis to warning. If Sections 1–3 presented the window, the architecture, and the forks, Section 4 introduces the long arc of consequences—the part nations always underestimate. Decline is rarely dramatic. It is silent, incremental, deceptively slow. It arrives not as an explosion but as a quiet erosion of potential. And 2035 becomes the moment when India either resets its trajectory—or locks itself into a curve that becomes impossible to reverse.

Decline Is Not a Fall—It Is a Drift

Nations don't wake up one morning and realize they have failed. They drift—inch by inch—into irrelevance. Talent leaves quietly. Foreign investors diversify quietly. Global supply chains skip a country quietly. Startups relocate quietly. Universities lose competitiveness quietly. Political noise escalates quietly. Institutions weaken quietly. Innovation slows quietly. Bureaucracies become ceremonial quietly. Nothing dramatic happens. The dashboard still shows growth, optimism, conferences, big statements. But the underlying architecture decays beneath the surface, unannounced. This is how nations miss their moment—not through crisis, but through comfort.

The Hard Truth: 2035 Is a One-Way Door

Some historical windows do not reopen. Once global compute hierarchies solidify, late entrants cannot renegotiate access. Once semiconductor clusters lock into regions, supply chains cannot be relocated easily. Once talent ecosystems settle, reversibility becomes nearly impossible. Once countries fall into middle-income stagnation, escaping requires miracles. 2035 is that kind of one-way door. Cross it with capability, and India gets a seat at the table. Cross it without capability, and India becomes a permanent consumer in a world of producers. In geopolitics, the most expensive mistakes are the ones nations don't notice in real time.

Dependency Deepens Quietly—and Permanently

If India misses the 2035 window, its compute will be rented, its AI second-hand, its chips restricted, its innovation derivative, its talent migrated, its foreign policy constrained, its economy a service outlet for architecture nations, its sovereignty negotiable. Dependency doesn't announce itself with humiliation. It arrives as convenience, affordability, partnerships—until one day, every pillar of national power is externally controlled. Dependency is not a failure of ambition. It is a failure of timing.

Opportunity Is Also a Curve—Not a Constant

Just as decline drifts, so does opportunity. If India invests now—seriously, structurally, strategically—its trajectory can bend upward beyond anything in its post-independence history. Because India's advantages are massive: demographic scale, economic momentum, global trust capital, diaspora leverage, strategic geography, political relevance, market depth, and cultural soft power. But these advantages are perishable. They expire if architecture does not convert them into compounding capability. In the compute century, potential has a short shelf life.

The Final Insight: History Rewards the Prepared, Not the Hopeful

History does not reward nations for wanting greatness. It rewards nations for preparing for it. 2035 is not India's deadline—it is India's mirror. What India sees in that mirror will depend entirely on what it builds before it arrives. Nations don't accelerate because the world gives them a chance. Nations accelerate because they build the capability to seize that chance.

The consequence curve is already forming. India must decide whether it bends upward—or downward—before 2035 locks it in.

18.5 — The Last Window: Why 2035 Decides India's Next 50 Years

Some windows in history open once, stay open briefly, and then close for generations. 2035 is that window for India—not because the calendar demands it, but because global architectures are converging into irreversible shapes. This is the moment India must confront with gravity, clarity, and urgency.

The Compute Century Will Freeze Into Place

Technological epochs are not fluid forever. They solidify. They crystallize. They lock in hierarchies that define global power. By 2035, AI leaders will be entrenched, chip supply chains geographically concentrated, cloud infrastructures monopolized, defense technologies reliant on compute pipelines already established, global labor markets sorted between creators and consumers, and innovation networks self-reinforcing. Once that architecture becomes rigid, late entrants cannot break in—not with ambition, not with diplomacy, not even with money. This is why 2035 matters. It is not prophecy. It is the natural closing of an architectural cycle.

Demography's Advantage Turns Into Burden After 2035

India's demographic dividend is a timer, not a guarantee. Right now, India's working-age population is expanding. By the early 2030s, it peaks. After that, the dependency ratio rises, and the dividend turns into a demographic tax. If India does not convert this vast young workforce into scientists, engineers, builders, researchers, innovators, creators, administrators, and leaders before 2035, the opportunity disappears. A young population without capability is not strength—it is pressure. History is unforgiving to nations that waste their youth window.

Economic Momentum Is Also a One-Time Gift

India grows today because global investors see potential, supply chains want diversification, geopolitical shifts favor India, and the world wants an alternative to China. But momentum is not permanent. If India fails to build capability, credibility, and stability by 2035, investors will move to Africa and Southeast Asia, manufacturers will settle elsewhere, research collaborations will bypass India, global supply chains will anchor in other regions, and capital will treat India as a market—not a maker. Nations rarely get a second momentum wave. Missing the first is often fatal.

If India Doesn't Rise Now, It Gets Locked Into Dependency

India's future is not between "rise" and "decline." It is between sovereignty and dependency. If India does not build compute, chips, talent depth, industrial backbone, institutional strength, research ecosystems, and predictable governance by 2035, it becomes structurally dependent for the next 50 years. Once critical technologies settle into fixed global monopolies, breaking them requires impossible effort. Dependency becomes architecture. Architecture becomes destiny. And destiny becomes irreversible.

History Remembers Nations by What They Did With Their Window

Every nation gets one defining moment. Japan had 1950–1970. South Korea had 1975–1995. China had 1990–2010. Europe had the post-war golden decades. America had the long 20th century. India's moment is 2025–2035. This is the only decade in which geopolitics favors India, demography favors India, global markets seek diversification, technology transitions are still fluid, supply chains are still movable, domestic optimism is still high, and international trust is still strong. After 2035, the curve hardens. What India builds becomes permanent. What India ignores becomes permanent.

"Nations do not rise because they are destined to. They rise because they recognize the moment meant for them— and act before it disappears."

Closing Reflection — Part V

The 2035 Equation Becomes a Blueprint

Part V brought the book to its sharpest edge. After tracing India's position in global architectures, its internal contradictions, and the tightening noose of time, this part finally answered the only question that matters: what must India build?

If Parts I–IV revealed the diagnosis, Part V delivered the prescription. Not slogans. Not sentiments. Not political fantasies. But architecture—cold, structural, foundational.

It unmasked the myth that national destiny is shaped by elections, personalities, or temporary economic spikes. Instead, it showed that sovereignty is engineered—stitched into courts that can deliver justice on time, bureaucracies that can execute without fear, regulators that can safeguard markets, universities that can produce knowledge, and state systems that can function with coherence.

Part V also revealed the truth that India's ambitions cannot sit on brittle institutions. A billion aspirations cannot live inside outdated architectures. And a global-power dream cannot survive on political memory, emotional nationalism, or borrowed technology.

It ended with a simple but profound realization: capability is not built by inspiration. Capability is built by institutions.

The message is unambiguous and heavy: India stands at the threshold of becoming a sovereign nation in the compute century—but only if it rebuilds the systems that carry its ambitions.

Part V stripped the conversation of illusions. It directed the reader's eyes to the scaffolding that actually holds a nation up—and warned what happens when that scaffolding cracks.

Now the journey shifts.

Part VI — The Architecture Of A Sovereign India

India has diagnosed its gaps. It understands global architectures. It knows the cost of chaos, dependency, and delay.

Now it must design—systematically, deliberately, uncompromisingly—the architecture that will carry it into 2035 and beyond.

Part V — The Architecture of a Sovereign India

"Nations do not rise by destiny. They rise by design." — Chavanian Maxim on Sovereignty

Overview

Part V is where ambition becomes engineering. After exposing India's structural vulnerabilities and the global race reshaping power, this section shifts from diagnosis to construction. It is the pivot from warning to blueprint, from critique to architecture.

Here, the reader is guided through the five foundational architectures that will determine whether India becomes a sovereign power or remains a dependent participant:

- **Institutional Resilience** — the scaffolding that ensures continuity, coherence, and credibility.
- **Leadership Maturity** — the discipline to govern beyond charisma, cycles, and noise.
- **Economic Design** — the structural frameworks that convert growth into durability and leverage.
- **Talent Systems** — the pipelines that transform demographic scale into intellectual sovereignty.
- **Digital Security** — the shield and backbone of sovereignty in the compute century.

Each chapter dismantles old assumptions and rebuilds the conceptual scaffolding for a 21st-century India—one capable of executing at scale, retaining its best minds, absorbing global shocks, and commanding respect in an architecture-driven world.

Part V is practical, strategic, and unforgiving in its clarity: India's future will be built, not inherited.

Chapter 19 — India's Institutional Rebuild

Courts, Bureaucracy, Regulation, and State Capacity

The Nation Trying to Build Skyscrapers on Sand

It's a bright morning in New Delhi. Television screens beam with confidence—another expressway is inaugurated, another space mission celebrated, another global summit staged with the polish of a rising power. India looks ready for the world, eager to prove it belongs among the giants.

But beneath the glitter, the foundation tells a different story. In a district court, a judge flips through a case file that has dragged on for two decades, knowing the verdict will likely come after he retires. A young IAS officer, transferred three times in two years, hesitates to take bold decisions because tomorrow's order might undo today's courage. A regulator drafts guidelines, but before they pass through logic, they must pass through politics, industry pressure, and bureaucratic caution. A state government struggles to coordinate with the Centre—not because of policy differences, but because of political score-keeping.

This is India's quiet contradiction: a skyline of ambition resting on a foundation of sand. We celebrate what rises at the top while ignoring what erodes at the bottom. We build taller, faster, louder—while the pillars meant to carry that height buckle under outdated processes, corruption-soaked incentives, judicial fatigue, and administrative overstretch.

The tragedy is not that India lacks brilliance. The tragedy is that brilliance must first fight its own institutions before it can serve the nation.

This chapter refuses to romanticize India's rise. Because in the compute century, no nation becomes a superpower if its institutions remain colonial in design, political in function, and exhausted in execution. Here, the façade ends—and the reconstruction begins.

19.1 — Courts: Justice That Arrives Too Late to Matter

India's courts are not just delayed—they are drowning. A century-old judicial architecture is trying to govern a billion-person society moving at digital speed. The mismatch is brutal. Step into any district courtroom and you see the slow violence of backlog: dusty files stacked like tombstones, litigants aging as their cases crawl forward, lawyers whose careers stretch across generations of hearings, and judges who work harder than the system allows but never fast enough to change the arithmetic. Justice here is not denied—it is deferred until it loses meaning.

This is not cynicism, but painful clarity. The judiciary was built for a different India—smaller, simpler, less complex. Today, it must handle everything from cybercrime to corporate fraud to constitutional battles with tools designed for a time when land disputes were the nation's biggest headache. Yet governments of every stripe have allowed judicial reform to remain ceremonial, not structural. Vacancies linger for years. Courtrooms lack modern research support. Digitalization exists as patchwork. And political interference—sometimes subtle, sometimes blunt—corrodes independence whenever power feels threatened.

The consequences are not confined to the legal sphere. They ripple across the economy, society, and strategy. Investors hesitate because disputes take decades to resolve. Startups avoid innovation that risks litigation. Citizens lose trust in the state's ability to protect them. Criminals and corrupt officials exploit delay as a shield. Every pending case bleeds quiet productivity from the nation.

The uncomfortable truth is simple: no country becomes powerful if its justice system moves slower than its criminals, its economy, or its crises. A court system that cannot enforce contracts cripples industry. A system that cannot punish wrongdoing encourages corruption. A system that cannot resolve disputes in time undermines its own legitimacy.

India's rise will not be determined by GDP figures or diplomatic summits alone. It will be determined by whether its courts can deliver justice before justice becomes irrelevant.

This section lands with a firm but empathetic indictment: India cannot leap into the future with a judiciary shackled to the past.

19.2 — Bureaucracy: A Machine Built for Control, Not Delivery

India's bureaucracy was designed to run an empire, not a modern nation-state. Its architecture still carries the DNA of colonial governance—layers of hierarchy, an obsession with files over outcomes, a culture of compliance rather than creativity, and an instinct to police instead of enable.

Picture the familiar scene: a young entrepreneur waiting outside a government office, clutching a folder thicker than their business plan, watching clerks move paper from one desk to another as though national growth depends on the choreography of signatures.

This is not incompetence—it is misalignment. India's bureaucracy is filled with intelligent, committed officers. But they operate inside a system engineered to slow, not accelerate. A system where approval matters more than execution, where avoiding mistakes is rewarded more than achieving impact, where transfers erase institutional memory, and where the most capable officers spend half their careers fighting internal sabotage.

The deep structural issues are clear:

- Promotion by seniority, not performance, creating incentives to wait rather than innovate.
- Turf battles between ministries, where coordination dies in paperwork and pride.
- Perverse incentives, where saying "no" is safer than attempting something new.
- Politicized postings, turning administrative careers into loyalty tests.
- Absence of specialization, forcing generalists to run complex modern sectors—AI, infrastructure, climate policy—with outdated toolkits.

The painful truth is this: India's bureaucracy is not underperforming because of its people—it is underperforming because of its structure. Even the brightest IAS officer cannot fix a broken supply chain system with a district-level mandate. Even the sharpest secretary cannot deliver national-scale reform when every decision is hostage to ten parallel departments.

The national cost is immense: delayed projects, paralyzed reforms, stalled innovations, regulatory confusion, investor distrust, and public frustration. Talent that could build the future ends up managing paperwork from the past.

And in a century defined by compute, AI, semiconductors, climate risk, and complex interdependence, India's administrative machinery is still optimized for maintaining order, not driving progress. The bureaucracy works tirelessly—but rarely toward the outcomes the century demands.

The conclusion is sharp yet hopeful: India does not need to replace its bureaucracy; it needs to repurpose it. Empower specialists. Redesign incentives. Protect autonomy. Digitize intelligently. Break silos. Mandate accountability. Build career pathways that reward delivery, not delay.

Without this transformation, India will remain a nation where brilliant policies die in mediocre execution—and where the potential of a billion people stays trapped inside a governance machine never built for the future.

19.3 — Regulation: When the Referee Becomes the Roadblock

India's regulators were meant to be the guardians of fairness, stability, and long-term national interest. Instead, too many have become gatekeepers of delay, confusion, and contradictory mandates.

Picture the moment: a tech founder receives two notices from two different regulatory bodies—one asking him to expand his service, the other asking him to shut it down—both signed on the same day. He laughs, not out of humor, but out of resignation. This is the cost of navigating a regulatory maze that cannot decide what it wants to protect or promote.

India's regulatory ecosystem is a patchwork—part colonial legacy, part 1990s reform attempt, part political battleground. Regulators often behave like micro-governments unto themselves, operating with unclear mandates, outdated frameworks, and little coordination.

The fault lines are visible:

- Overlapping jurisdictions that compete for influence rather than collaborate for clarity.
- Rules designed for a previous technological era, incapable

of handling digital markets, AI, fintech, biotech, or modern manufacturing.

- Politically appointed leadership, compromising autonomy, continuity, and credibility.
- Reactive policy-making, swinging between extremes based on headlines, scandals, or electoral cycles instead of long-term strategy.
- Opaque processes, leaving businesses unable to predict how regulators will interpret the rules they themselves have written.

Regulation should be the scaffolding that holds innovation safely—not the cage that suffocates it. But in India, regulation often swings between two damaging modes: excessive policing and complete abdication. When regulators crack down, they cripple industry. When they look away, they invite chaos. Both outcomes erode trust.

The impact on national progress is profound. Startups scale slower because compliance becomes a second full-time job. Global companies hesitate because India's regulatory signals oscillate. Investors demand risk premiums for unpredictability. Innovation dies before it reaches the market because regulatory timelines exceed business timelines.

And in a world where technology evolves in months, India's regulatory cycle still runs on multi-year deliberations, consultations, and committee reports. The referee has fallen behind the game.

Yet the tone here is constructive, not cynical. Effective regulation could become India's strategic advantage—if redesigned for speed, clarity, transparency, and modernity. Regulators need expertise, autonomy, digital competence, and a clear mandate to facilitate national capability, not political theatrics.

A nation cannot build sovereignty on systems that fear innovation. Regulation must become India's launchpad, not its leash.

19.4 — State Capacity: The Missing Engine of a Billion-Person Nation

State capacity is the quiet force that determines whether a country actually works. Not the speeches, not the slogans, not the press conferences—but the ability of government machinery to deliver services, enforce laws, implement reforms, manage crises, and coordinate across vast complexity. And here lies India's stark contrast: it dreams like a continental superpower but often executes like a scattered federation of disjointed offices, uneven capabilities, and fragile administrative bandwidth.

Picture the reality. A flood in one state where rescue teams fail to coordinate. A digital service crash in another because servers were never upgraded. An infrastructure project in a third that stalls because local officials weren't trained to manage contractors. A national scheme delayed because last-mile data was wrong. This patchwork becomes the face of India's governance—not because people don't care, but because the state simply lacks the muscle to act coherently at scale.

The breakdown is structural:

- State governments with wildly uneven competencies, creating a country where public service quality depends on geography, not citizenship.
- Local administrations starved of funds, technology, and trained personnel, forced to improvise with obsolete tools.
- Central ministries issuing directives faster than states can absorb them, turning reform into paperwork.
- Coordination failures, where vital information stops at bureaucratic borders or dies in departmental silos.

- Emergency systems designed for a smaller, slower India, unable to respond to climate shocks, cyber threats, or large-scale disruptions.

The deeper injury is this: state capacity has never been treated as a national project. Political cycles favor announcements over administration. Bureaucratic reform is avoided because it threatens entrenched interests. Capacity-building institutions are underfunded, understaffed, and politically sidelined. As a result, India relies not on system strength but on individual heroism—officers who stretch beyond human limits to compensate for broken machinery. But individuals cannot carry architectural deficits forever.

The national cost is immense. Reforms collapse between vision and execution. Crises turn into tragedies instead of manageable events. Citizens lose faith in governance. Businesses lose trust in regulatory consistency. Foreign partners hesitate because they cannot predict delivery. Talent avoids public service because the system punishes initiative.

State capacity is not bureaucracy. It is the operating system that makes everything else possible—economic growth, security, digital transformation, social welfare, global credibility. India cannot enter the compute century with an execution engine designed for an agrarian nation.

If India wants to rise, it must rebuild not just policies, but the very machinery that turns policies into reality. The world's largest democracy cannot afford the world's most overburdened state. Sovereignty is not won through speeches—it is built through the patient, disciplined construction of a state that can deliver for a billion people, every single day.

Chapter 20 — Leadership Architecture for a Billion People

Why the next decade demands teams, not icons.

The Nation Waiting for a Superhero Who Will Never Arrive

India has always looked upward when it dreams of transformation. Crowds gather in stadiums, chanting the names of leaders as though one voice could bend the arc of history. Political narratives revolve around individuals—heroes who promise to cut through the noise, reformers who vow to sweep away corruption, saviors who claim they can carry the weight of a billion people on their shoulders. Television screens magnify their gestures, newspapers amplify their words, and social media turns them into symbols of destiny.

It is a cinematic scene: a nation waiting for a superhero. Waiting for the one leader who will solve the contradictions, accelerate the economy, modernize the bureaucracy, reform the courts, stabilize the politics, and integrate India into global architectures—all at once, all alone. The expectation is intoxicating, but it is also a trap.

Because beneath the spectacle, the real machinery of progress remains neglected. Teams of civil servants who must execute reforms. Institutions that must endure beyond electoral cycles. Experts who must design policy with technical precision. Continuity that must survive the churn of politics. These are the engines of sovereignty, but they rarely make headlines. They are invisible in the glare of personality-driven politics.

The truth is sharp: no single leader can carry a billion-person nation into the compute century. The scale is too vast, the complexity too deep, the challenges too interconnected. Sovereignty in this century will not be won by charisma or speeches—it will be engineered by coordinated leadership architecture. By systems that reward collaboration over ego, by teams that blend political vision with administrative execution, by institutions that protect continuity when personalities fade.

India's rise will not come from waiting for a superhero who will never arrive. It will come from building a leadership design that multiplies competence, distributes responsibility, and sustains progress across decades. The next decade demands teams, not icons.

20.1 — The Failure of One-Man Models: Why Icons Cannot Scale

India has a recurring habit: when faced with complexity, it looks for a single figure to embody the solution. The nation bets on individuals instead of systems, icons instead of institutions. Crowds cheer leaders as if charisma alone can substitute for architecture. Political campaigns promise transformation through personality. Media narratives elevate reformers as saviors. And governance itself often bends toward the gravitational pull of one office, one voice, one decision-maker.

This personality-driven governance creates a dangerous illusion. It suggests that national progress can be scripted by speeches, rallies, or symbolic gestures. But the machinery of a billion-person nation cannot be powered by charisma. Charisma inspires; it does not execute. Capability requires systems. Continuity requires institutions. Scale requires teams.

Over-centralization compounds the problem. Decisions that should flow through ministries, regulators, and state governments are pulled upward into a single node of authority. Ministers are often chosen for loyalty rather than competence, reducing them to extensions of personality rather than engines of expertise. Policy becomes hostage to political calculation, and execution slows under the weight of bottlenecks. The exhaustion of single-node decision-making is visible everywhere: files waiting for signatures, reforms delayed until approval, crises managed reactively because one office cannot process the volume of complexity pouring in from every corner of the nation.

The illusion that charisma equals capability is perhaps the most seductive trap. A leader may command crowds, dominate headlines, and project confidence—but none of that translates into semiconductor ecosystems, AI governance frameworks, climate resilience strategies, or supply-chain modernization. These are domains that demand distributed expertise, technical mastery, and institutional depth. No single mind, however brilliant, can manage the interlocking challenges of the compute century.

Modern complexity is unforgiving. AI requires coordinated research corridors, ethical frameworks, and compute infrastructure. Climate risk demands multi-level governance, from local disaster response to national energy transitions. Supply chains depend on ports, logistics, contracts, and global trust—all requiring thousands of decisions executed coherently. Semiconductor ecosystems are intricate webs of design, fabrication, packaging, and testing, spread across continents. To imagine that one leader, one office, or one personality can orchestrate this is to mistake theater for architecture.

India's repeated reliance on one-man models has left it vulnerable to cycles of exhaustion. Each leader promises acceleration, but without systems, the promise collapses into noise. Each reformer vows transformation, but without institutions, the transformation stalls. Each icon inspires hope, but without teams, the hope dissipates.

The reality is sharp: nations scale through architecture, not icons. Sovereignty in the compute century will not be won by the charisma of individuals but by the maturity of systems. India must move beyond the myth of the superhero leader. It must design leadership as a distributed architecture—teams that multiply competence, institutions that sustain continuity, and systems that absorb complexity. Only then can ambition translate into execution, and execution into sovereignty.

20.2 — The Architecture of Team Leadership: How Strong Nations Actually Govern

Strong nations do not rise on the shoulders of single leaders. They rise on the scaffolding of leadership architectures—systems that distribute responsibility, embed expertise, and ensure continuity beyond electoral cycles or political personalities. The contrast across the world is instructive, and it reveals why India must shift from hero-driven governance to architecture-driven leadership.

In the United States, decision-making is deliberately distributed. Cabinet secretaries, independent agencies, congressional committees, and state governments all share power. The system is messy, often slow, but it is resilient. No single leader can dictate the nation's trajectory alone. The architecture forces collaboration, checks excess, and ensures that expertise—whether in defense, finance, or technology—has institutional weight. America's strength lies not in the charisma of its presidents but in the depth of its leadership layers.

China offers a different model: technocratic layering. Its governance is built on councils of engineers, economists, and planners who rise through decades of specialized experience. Leadership is not just political—it is technical. Five-year plans are not slogans; they are execution blueprints crafted by teams of experts embedded in the state machinery. The system is authoritarian, but its technocratic depth allows China to mobilize resources at scale and sustain long-term projects without being hostage to individual charisma.

Europe demonstrates the power of institutional leadership. The European Union, with its commissions, councils, and parliaments, is designed to outlast political cycles. National governments operate within frameworks that emphasize process, negotiation, and continuity. Leadership here is not about icons but about institutions that absorb shocks, mediate conflicts, and sustain collective progress. Europe's resilience comes from the fact that no single leader can dismantle the architecture—it is too embedded, too layered, too institutionalized.

South Korea and Taiwan showcase expert-led councils. Their rise in technology and manufacturing was not driven by singular personalities but by leadership teams that blended political will with technical mastery. Councils of scientists, engineers, and industrial strategists guided national priorities, ensuring that semiconductor ecosystems, research clusters, and industrial policies were executed with precision. Their leadership architecture was cross-functional, data-driven, and deeply strategic—designed to survive beyond the tenure of any one government.

The lesson is clear: sovereign nations build leadership teams, not cults of personality. They design cross-functional structures that integrate domain experts, data systems, and institutional continuity. They embed competence into the architecture so that progress does not depend on charisma, and reforms do not collapse when personalities fade.

India must make this shift. Hero-driven governance cannot scale to the complexity of AI ecosystems, climate resilience, semiconductor alliances, or supply-chain modernization. These are challenges that demand distributed expertise, coordinated execution, and institutional maturity. Competence must matter more than charisma. Architecture must matter more than applause.

The future of India's sovereignty will not be decided by the strength of one leader's voice but by the strength of the teams, institutions, and systems that carry the nation forward. To govern a billion people in the compute century, India must build leadership as architecture—resilient, expert-driven, and designed to outlast the noise of politics.

20.3 — Competence Over Loyalty: The Next Decade's Leadership Mandate

India's internal reality is sobering. Ministers often manage portfolios they do not understand. Energy policy is overseen by politicians with no grounding in science. Digital ministries are led by those unfamiliar with technology. Finance portfolios are sometimes entrusted to individuals without deep economic training. Education is guided by leaders who have never worked inside a classroom or research institution. The mismatch is glaring: a billion-person nation navigating the most complex century in history with leadership pipelines that reward loyalty over competence.

Civil servants fare little better. Transfers arrive before they can learn the intricacies of a sector. Officers who begin to understand infrastructure are suddenly moved to agriculture. Those who grasp health policy are reassigned to transport. Institutional memory evaporates with every reshuffle, leaving ministries perpetually in training mode. Political appointees, often chosen for allegiance rather than expertise, compound the problem. Bureaucratic silos block interdisciplinary leadership, ensuring that climate policy, digital transformation, and industrial modernization remain fragmented instead of integrated.

This is not a critique of individuals—it is a critique of the system. A system that confuses loyalty with capability, that prizes obedience over knowledge, that treats governance as a political reward rather than a professional responsibility. The result is predictable: policies that sound ambitious but collapse in execution, reforms that look visionary but stall in delivery, and institutions that remain brittle because they are never led by those who understand their complexity.

Modern governance cannot be managed this way. The compute century demands competence at the helm. Scientists must lead energy ministries, because energy transitions are technical, not rhetorical. Technologists must guide digital ministries, because AI, cybersecurity, and cloud infrastructure cannot be managed by generalists. Economists must shape finance portfolios, because fiscal stability and global capital flows require precision. Educationists must direct human resource development, because the future of talent cannot be scripted by those unfamiliar with pedagogy or research.

Professionalized leadership pipelines are no longer optional—they are the mandate of sovereignty. Nations that embed expertise into governance scale faster, execute better, and command greater trust. Nations that confuse charisma with competence drift into dependency. India cannot afford to remain in the latter category.

The next decade must be unapologetically honest: loyalty cannot be the currency of leadership. Competence must be. India must design systems where ministers are chosen for mastery, civil servants are retained long enough to build institutional depth, and interdisciplinary councils break silos to integrate expertise across domains.

The stakes are clear. Without competence, India will remain a nation of announcements. With competence, it can become a nation of execution. Sovereignty in the compute century will not be won by loyalty—it will be won by knowledge, discipline, and professionalized leadership.

20.4 — Leadership as Infrastructure: The Operating System India Must Build

Leadership is not a person. It is a system. This is the philosophical punchline India must absorb before the 2035 window closes. Nations that confuse leaders for leadership drift into fragility; nations that design leadership as infrastructure build sovereignty that endures.

India's political imagination has long been dominated by individuals—icons who inspire, reformers who promise, saviors who symbolize. But the compute century is not built on symbols. It is built on operating systems: architectures of leadership that ensure continuity, reliability, neutrality, quality, and scale.

Teams ensure continuity. No single leader can outlast the churn of politics, but well-designed teams can carry reforms across decades. When ministries embed cross-functional leadership groups, when councils of experts sustain national missions, when institutional memory is preserved through collective stewardship, the nation gains resilience. Continuity is not charisma—it is architecture.

Processes ensure reliability. Leadership cannot depend on improvisation or personal instinct. It must be encoded in processes that guarantee predictable outcomes. Whether in disaster response, industrial policy, or digital regulation, reliability comes from systems that work the same way regardless of who occupies the office. Nations rise when their processes deliver results without drama.

Institutions ensure neutrality. Leadership must be shielded from the volatility of politics. Courts, regulators, universities, and scientific bodies must operate as neutral guardians of long-term interest. When institutions are strong, leadership becomes impartial, credible, and trusted. Neutrality is not weakness—it is the foundation of legitimacy.

Expertise ensures quality. Leadership in the compute century cannot be generic. Energy transitions require scientists. Digital ecosystems require technologists. Finance requires economists. Education requires educationists. Quality comes from embedding domain mastery into leadership pipelines. Without expertise, leadership becomes rhetoric. With expertise, it becomes execution.

Coordination ensures scale. A billion-person nation cannot be governed through isolated silos. Leadership must be designed as a network—ministries, states, regulators, and councils working in sync. Coordination multiplies capacity, prevents duplication, and ensures that national missions move forward as coherent strategies rather than fragmented projects. Scale is not achieved by speeches—it is achieved by synchronized systems.

The quiet but powerful truth is this: nations fall when they confuse leaders for leadership. Nations rise when leadership becomes architecture.

India must stop waiting for superheroes and start building operating systems. Leadership must be treated as infrastructure—designed deliberately, maintained continuously, and upgraded relentlessly. Just as roads carry commerce and grids carry electricity, leadership architecture must carry sovereignty. Without it, ambition collapses into noise. With it, ambition becomes execution.

The century will not reward nations that rely on personalities. It will reward nations that build leadership as infrastructure—an operating system capable of carrying a billion people into the future.

Chapter 21 — Economic Architecture for Compute Power

Designing sectors that shape sovereignty

The Economy Built on Borrowed Engines

India's dashboards glow with confidence. GDP charts climb upward, exports tick higher, startups announce record valuations, and global headlines celebrate the country as the next great growth story. On the surface, the picture is dazzling: a nation rising, a market expanding, an economy seemingly unstoppable.

But beneath the glow lies a quieter, more unsettling truth. The engines powering this rise—chips that drive devices, cloud infrastructures that host data, algorithms that shape commerce, advanced manufacturing systems that produce precision goods, research tools that enable discovery—belong largely to other nations. India's ambition is domestic, but its architecture is imported. The scaffolding of its economic success rests on foundations designed elsewhere.

Picture the contrast. A startup founder in Bengaluru builds an app celebrated worldwide, but the servers run on foreign cloud platforms. A factory in Gujarat produces automobiles at scale, but the semiconductors inside are shipped from Taiwan or South Korea. A research lab in Pune publishes breakthrough papers, but the instruments are sourced from Europe. Even India's booming digital economy—its payments, logistics, and e-commerce—rides on algorithms and architectures conceived outside its borders.

The scene is cinematic but sobering: a nation sprinting forward, powered by engines it does not own. The dashboards look impressive, but the levers of sovereignty remain external. India celebrates growth, yet the architecture of that growth is borrowed.

This is the paradox of the present moment. Economic ambition is real, but economic architecture is fragile. Sovereignty in the compute century will not be measured by GDP alone. It will be measured by who owns the engines of growth—who designs the chips, who controls the clouds, who writes the algorithms, who builds the manufacturing ecosystems, who develops the research tools.

And here the truth lands with quiet force: in the compute century, an economy built on someone else's architecture is an economy built on sand.

21.1 — The Hard Truth: Services Cannot Carry a Compute Century Nation

India's economic story of the last three decades has been written in code and call centers. IT services, business process outsourcing, and low-value global contracts became the engines of growth, lifting millions into the middle class and projecting India onto the global stage as the "back office of the world." For a time, this model worked brilliantly. Labour arbitrage—offering skilled workers at lower costs—was India's comparative advantage. But in the compute century, this advantage is no longer enough.

The limits of labour arbitrage are now visible. What once seemed infinite—global demand for outsourced services—has begun to plateau. Contracts that once flowed steadily are now contested by automation, AI, and cheaper competitors in Africa and Southeast Asia. The promise of endless IT exports has flattened because services without deep technology cannot scale into sovereignty. India's IT sector remains impressive in size, but its architecture is shallow: it delivers tasks, not platforms; contracts, not ecosystems; execution, not ownership.

The fragility of service-led growth becomes sharper in a world shifting to automation. Algorithms now perform routine coding. AI systems handle customer queries once managed by call centers. Cloud-based platforms reduce the need for outsourced infrastructure management. The very foundation of India's service economy—human labour performing repetitive tasks—is being eroded by machines that do the same work faster, cheaper, and more reliably. What was once India's strength risks becoming its vulnerability.

Meanwhile, value creation has migrated back to countries that own compute and intellectual property. The nations that design chips, build cloud infrastructures, and control AI frameworks capture the lion's share of profits. India, by contrast, remains a consumer of these architectures. Its companies deliver services on top of platforms they do not own, creating revenue but not sovereignty. The deeper wealth—the patents, the algorithms, the semiconductor clusters, the research breakthroughs—belongs elsewhere.

This is not a dismissal of India's achievements. The IT services revolution transformed the nation's trajectory, created jobs, and built global credibility. But the hard truth is that services alone cannot carry a billion-person nation into the compute century. They cannot deliver the kind of compounding capability that chips, AI, and advanced manufacturing provide. They cannot anchor sovereignty in a world where power is defined by who controls the engines of computation.

India must evolve beyond its comfort zone. It must move from being the world's service provider to being a world-class architect of technology. That means investing in semiconductor ecosystems, building indigenous cloud infrastructures, nurturing deep-tech startups, and embedding research into the core of its economic design. Services can remain part of the story, but they cannot be the whole story.

The diagnosis is sharp but empathetic: India's service-led growth was a remarkable chapter. But the next chapter must be written in compute, not contracts. Without this shift, India risks building its future on sand—an economy impressive in dashboards but fragile in architecture.

21.2 — The Five Sectors That Shape Sovereignty

In the compute century, sovereignty will not be decided by slogans or GDP charts. It will be decided by which nations control the engines of capability—the sectors that define military strength, economic resilience, technological leadership, and innovation frontiers. These are not "industries" in the conventional sense. They are strategic pillars of sovereignty, the scaffolding upon which nations either rise into leadership or drift into dependency.

Semiconductors — The Foundation of Sovereignty

Every modern system—missiles, smartphones, satellites, medical devices, AI platforms—runs on chips. Semiconductors are the invisible currency of power. Nations that design, fabricate, and package chips control the arteries of the global economy. Those that depend on imports remain vulnerable to supply shocks, geopolitical leverage, and technological ceilings. For India, sovereignty begins with silicon. Without indigenous semiconductor ecosystems, every ambition—military, economic, digital—rests on borrowed foundations.

AI & Algorithms — The Engines of Industry and Governance

Artificial intelligence is not just software; it is the operating system of the future. Algorithms will decide how factories run, how cities are managed, how healthcare is delivered, how wars are fought. Nations that own AI frameworks will shape industries and governance alike. Those that consume second-hand algorithms will live under invisible dependencies. Sovereignty in the 21st century will be measured by who writes the code that governs society.

Advanced Manufacturing — Precision Industries That Anchor Resilience

Manufacturing is no longer about scale alone—it is about precision, integration, and resilience. Nations that master advanced manufacturing—robotics, additive technologies, high-precision engineering—anchor their economies against shocks. They can produce critical goods domestically, absorb disruptions in supply chains, and sustain industrial depth. Without advanced manufacturing, economies remain fragile, dependent on imports for their most strategic needs.

Energy Systems & Green Tech — The Backbone of Sustainable Growth

Energy is the bloodstream of sovereignty. Nations that control clean, reliable, and scalable energy systems will power their industries, cities, and militaries without external dependence. Green technologies—solar, wind, hydrogen, storage—are not just environmental choices; they are strategic imperatives. In a century defined by climate risk, energy sovereignty will separate nations that thrive from those that collapse under scarcity and volatility.

Biotech & Frontier Science — The Innovation Frontier

The next breakthroughs—genomics, synthetic biology, quantum computing, space exploration—will redraw the map of power. Biotech in particular will determine food security, healthcare resilience, and even defense capabilities. Nations that lead in frontier science will set the pace of innovation. Those that lag will consume discoveries made elsewhere, forever dependent on external intellectual property.

Together, these five sectors form the architecture of sovereignty. They are not optional industries to be "developed" when convenient. They are the pillars upon which national destiny rests. Nations that build them will lead. Nations that neglect them will follow.

India must recognize this truth: in the compute century, sovereignty is not inherited—it is engineered. And engineering begins with these five sectors.

21.3 — India's Economic Misalignment: Ambition Without Industrial Depth

India speaks the language of ambition fluently. Policy documents announce visions of global leadership. Summits showcase India as the next manufacturing hub. Memorandums of understanding are signed with fanfare, ribbon-cuttings are broadcast as proof of progress, and headlines celebrate the promise of transformation. Yet beneath the spectacle lies a sobering reality: ambition without industrial depth is architecture without foundations.

Policies are announced without execution ecosystems. A semiconductor mission is declared, but fabrication plants remain on paper. A defense modernization plan is unveiled, but procurement pipelines stall in bureaucracy. A renewable energy target is set, but transmission infrastructure lags behind. India's economic narrative is filled with declarations, but the machinery to translate them into reality is fragile, fragmented, and often absent.

Supply chain integration remains weak. Factories operate in isolation, disconnected from logistics networks, research clusters, and global value chains. Components travel across states with delays and inefficiencies, eroding competitiveness. High logistics costs—among the highest in the world—drag down productivity, making Indian goods less competitive even when labor costs are low. The arteries of industrial growth are clogged, and without integration, scale collapses into inefficiency.

Domestic intellectual property and R&D investment remain shallow. India produces talent but not enough patents. Universities generate graduates but not enough breakthroughs. Research institutions struggle with funding, autonomy, and continuity. As a result, India consumes technologies designed elsewhere, embedding dependency into its economic DNA. Without indigenous IP, India cannot anchor sovereignty in the compute century.

Industrial zones are inconsistent. Some regions thrive with infrastructure, skilled labor, and investor confidence. Others remain stuck in outdated frameworks, plagued by unreliable power, poor connectivity, and weak governance. The unevenness creates a patchwork economy where geography determines opportunity, and national ambition fractures into local limitations.

Overreliance on imports for critical components compounds the vulnerability. Chips, sensors, advanced machinery, research instruments—all flow in from abroad. India assembles but does not design. It manufactures but does not own. It exports services but imports sovereignty. The imbalance is stark: a nation aspiring to lead, yet tethered to external supply chains for its most strategic needs.

The critique must be severe because the stakes are existential. Political theatrics—summits, MoUs, ribbon-cuttings—create headlines but rarely translate into deep capability. They project ambition without building architecture. They celebrate announcements while ignoring execution. They create the illusion of progress while the foundations remain brittle.

India's economic misalignment is not about lack of ambition—it is about lack of depth. Sovereignty in the compute century will not be won by declarations. It will be won by industrial ecosystems that integrate supply chains, reduce logistics costs, generate domestic IP, professionalize R&D, and anchor manufacturing in resilient zones. Without this depth, India risks becoming a nation of promises without platforms, ambition without architecture, growth without sovereignty.

21.4 — The Compute-Centric Economy: Designing for Power, Not Just Growth

India's economic story must now move beyond dashboards of GDP growth and startup valuations. Growth alone is no longer the measure of sovereignty. In the compute century, the true test is whether a nation owns the architecture of its economy—the engines of chips, algorithms, manufacturing, energy, and research. Without this architecture, growth is fragile. With it, growth becomes power.

The first pillar is a *national semiconductor mission with real autonomy*. India cannot afford to treat chip design and fabrication as ceremonial projects. It must build end-to-end ecosystems—design, fabrication, packaging, testing—anchored in domestic capability. Autonomy here means freedom from political cycles, continuity across decades, and insulation from short-term pressures. Chips are not just an industry; they are the foundation of military, economic, and digital sovereignty.

The second pillar is *AI infrastructure with domestic compute*. India's digital economy cannot rely indefinitely on rented servers and foreign algorithms. Sovereignty demands indigenous compute clusters, national AI frameworks, and ethical governance designed at home. Without domestic compute, India's innovation will remain derivative. With it, India can shape industries, governance, and society on its own terms.

The third pillar is *manufacturing clusters aligned with global supply chains*. India must move beyond fragmented industrial zones into integrated ecosystems that connect ports, logistics, research hubs, and skilled labor. Precision manufacturing—robotics, additive technologies, advanced engineering—must anchor resilience. Only then can India absorb shocks, scale exports, and embed itself into global supply chains as a maker, not just a market.

The fourth pillar is *export-led precision industries*. India's economic architecture must be designed not just for domestic consumption but for global competitiveness. Precision industries—pharmaceuticals, aerospace, electronics, green technologies—must be scaled for export, embedding India into the arteries of global commerce. Sovereignty is strengthened when the world depends on your products, not when you depend on theirs.

The fifth pillar is *R&D hubs with world-class autonomy*. India's universities and research institutions must be liberated from bureaucratic micromanagement and political interference. They must be funded, professionalized, and empowered to produce breakthroughs. Without indigenous IP, India will remain a consumer of discoveries made elsewhere. With world-class R&D autonomy, India can set the pace of frontier science.

Finally, *policy stability that lasts beyond political cycles* is essential. Economic architecture cannot be rebuilt every five years. It requires continuity, predictability, and insulation from electoral volatility. Nations that embed stability into their economic design attract investment, sustain reforms, and build credibility.

The powerful truth emerges: growth is not enough. Economic architecture is the new national defense. In the compute century, sovereignty will not be won by GDP charts or startup headlines.

It will be won by nations that design their economies as strategic operating systems—resilient, autonomous, and aligned with the engines of global power.

India's choice is clear: remain a service-led economy built on borrowed engines, or construct a compute-centric architecture that transforms growth into sovereignty.

21.5 — The Economic OS for 2035: Coordination Over Chaos

India's economic journey has often resembled a patchwork quilt—schemes launched in isolation, policies announced without integration, reforms celebrated as events rather than embedded as systems. The result is momentum without coherence, ambition without architecture. If India is to rise as a sovereign power in the compute century, it must abandon this fragmented approach and build a coherent economic operating system—an OS designed not for slogans, but for sovereignty.

This OS must synchronize the nation's core engines. *Finance, industry, research, and regulation must move in sync.* Today, they often operate as parallel silos: banks fund projects without aligning with industrial strategy, regulators issue directives disconnected from research realities, and industry scales without embedding innovation. A true economic OS integrates these functions, ensuring that capital flows into strategic sectors, regulation enables rather than obstructs, and research translates into industrial depth.

It must also rewire the relationship between *states and the Centre.* India's federal architecture too often turns partners into rivals, with states competing for resources and the Centre imposing directives without local alignment. In a compute-driven world, this rivalry is a liability. Coordination must replace competition. States must be empowered as laboratories of innovation, while the Centre provides continuity, scale, and national coherence. Sovereignty demands partnership, not fragmentation.

The OS must channel *talent and capital toward strategic sectors.* India produces extraordinary talent, but much of it migrates abroad or dissipates into low-value work. Capital, meanwhile, often flows into speculative ventures rather than long-term capability. A coherent architecture directs both talent and capital into the five sovereignty sectors—semiconductors, AI, advanced manufacturing, energy, and biotech—ensuring that India builds engines of power rather than bubbles of growth.

Finally, the OS must embed *long-term planning that outlives short-term politics.* India's economic story has been repeatedly disrupted by electoral cycles, with policies reversed, priorities reshuffled, and continuity sacrificed. Sovereignty cannot be built on five-year horizons. It requires decades of sustained investment, policy stability, and institutional memory. Nations that endure treat economic architecture as a generational project, not a political instrument.

The philosophical punchline is clear: India does not need more schemes, announcements, or dashboards. It needs an operating system—a coherent architecture that integrates finance, industry, research, regulation, states, talent, and capital into a single rhythm. Coordination must replace chaos. Architecture must replace improvisation.

And the quiet, visionary truth with which this chapter closes:

A sovereign India will not emerge from GDP curves or slogans—it will emerge from the architecture it builds beneath them.

Chapter 22 — The Talent Infrastructure of the Future

From brain drain to brain networks

The Nation That Trains the World but Cannot Retain Its Own

Every night, flights lift off from India's airports carrying its brightest minds. Students bound for American universities, researchers heading to European labs, engineers recruited by global firms, founders chasing venture capital in foreign hubs. The departure gates are filled with ambition, energy, and brilliance. Families wave proudly, knowing their children will thrive abroad. The nation applauds their success—yet beneath the applause lies a quiet ache.

India has become the world's greatest talent factory. Its classrooms, coaching centers, and universities produce millions of skilled professionals every year. Its diaspora powers Silicon Valley, staffs NASA, leads global corporations, and drives breakthroughs in medicine, finance, and technology. The world celebrates Indian talent. But India itself struggles to retain it. The paradox is stark: a nation that trains the world cannot keep its own.

The pride of exporting talent collides with the pain of importing capability. India's hospitals rely on foreign medical devices. Its factories depend on imported chips. Its research institutions purchase instruments designed elsewhere. Even as Indian minds design algorithms for global giants, India's own digital infrastructure runs on platforms it does not own. The imbalance is unsettling: India supplies brains but consumes architectures.

The sharp insight emerges: India's true challenge is not talent generation—it is talent circulation, retention, and deployment. The nation does not lack brilliance; it lacks the systems to channel brilliance into domestic capability. Talent flows outward because networks abroad are stronger, opportunities deeper, and ecosystems more coherent. The world has built networks using Indian minds. India must now build networks of its own.

This chapter begins with that truth. Sovereignty in the compute century will not be won by producing talent alone. It will be won by designing infrastructures that keep talent engaged, connected, and deployed at home. India must evolve from being a talent exporter to being a talent architect—transforming brain drain into brain networks, and brilliance into sovereignty.

22.1 — The End of Brain Drain: Talent No Longer Leaves... It Relocates Its Potential

For decades, the phrase "brain drain" has haunted India's imagination—a lament for the engineers, doctors, scientists, and entrepreneurs who left the country in search of opportunity abroad. It carried the tone of abandonment, as though talent had betrayed the nation by choosing foreign shores. But in the compute century, this framing is outdated. Talent does not simply leave; it relocates its potential. It plugs into ecosystems where opportunity, funding, mentorship, and infrastructure exist—ecosystems India has not yet built at scale.

Consider the researcher. A young scientist in Delhi may dream of pioneering work in genomics or quantum computing. At home, she faces underfunded labs, bureaucratic procurement delays, and limited access to cutting-edge instruments. Abroad, she finds world-class facilities, generous grants, and collaborative networks that accelerate discovery. Her choice is not abandonment—it is alignment with velocity. She relocates her potential to where it can thrive.

Consider the engineer. India produces some of the finest technical talent in the world, yet many of its brightest join unicorns in Silicon Valley, Berlin, or Singapore. Why? Because those ecosystems offer not just salaries, but exposure to frontier problems, mentorship from global leaders, and pathways to scale ideas into products. The engineer is not rejecting India; he is seeking the architecture that India has not yet enabled.

Consider the founder. India's startup scene is vibrant, but many ambitious entrepreneurs still relocate to ecosystems where venture capital is deeper, regulatory frameworks are clearer, and infrastructure is more reliable. A founder who moves her company to Boston or London is not abandoning India—she is escaping the friction that slows innovation at home. She is choosing continuity over chaos, velocity over stagnation.

The pattern is consistent: domestic institutions cannot match global velocity. India's universities remain burdened by bureaucracy. Its research centers struggle with autonomy. Its funding pipelines are shallow and inconsistent. Its regulatory frameworks often confuse rather than enable. Talent flows outward not because it lacks patriotism, but because it lacks pathways.

This reframing matters. Talent is not abandoning India; India is not enabling talent. The diaspora's success is proof of India's brilliance, but also proof of India's infrastructural deficit. The world has built networks using Indian minds. India must now build networks of its own—ecosystems where researchers, engineers, and founders can thrive without leaving, where potential is circulated and deployed domestically, where ambition does not require relocation.

The quiet but piercing truth is this: India's challenge is not brain drain. It is brain deployment. Sovereignty in the compute century will depend not on how many minds India produces, but on how many it retains, circulates, and empowers at home.

22.2 — The New Paradigm: Brain Networks, Not Brain Drain

The old narrative of "brain drain" belongs to a different century. It imagined talent as a finite resource that, once lost to migration, weakened the nation. But in the compute century, talent need not be physically present to contribute. Networks, not geography, define capability. Sovereign nations no longer lament migration—they design architectures that harness their diaspora, circulate expertise, and integrate global talent footprints into domestic strength.

India's diaspora is vast, diverse, and deeply embedded in global ecosystems. Its researchers lead laboratories in Boston, Berlin, and Tokyo. Its engineers design systems in Silicon Valley and Shenzhen. Its founders build companies in London, Singapore, and Toronto. This is not a loss—it is an opportunity. India can transform its global footprint into a distributed brain network, where talent abroad remains connected to missions at home.

Distributed research teams are the first frontier. Indian scientists working in global labs can collaborate seamlessly with domestic institutions through digital platforms, shared datasets, and joint projects. Instead of lamenting their departure, India can design mechanisms for their continued contribution—turning distance into advantage.

Global innovation clusters linked to India can become bridges of capability. Diaspora-led hubs in California, Berlin, or Seoul can be formally connected to Indian universities, startups, and ministries.

These clusters can serve as outposts of Indian innovation, channeling knowledge, capital, and mentorship back into domestic ecosystems.

Co-development labs across continents can anchor sovereignty. Imagine AI research centers jointly operated in Bengaluru and Boston, or biotech labs spanning Pune and Cambridge. Such collaborations embed India into global innovation chains while ensuring that breakthroughs are shared, not outsourced.

Reverse mentoring from diaspora experts can accelerate domestic capability. Senior scientists, entrepreneurs, and technologists abroad can mentor younger talent in India, transferring frontier knowledge directly into the nation's bloodstream. This is not charity—it is architecture: a deliberate system of knowledge circulation.

Academic-industrial fellowships can institutionalize the flow. Professors abroad can spend sabbaticals in Indian universities; industry leaders can rotate through Indian research centers; Indian scholars can embed themselves in global labs with guaranteed pathways back home. These fellowships transform migration into circulation, ensuring that talent flows both ways.

Cross-border entrepreneurial networks can multiply India's startup ecosystem. Diaspora founders can co-invest, co-develop, and co-scale ventures with domestic entrepreneurs, embedding Indian startups into global markets from inception. Sovereignty here is not isolation—it is integration with advantage.

The paradigm shift is clear: sovereign nations build talent networks—integrated, global, resilient. They do not lament migration; they design architectures that convert migration into strength. India's challenge is not to stop its talent from leaving, but to ensure that wherever it goes, it remains connected, contributing, and coordinated.

The optimistic truth is this: India already trains the world. Its next step is to network the world—transforming brain drain into brain circulation, and diaspora pride into domestic capability. In the compute century, talent networks are the new infrastructure of sovereignty.

22.3 — Rebuilding the Domestic Talent Engine: From Escape to Return

India's challenge is not producing talent—it is keeping it. The nation trains millions of engineers, scientists, and innovators every year, yet too many of them look outward for opportunity. The reason is not lack of patriotism; it is lack of architecture. Talent stays where it sees purpose, not pressure; opportunity, not obstruction. If India wants to convert leakage into magnetism, it must rebuild its domestic talent engine—an ecosystem that makes staying not just possible, but irresistible.

The first step is to *free research institutions from political interference.* India's laboratories and councils cannot thrive if their agendas shift with electoral cycles or ministerial whims. They need autonomy to set priorities, continuity to pursue long-term projects, and insulation from political turbulence. Only then can they attract and retain researchers who want to build careers in discovery rather than navigate bureaucracy.

Next, *universities must be granted world-class autonomy.* India's higher education system is vast, but too often constrained by rigid regulations, outdated curricula, and micromanagement. Universities must be empowered to design programs, attract global faculty, and compete internationally. Autonomy is not indulgence—it is infrastructure. Without it, India's brightest students will continue to seek institutions abroad that offer freedom to explore, innovate, and excel.

Industry-academia integration is another critical pillar. Research must not remain trapped in journals; it must flow into factories, startups, and national missions. Universities should partner with industries to co-develop technologies, while industries should invest in academic research as part of their growth strategy. This integration creates pathways where talent sees its work translated into impact, anchoring purpose at home.

India must also design *innovation corridors and deep-tech clusters.* These are ecosystems where startups, labs, investors, and regulators co-exist, accelerating breakthroughs in AI, biotech, semiconductors, and green technologies. Corridors provide infrastructure, mentorship, and scale; clusters create density of talent and ideas. Together, they transform isolated ambition into collective capability.

Regulatory frameworks that reward experimentation are essential. Today, innovators often face obstruction—licenses delayed, approvals uncertain, compliance confusing. India must flip this script. Regulations should enable risk-taking, protect experimentation, and provide clear pathways for scaling. Talent thrives where failure is tolerated and learning is rewarded.

Finally, India must build *career pathways that retain scientists and innovators.* Too often, researchers face stagnant salaries, limited recognition, and unclear progression. Innovators struggle to find long-term support. India must professionalize these pathways—competitive funding, global exposure, recognition systems, and structured careers that make science and innovation as attractive as corporate jobs.

The developmental truth is clear: India cannot stop its talent from dreaming globally, but it can create ecosystems that make returning—or never leaving—the more compelling choice. Talent will stay where it sees purpose, opportunity, and impact. India's task is to build that architecture: research institutions with autonomy, universities with freedom, industries integrated with academia, corridors of innovation, clusters of deep tech, regulations that enable, and careers that inspire.

Escape must become return. Leakage must become magnetism. Only then will India's talent engine power sovereignty in the compute century.

22.4 — The Talent OS 2035: Networks, Platforms, and Circulation

India must stop imagining talent as a pipeline—linear, one-directional, and finite. In the compute century, talent is not a stream to be contained; it is an operating system to be designed. The difference is profound. A pipeline produces graduates, exports workers, and counts numbers. An operating system circulates minds, connects networks, and multiplies capability. Sovereignty will not be won by how many engineers India trains, but by how effectively it integrates them into a living architecture of power.

This operating system requires *mobility*. Talent must be able to move fluidly across institutions, industries, and geographies without being trapped in bureaucratic silos. Researchers should shift seamlessly between labs and startups; engineers should rotate across sectors; entrepreneurs should access global markets without friction. Mobility ensures that knowledge flows, not stagnates.

It requires *mentorship networks*. Talent thrives when guided by those who have already navigated complexity. India must design systems where diaspora experts mentor domestic innovators, senior scientists guide younger researchers, and industry leaders coach emerging entrepreneurs. Mentorship is not incidental—it is infrastructure.

It requires *continuous upskilling*. In a century where technologies evolve faster than curricula, talent must be constantly refreshed. Universities must become lifelong learning platforms, industries must embed training into careers, and digital systems must provide on-demand education. Upskilling is not optional—it is survival.

It requires *global linkages.* Talent cannot be confined within borders. India must embed itself into global research corridors, innovation clusters, and entrepreneurial networks. Talent abroad must remain connected to missions at home, and talent at home must have pathways into global ecosystems. Sovereignty is strengthened not by isolation, but by integration with advantage.

It requires *compute access.* Talent cannot innovate without infrastructure. Researchers need high-performance computing, startups need cloud platforms, and engineers need simulation tools. Compute is the oxygen of modern talent. Without it, brilliance suffocates. With it, brilliance scales.

It requires *leadership ecosystems.* Talent must be guided by architectures that reward competence, collaboration, and vision. Councils of scientists, technologists, and entrepreneurs must shape national missions, ensuring that talent is deployed strategically rather than wasted in fragmentation. Leadership is not charisma—it is orchestration.

Finally, it requires *institutions that evolve faster than industries.* In India today, industries often outpace institutions. Startups innovate while universities lag; markets shift while regulators stall. The Talent OS must reverse this imbalance. Institutions must be agile, adaptive, and anticipatory—evolving faster than the sectors they serve.

The philosophical punchline is clear: talent is not a pipeline to be managed; it is an operating system to be designed.

And the visionary truth with which this chapter closes:

India will rise not by keeping its talent at home, but by connecting every Indian mind—wherever it lives—into the nation's architecture of power.

Chapter 23 — Security, Intelligence, and the Digital State

The new national security framework

The Nation Protected by Walls, But Exposed by Wires

India proudly showcases its strength in the language of steel and spectacle. Tanks roll across parade grounds, missiles arc into the sky, border fencing stretches across rugged terrain, and military formations march in perfect synchrony. The nation's physical preparedness is visible, tangible, and celebrated. It projects confidence: a country shielded by walls, armed with weapons, and defended by soldiers.

Yet beneath this display lies a quieter, more unsettling reality. The vulnerabilities that matter most today are not visible in parades. They exist in unsecured data lakes where citizen information leaks without trace. They exist in ministries breached by cyber intrusions, where sensitive files are siphoned off by invisible adversaries. They exist in outdated surveillance systems that cannot keep pace with modern threats, and in fragmented intelligence networks that fail to coordinate across agencies. They exist in cloud infrastructures controlled by foreign firms, where India's digital sovereignty is hostage to external architectures.

The cinematic contrast is stark: physical preparedness versus digital fragility. India has built walls, but its wires remain exposed. It has invested in missiles, but its algorithms remain vulnerable. It has fortified borders, but its data flows remain porous. The nation's greatest risks no longer cross terrain—they cross cables. They no longer march in formation—they infiltrate through code. They no longer announce themselves with noise—they arrive silently, through compromised systems.

This is the new battlefield: invisible, continuous, and unforgiving. Cyber warfare, data theft, algorithmic manipulation, and digital espionage now define the frontlines of sovereignty. A nation that secures its borders but neglects its networks is not secure—it is exposed.

The hook lands hard: India's greatest risks no longer cross borders—they enter through cables, code, and compromised systems.

A new security architecture is not optional; it is existence.

23.1 — The Collapse of Old Security Models: Guns Cannot Stop Algorithms

For most of the 20th century, national security was defined by visible strength—armies on borders, fleets at sea, missiles in silos, and tanks on parade. Sovereignty was measured in divisions and battalions, in the ability to defend territory with steel and firepower. But in the compute century, this model has collapsed. Guns cannot stop algorithms. Borders cannot block cables. Missiles cannot intercept misinformation.

India's threats today arrive in forms the old security architecture cannot contain. *State-backed cyberattacks* infiltrate ministries, banks, and defense networks, siphoning sensitive data without a single soldier crossing a border. *AI-generated misinformation* floods social media, manipulating public opinion, destabilizing elections, and eroding trust in institutions. *Digital sabotage of infrastructure* targets power grids, transport systems, and healthcare networks, where a single breach can paralyze entire cities.

Even supply chains have become weapons. *Supply chain weaponization* allows adversaries to embed vulnerabilities into imported chips, sensors, or software, creating backdoors into critical systems. Sovereignty is compromised not by invasion, but by dependence.

Markets themselves are no longer immune. *Algorithmic manipulation of financial systems* can trigger volatility, distort trade flows, and undermine investor confidence. Public opinion, too, is vulnerable—shaped by invisible algorithms that amplify division, polarize societies, and weaken democratic coherence.

And perhaps most dangerously, India's digital backbone rests on *cloud-level vulnerabilities.* Much of the nation's data, commerce, and governance runs on infrastructures controlled by foreign firms. This dependency creates exposure: sovereignty is hostage to architectures India does not own.

The battlefield has shifted. It is no longer fought on land, sea, or air alone. It is fought in code, in networks, in architectures of data and compute. Territory is still important, but architecture is decisive. A nation may defend its borders with tanks and missiles, yet remain exposed if its algorithms are compromised, its data stolen, its networks infiltrated.

Traditional military strength remains necessary—it deters aggression, secures borders, and projects power. But it is no longer sufficient. Security in the compute century requires a new architecture: cyber defense systems as robust as missile shields, intelligence networks as integrated as armies, and digital sovereignty as central as territorial sovereignty.

India must dismantle the illusion that old models can protect against new threats. Guns cannot stop algorithms. Walls cannot block wires. Sovereignty today is not defended only by soldiers—it is defended by systems.

The globally aware truth is clear: nations rise or fall not by the size of their armies, but by the resilience of their architectures. The battlefield has moved from land to code, from territory to architecture. India must move with it—or risk being left exposed in a century where wars are fought invisibly, continuously, and without warning.

23.2 — Intelligence in the Compute Century: From Surveillance to Prediction

The architecture of intelligence must evolve. For much of the 20th century, agencies were designed to monitor—collecting information, surveilling suspects, and investigating threats after they appeared. But in the compute century, this reactive model is dangerously inadequate. Threats now move at digital velocity. Cyberattacks unfold in milliseconds, misinformation campaigns spread in hours, and supply chain sabotage can ripple across industries in days. Surveillance alone cannot protect sovereignty. Intelligence must shift from monitoring to modelling, from investigation to prediction, from reaction to anticipation.

India's current intelligence ecosystem remains fragmented. Agencies operate in silos, each guarding its own data, reluctant to share insights across institutional boundaries. This fragmentation slows response and prevents the nation from seeing the full picture of emerging threats. Outdated tools compound the problem. Systems built for analog surveillance cannot process the torrents of digital signals—social media flows, encrypted communications, algorithmic manipulations—that define modern conflict.

Bureaucratic turf wars further weaken agility. Agencies compete for jurisdiction, resources, and recognition, often duplicating efforts while leaving gaps unaddressed. Threats slip through the cracks not because they are invisible, but because institutions are too busy defending their turf to defend the nation. The absence of integrated data systems means intelligence remains scattered, uncoordinated, and incomplete. And without sufficient *AI-backed analytics*, India cannot keep pace with adversaries who already deploy machine learning to detect vulnerabilities, manipulate narratives, and automate attacks.

The solution is clear: India must build a new intelligence architecture designed for the compute century. At its core must be *unified intelligence grids*—platforms that integrate data across agencies, states, and sectors, creating a single, coherent view of threats. These grids must be powered by *AI-driven threat detection*, capable of identifying patterns invisible to human analysts, predicting risks before they materialize, and flagging anomalies in real time.

Cross-agency data interoperability is essential. Intelligence cannot remain locked in silos; it must flow seamlessly across institutions. Shared protocols, standardized formats, and secure communication channels must ensure that insights travel faster than threats. Sovereignty demands speed, and speed demands interoperability.

Finally, India must establish *cyber defense corps staffed by top-tier talent.* Just as armies recruit the best soldiers, intelligence must recruit the best minds—data scientists, AI engineers, cybersecurity experts, behavioral analysts. These corps must be empowered with autonomy, resources, and cutting-edge tools, ensuring that India's defense is not just physical but digital, not just reactive but predictive.

The urgency is undeniable. In the compute century, intelligence is not about watching—it is about anticipating. Nations that cling to surveillance will remain exposed. Nations that build predictive intelligence architectures will remain sovereign.

India's choice is stark: continue with fragmented silos and outdated tools, or design intelligence as a unified, AI-powered operating system. The battlefield has already shifted. The question is whether India's intelligence will shift with it.

23.3 — The Digital State: Architecture as National Defense

The idea of the state must now be redefined through an architectural lens. In the compute century, sovereignty is not secured only by armies or borders—it is secured by the architecture of the digital state. A nation's resilience depends on whether its digital foundations are sovereign, secure, and adaptive. Without this architecture, even the strongest military becomes vulnerable to invisible incursions.

A sovereign digital state requires *domestic cloud infrastructure.* India cannot afford to anchor its governance, commerce, and citizen data on foreign-controlled platforms. Domestic clouds are not simply storage—they are sovereignty. They ensure that the nation's most sensitive information remains within its own jurisdiction, immune to external leverage or geopolitical shocks.

It requires *secure digital identity frameworks.* In a billion-person nation, identity is the backbone of governance. Aadhaar and other systems must evolve into architectures that are secure, encrypted, and interoperable, protecting citizens from fraud, surveillance abuse, and data theft. Identity must empower, not expose.

It requires *encrypted governance systems.* Ministries, courts, and public offices must operate on infrastructures where communication, documentation, and decision-making are shielded from intrusion. Encryption is not a technical detail—it is the architecture of trust. Without it, governance becomes porous, vulnerable to manipulation and espionage.

It requires *resilient public data infrastructure.* Health records, financial flows, transport systems, and energy grids must be designed to withstand cyberattacks, outages, and sabotage. Resilience means redundancy, backup, and continuity—ensuring that critical services never collapse under pressure.

It requires *real-time analytics for crisis management.* Pandemics, floods, cyberattacks, and financial shocks demand immediate response. A sovereign digital state must embed analytics into its architecture, enabling leaders to see crises as they unfold, predict their trajectories, and act decisively. Delay is vulnerability; velocity is defense.

It requires *cyber-secure supply chains.* Chips, sensors, and software imported without scrutiny create backdoors into national systems. India must design supply chains that are verified, monitored, and secured end-to-end. Sovereignty cannot rest on components that carry hidden vulnerabilities.

The critique is sharp. India's current vulnerabilities are systemic. Government offices still operate on outdated systems, where files are stored on unsecured servers and communication flows through obsolete channels. Critical infrastructure—from power grids to transport networks—relies on foreign software, embedding dependency into the nation's core. Citizen data is poorly protected, exposed to breaches that erode trust and compromise privacy. Ministries lack digital hygiene, with weak protocols, inconsistent practices, and fragmented standards.

The diagnosis is clear: India's digital state is fragile because its architecture is incomplete. Sovereignty in the compute century will not be defended by parades or declarations—it will be defended by systems. Domestic clouds, secure identities, encrypted governance, resilient data, real-time analytics, and cyber-secure supply chains are not optional—they are the infrastructure of national defense.

The elegant truth is this: the state is no longer defined only by territory. It is defined by architecture. And in the compute century, architecture is defense.

23.4 — Security as Coordination: The Missing Operating System

India does not lack security agencies. It has armies, paramilitary forces, intelligence bureaus, cyber cells, diplomatic corps, and regulatory authorities. Each operates with dedication, each defends its mandate. Yet the nation remains exposed. The problem is not absence of institutions—it is absence of architecture. India has nodes of power, but no operating system to connect them.

National security in the compute century cannot be fragmented. It requires synchronized layers, each reinforcing the other, each moving in rhythm. *Defense* must protect borders and project deterrence. *Diplomacy* must secure alliances, negotiate technology access, and shape global norms. *Intelligence* must anticipate threats before they materialize. *Cyber capability* must shield networks, detect intrusions, and neutralize digital sabotage. *Domestic security* must ensure resilience against terrorism, misinformation, and internal destabilization. *Economic architecture* must protect supply chains, secure critical industries, and prevent dependency. *Digital networks* must be sovereign, encrypted, and resilient. *Public communication systems* must counter misinformation, sustain trust, and unify society in moments of crisis.

Today, these layers exist in isolation. Defense operates without full integration with cyber. Diplomacy negotiates without real-time intelligence inputs. Economic policy is designed without embedding security considerations. Public communication is reactive, fragmented, and often politicized. The result is a nation with strength in parts but weakness in whole.

The truth is stark: India does not lack security agencies—it lacks a security architecture.

What India needs is a *National Security Operating System (NSOS)*—an integrated framework that connects all nodes of power. This OS would unify defense, diplomacy, intelligence, cyber, domestic security, economic design, digital networks, and communication into a single architecture. It would ensure interoperability, real-time coordination, and shared situational awareness. It would replace fragmentation with rhythm, silos with synchronization, improvisation with design.

The NSOS must be visionary yet implementable. It must be designed as infrastructure, not as event. It must embed protocols for crisis management, channels for cross-agency communication, and platforms for data integration. It must be staffed by top-tier talent, empowered with autonomy, and insulated from political turbulence. Above all, it must be treated as permanent architecture—continuously upgraded, relentlessly maintained, and never allowed to decay into bureaucracy.

Philosophically, the insight is profound: security is no longer about strength in isolation. It is about coordination across systems. A missile shield without cyber defense is incomplete. Intelligence without diplomacy is impotent. Economic architecture without digital sovereignty is fragile. Public communication without credibility is dangerous. Only when these layers move together does sovereignty become resilient.

The visionary truth is this: India's survival in the compute century depends not on the number of agencies it has, but on the operating system it builds to connect them. Security is coordination. Architecture is defense. The missing OS must now be designed.

23.5 — The Sovereignty Blueprint: From Vulnerable to Vigilant

India's security in the compute century will not be defined by what it defends, but by what it builds. Tanks, missiles, and border walls remain necessary, but they are no longer sufficient. Sovereignty now rests on architecture—on the depth of systems, the resilience of networks, and the coherence of infrastructures that cannot be breached by cables, code, or compromised algorithms. The blueprint for vigilance is not about fortification; it is about construction.

India must **build depth, not dependence.** Depth means indigenous semiconductor ecosystems, sovereign clouds, encrypted governance, and resilient supply chains. Dependence means importing chips, renting platforms, and outsourcing security to foreign firms. Depth anchors sovereignty; dependence erodes it. A nation that builds depth can withstand shocks. A nation that relies on others remains perpetually exposed.

India must **build networks, not silos.** Security cannot remain fragmented across ministries, agencies, and states. It must be orchestrated as a single rhythm—defense, diplomacy, intelligence, cyber, economic, and communication systems moving in sync. Silos slow response, weaken resilience, and create blind spots. Networks accelerate coordination, multiply capability, and ensure that threats are met with unified force.

India must **build capabilities, not narratives.** Summits, declarations, and parades project ambition but do not deliver sovereignty. Capabilities are built in labs, factories, and data centers—where talent is deployed, research is funded, and architectures are designed. Narratives inspire, but capabilities endure. A nation that builds capabilities commands respect; a nation that relies on narratives risks illusion.

India must **build a digital state worthy of a billion-strong democracy.** This means secure digital identities, encrypted governance, resilient public data infrastructures, and cyber-secure supply chains. It means treating citizen data as sacred, protecting it with the same seriousness as territorial borders. It means designing systems that empower citizens while shielding them from manipulation, surveillance abuse, and breaches. A billion-strong democracy cannot survive on outdated systems; it must be anchored in architectures that match its scale.

The philosophical punchline is clear: sovereignty is no longer defended only by soldiers—it is defended by systems. India's security will depend not on the walls it strengthens, but on the wiring it builds.

And the quiet but electrifying truth with which this chapter closes:

A nation becomes sovereign not when it strengthens its walls, but when it strengthens its wiring.

Closing Reflection — Part V

Architecture as Sovereignty

Part V has carried us through the scaffolding of India's survival in the compute century. We have dismantled illusions and rebuilt clarity: leadership is not charisma but infrastructure; economic growth is not dashboards but architecture; talent is not a pipeline but an operating system; security is not walls but wiring. Each chapter has revealed the same truth in different domains—sovereignty is no longer defended by spectacle, but by systems.

India's vulnerabilities are not hidden. They are visible in the fragility of services without depth, in the dependence on borrowed engines, in the leakage of talent, in the fragmentation of security. Yet India's possibilities are equally visible: the capacity to design semiconductor ecosystems, to orchestrate predictive intelligence, to magnetize talent, to build economic and digital states worthy of a billion-strong democracy.

The philosophical punchline of Part V is simple but decisive: *architecture is destiny.* Nations rise when they design coherent operating systems across leadership, economy, talent, and security. Nations fall when they confuse announcements for execution, walls for wiring, or leaders for leadership.

India now stands at the threshold. The scaffolding has been diagnosed, the blueprint outlined. What remains is choice. Will

India accelerate into sovereignty by building the architectures we have mapped—or will it drift into entropy by delaying, fragmenting, and depending?

This is the pivot into Part VI. Here, the narrative shifts from diagnosis to destiny. Two futures unfold:

- **Future A: The Ascending India** — if the nation solves its internal chaos and builds capability.
- **Future B: The Dependent India** — if the nation delays, disorders itself, and drifts into reliance.
- **The Point of No Return** — the year after which recovery becomes impossible.
- **Resetting India's Trajectory** — a prescription for policymakers and citizens to choose acceleration over entropy.

Part V has shown us what must be built. Part VI will show us what happens if we build—or if we fail.

Part VI: The Two Futures

Acceleration or Entropy

"The future is not inherited. It is engineered. Nations rise not by chance, but by the architectures they choose to build—or neglect."

Overview

Overview Part VI is the book's decisive pivot. After diagnosing India's vulnerabilities across leadership, economy, talent, and security, we now confront the horizon. The future splits into two paths: **Future A — Ascending India**, a nation that builds depth and coherence; and **Future B — Dependent India**, where drift and delay erode sovereignty. Between them lies the **Point of No Return**, beyond which recovery is impossible.

The closing chapter, *Resetting India's Trajectory*, prescribes acceleration over entropy, architecture over improvisation, sovereignty over dependence. Part VI is not prediction—it is choice, the blueprint of destiny India must decide before time decides for it.

Chapter 24 — Future A: The Ascending India

If India solves internal chaos and builds capability

The Nation That Turns Disorder Into Design

Imagine an India where the noise of fragmented schemes has given way to the rhythm of coherence. Ministries no longer compete in silos but move in sync; universities no longer lose talent but magnetize it; industries no longer depend on imports but anchor global supply chains. The chaos that once drained energy has been replaced by architecture that multiplies it.

Flights that once carried India's brightest minds outward now bring them back, drawn by ecosystems that rival the world's best. Research labs hum with breakthroughs, factories pulse with precision manufacturing, and digital networks operate on sovereign clouds. The nation's security is not only defended at borders but embedded in its wiring.

This is the cinematic vision of **Future A: The Ascending India**—a country that has solved its internal disorder and built capability across leadership, economy, talent, and security. It is not a fantasy; it is a blueprint. The possibility exists if India chooses architecture over improvisation, depth over dependence, and coherence over chaos.

The hook lands with clarity: India's rise will not be the result of slogans or chance. It will be the consequence of design.

24.1 — Leadership as Architecture: From Personality to System

In the ascending future, India's leadership is no longer defined by personalities—it is defined by architecture. For too long, the nation has relied on charisma, slogans, and symbolic gestures to project strength. Leaders have been celebrated for their image rather than their ability to design systems. But in the compute century, sovereignty cannot rest on personality. It must rest on operating systems of governance that endure beyond individuals, beyond cycles, beyond spectacle.

Leadership as architecture means building frameworks that outlast the leader. It means designing institutions that are resilient, policies that are coherent, and processes that are transparent. Charisma may inspire, but architecture sustains. A nation rises not when its leaders dominate headlines, but when its systems deliver outcomes consistently, predictably, and at scale.

India's current challenge is fragmentation. Ministries often operate in silos, competing for resources and recognition rather than collaborating for coherence. Policies shift with political cycles, leaving long-term projects vulnerable to disruption. Decision-making is slowed by bureaucracy, while accountability is blurred across layers of governance. This is leadership as improvisation—reactive, episodic, and fragile.

The ascending India must replace improvisation with design. Leadership must be understood as the ability to orchestrate complexity, to align ministries, states, industries, and institutions into a single rhythm. It must embed continuity into national missions, ensuring that semiconductor ecosystems, AI infrastructures, and security architectures are pursued across decades, not abandoned after elections.

This requires leaders who treat governance as system-building. They must design coordination platforms that integrate ministries, policy frameworks that survive political transitions, and decision protocols that accelerate response without sacrificing accountability. Leadership must be measured not by speeches, but by the coherence of systems.

In this paradigm, the leader is not the architect alone—they are the conductor of an orchestra. Their role is to ensure that defense, economy, talent, and security move in sync, that ministries do not compete but collaborate, that states are empowered as laboratories of innovation while the Centre provides continuity and scale. Leadership becomes less about command and more about coordination.

The philosophical shift is profound: leaders are temporary, but architecture is permanent. A leader who builds systems leaves behind resilience. A leader who relies on personality leaves behind fragility. The ascending India will be defined by leaders who understand this distinction, who design operating systems of governance that endure beyond their tenure.

The constructive truth is clear: India's rise will not be powered by personalities—it will be powered by architectures. Leadership must evolve from spectacle to system, from charisma to coherence, from improvisation to design. Only then will India's governance become the foundation of sovereignty in the compute century.

24.2 — Economic Depth: From Growth to Architecture

In the ascending future, India's economy is no longer measured only by growth charts or quarterly headlines. GDP curves may signal momentum, but they do not guarantee sovereignty. True resilience comes from depth—an economic architecture that embeds capability into the nation's foundations. Growth without depth is fragile; growth with architecture becomes power.

For decades, India has celebrated its service-led economy, its IT exports, and its startup ecosystem. These achievements are real, but they remain surface-level. Beneath them lies dependency: imported chips, rented compute, foreign-controlled platforms, and fragmented supply chains. The ascending India must move beyond this surface to build depth—systems that anchor sovereignty in the compute century.

Depth begins with **semiconductor ecosystems.** India cannot remain dependent on chips fabricated abroad. It must design, manufacture, and package semiconductors domestically, embedding autonomy into its technological backbone. Chips are not just components; they are the currency of modern power.

Depth requires AI infrastructure with domestic compute. India's digital economy cannot thrive on borrowed servers. Sovereign compute clusters, national AI frameworks, and ethical governance designed at home will ensure that India's innovation is not derivative but original. Compute is the oxygen of modern industry; without it, brilliance suffocates.

Depth demands manufacturing clusters aligned with global supply chains. India must evolve from fragmented industrial zones into integrated corridors where logistics, research, and skilled labor converge. Precision manufacturing—robotics, additive technologies, advanced engineering—must anchor resilience. Sovereignty is strengthened when India is a maker, not just a market.

Depth also means export-led precision industries. Pharmaceuticals, aerospace, electronics, and green technologies must be scaled for global competitiveness. When the world depends on India's products, India's sovereignty is reinforced. Dependency is reversed; capability becomes leverage.

Depth requires R&D hubs with world-class autonomy. India's universities and research institutions must be liberated from bureaucratic micromanagement. They must be funded, professionalized, and empowered to produce breakthroughs. Without indigenous IP, India remains a consumer of discoveries made elsewhere. With autonomy, India becomes a producer of frontier science.

Finally, depth demands policy stability that outlives political cycles. Economic architecture cannot be rebuilt every five years. Continuity, predictability, and insulation from electoral volatility are essential. Nations that embed stability into their economic design attract investment, sustain reforms, and build credibility.

The philosophical shift is decisive: growth is not enough. Economic depth is the new defense. India's sovereignty will not be secured by GDP dashboards or startup headlines, but by the architecture it builds beneath them.

The constructive truth is this: the ascending India will be defined not by how fast it grows, but by how deeply it builds. Depth transforms growth into sovereignty. Architecture transforms ambition into power.

24.3 — Talent Magnetism: From Brain Drain to Brain Networks

In the ascending future, India is no longer haunted by the phrase "brain drain." The nation has transformed its talent story from escape to magnetism, from leakage to circulation. Talent does not leave because opportunity is absent; it stays because ecosystems are abundant. And when talent does move abroad, it remains connected—circulating knowledge, capital, and networks back into India's architecture of power.

For decades, India's brightest minds boarded flights to foreign universities, labs, and firms, drawn by infrastructure, mentorship, and velocity unavailable at home. This outward flow was celebrated as diaspora pride but lamented as domestic loss. In Future A, that paradox dissolves. India builds ecosystems that rival the world's best, turning departure into circulation and return into magnetism.

The transformation begins with research institutions freed from political interference. Scientists no longer struggle under bureaucratic micromanagement; they operate in labs with autonomy, funding, and continuity. Breakthroughs in AI, biotech, and quantum computing emerge not abroad but in Bengaluru, Pune, and Delhi. Talent stays where discovery is possible.

It continues with universities granted world-class autonomy. Curricula evolve at digital velocity, faculty are recruited globally, and students are trained not just for jobs but for innovation. India's universities become magnets, attracting international scholars while retaining domestic brilliance.

Industry-academia integration anchors this magnetism. Research flows seamlessly into startups and factories, while industries invest in academic labs. Talent sees its work translated into products, patents, and national missions. Purpose replaces frustration; impact replaces stagnation.

India designs innovation corridors and deep-tech clusters where startups, labs, investors, and regulators co-exist. These corridors provide infrastructure, mentorship, and scale; clusters create density of ideas and talent. Together, they transform isolated ambition into collective capability.

Regulatory frameworks evolve to reward experimentation. Innovators no longer face obstruction; they find clear pathways to scale, protection for risk-taking, and recognition for breakthroughs. Talent thrives where failure is tolerated and learning is rewarded.

Finally, India builds career pathways that retain scientists and innovators. Competitive funding, global exposure, recognition systems, and structured progression make science and innovation as attractive as corporate careers. Talent sees not just opportunity but longevity.

The philosophical shift is profound: talent magnetism is not about preventing departure—it is about creating ecosystems so compelling that staying, returning, and circulating become natural choices. India's diaspora remains connected through distributed research teams, co-development labs, and entrepreneurial networks. Domestic talent thrives in corridors of innovation. Together, they form a brain network—global, resilient, and sovereign.

The constructive truth is clear: in Future A, India rises not by lamenting brain drain but by designing brain magnetism. Talent stays where it sees purpose, circulates where it sees networks, and returns where it sees architecture. Sovereignty in the compute century will be powered not by numbers of graduates, but by the coherence of talent ecosystems.

24.4 — Security and Sovereignty: From Walls to Wiring

In the ascending future, India's sovereignty is no longer imagined as walls, fences, and parades. It is imagined as wiring—secure networks, resilient architectures, and coordinated systems that protect the nation from invisible incursions. Tanks and missiles remain necessary, but they are no longer sufficient. The battlefield has shifted from land to code, from territory to architecture. India rises when it secures not only its borders, but its systems.

Security in Future A begins with domestic cloud infrastructure. India no longer anchors its governance and commerce on foreign-controlled platforms. Sovereign clouds ensure that citizen data, government records, and industrial flows remain within national jurisdiction. Dependency is replaced by depth; exposure is replaced by resilience.

It extends into encrypted governance systems. Ministries, courts, and public offices operate on secure channels where communication and documentation are shielded from intrusion. Encryption becomes the architecture of trust, ensuring that governance cannot be manipulated by external actors.

India builds predictive intelligence grids powered by AI. Threats are not merely monitored—they are anticipated. Cyberattacks are detected before they unfold, misinformation campaigns are neutralized before they spread, and vulnerabilities are patched before they are exploited. Intelligence evolves from surveillance to modelling, from reaction to anticipation.

Security also requires cyber defense corps staffed by top-tier talent. Just as armies recruit the best soldiers, India recruits the best minds—data scientists, cybersecurity experts, behavioral analysts. These corps defend networks, neutralize intrusions, and design architectures that evolve faster than adversaries. Talent becomes the frontline of sovereignty.

Economic resilience is embedded into security. Supply chains are verified, monitored, and secured end-to-end. Chips, sensors, and software imported into India are scrutinized for hidden vulnerabilities. Sovereignty is no longer hostage to dependency; it is anchored in secure economic architecture.

Finally, public communication systems are treated as part of national defense. Misinformation is countered with credibility, disinformation campaigns are neutralized with transparency, and citizens are unified through trusted channels. Sovereignty is not only about protecting systems—it is about protecting coherence.

The philosophical shift is decisive: security is no longer about walls, but about wiring. A nation may defend its borders with tanks, but if its networks are porous, its sovereignty is fragile. A nation may parade missiles, but if its data is compromised, its power is hollow.

The constructive truth is clear: in Future A, India rises because it designs security as architecture. Defense, diplomacy, intelligence, cyber capability, economic resilience, and communication systems move in sync, orchestrated by a National Security Operating System. Walls remain, but wiring defines sovereignty.

The visionary insight is this: India's sovereignty will not be secured by what it defends—it will be secured by what it builds. And in the ascending future, India builds wiring strong enough to carry the weight of a billion-strong democracy.

Chapter 25 — Future B: The Dependent India

If India delays, drifts, or disorders itself

The Nation That Mistook Motion for Progress

Picture an India that still celebrates parades, still announces schemes, still publishes dashboards of growth—but beneath the spectacle, the foundations are hollow. Ministries remain locked in turf wars, universities continue to lose their brightest minds, industries depend on imported chips and rented compute, and security agencies operate in silos while adversaries infiltrate through cables and code.

This is the cinematic vision of **Future B: The Dependent India**—a nation that mistakes activity for architecture, slogans for systems, and improvisation for design. Talent continues to escape, innovation corridors remain unfinished, and economic depth is replaced by dependency on foreign supply chains. Sovereignty erodes not through invasion, but through inertia.

The fragility is quiet but relentless. Data leaks become routine, misinformation corrodes trust, and critical infrastructure is hostage to foreign platforms. India drifts, delays, disorders itself—and in doing so, forfeits the chance to rise.

The hook lands with urgency: dependence is not destiny, but it is the consequence of delay. Future B is the mirror India must refuse to inhabit.

25.1 — Leadership in Drift: From Architecture to Improvisation

In the dependent future, India's leadership does not collapse—it drifts. It continues to announce programs, launch initiatives, and celebrate milestones, but beneath the surface, coherence is absent. Leadership becomes improvisation: reactive, episodic, and fragmented. The nation mistakes motion for progress, activity for architecture, and spectacle for sovereignty.

The first fault line is fragmented governance. Ministries operate as silos, each pursuing its own agenda, competing for recognition rather than collaborating for coherence. National missions—semiconductors, AI, cybersecurity, energy—remain scattered across departments with little synchronization. Projects stall not because of lack of talent, but because of lack of orchestration.

The second fault line is policy volatility. Initiatives are launched with fanfare but abandoned with elections. Long-term projects lack continuity, leaving infrastructure half-built and ecosystems unfinished. Investors hesitate, innovators lose confidence, and citizens grow weary of promises that dissolve into delays. Leadership becomes a cycle of announcements without architecture.

The third fault line is bureaucratic inertia. Decision-making slows under layers of approvals, turf wars, and procedural rigidity. Threats that demand velocity—cyberattacks, misinformation campaigns, supply chain sabotage—are met with sluggish response. Agencies duplicate efforts while leaving gaps unaddressed. Leadership becomes trapped in process rather than empowered by design.

The fourth fault line is personality-driven governance. Leaders rely on charisma, slogans, and symbolic gestures to project strength. But charisma cannot substitute for systems. Speeches inspire, but they do not build semiconductor fabs, secure networks, or orchestrate intelligence grids. Leadership becomes spectacle, disconnected from architecture.

The dependent India suffers from lack of institutional depth. Universities remain constrained by outdated regulations, research institutions remain politicized, and industries remain dependent on imports. Leadership fails to design frameworks that empower institutions to evolve faster than industries. The result is stagnation masked by rhetoric.

The philosophical diagnosis is clear: leadership in drift is not collapse—it is erosion. It does not destroy overnight; it weakens gradually, leaving the nation exposed to shocks it cannot absorb. Sovereignty erodes not through invasion, but through improvisation.

The cautionary truth is this: in Future B, India's leadership continues to move, but without architecture. It announces, but does not design. It improvises, but does not orchestrate. It inspires, but does not sustain. The nation drifts, delays, disorders itself—and in doing so, forfeits the coherence required for sovereignty in the compute century.

25.2 — Economic Fragility: From Depth to Dependence

In the dependent future, India's economy does not collapse—it stagnates. Growth continues to be reported, startups continue to be celebrated, and services continue to expand. Yet beneath the surface, the architecture is fragile. The nation mistakes activity for depth, headlines for resilience, and consumption for sovereignty. Economic fragility becomes the second fault line of Future B.

The first weakness is dependency on imported semiconductors and compute. India's industries—from defense to healthcare—remain reliant on chips fabricated abroad. Cloud infrastructures are rented from foreign firms, leaving critical data flows hostage to external architectures. Sovereignty is compromised not by invasion, but by dependency embedded into the nation's technological backbone.

The second weakness is manufacturing without resilience. Industrial corridors remain fragmented, logistics remain inefficient, and supply chains remain vulnerable to disruption. India continues to assemble but not design, to consume but not create. Precision manufacturing—robotics, aerospace, advanced engineering—fails to scale, leaving India dependent on imports for critical technologies.

The third weakness is innovation without continuity. Startups emerge with energy but lack ecosystems to sustain growth. Research institutions remain politicized, universities remain constrained, and intellectual property continues to be generated abroad. India consumes global breakthroughs but produces few of its own. Innovation becomes episodic rather than systemic.

The fourth weakness is policy volatility. Economic reforms are announced but rarely embedded. Tax regimes shift unpredictably, regulatory frameworks remain inconsistent, and long-term projects are disrupted by electoral cycles. Investors hesitate, industries stall, and infrastructure projects remain unfinished. Growth becomes fragile, dependent on external confidence rather than internal depth.

The fifth weakness is export fragility. India's global competitiveness remains limited to services and low-cost manufacturing. Pharmaceuticals, aerospace, electronics, and green technologies fail to scale into global dominance. The world does not depend on India's products; India depends on the world's supply chains. Dependency erodes leverage, leaving sovereignty exposed.

The philosophical diagnosis is clear: economic fragility is not about lack of growth—it is about lack of architecture. GDP dashboards may rise, but without depth, they mask vulnerability. Sovereignty cannot be secured by consumption; it must be secured by capability.

In Future B, India's economy drifts into dependency. Chips are imported, compute is rented, supply chains are fragile, innovation is episodic, policies are volatile, and exports are limited. The nation remains active but not sovereign, busy but not resilient.

The cautionary truth is this: economic fragility is not collapse—it is erosion. It weakens the nation gradually, leaving it exposed to shocks it cannot absorb. Sovereignty erodes not through poverty, but through dependency.

25.3 — Talent Drain: From Magnetism to Leakage

In the dependent future, India's greatest strength—its people—becomes its greatest vulnerability. Talent does not stay, it escapes. The nation continues to produce millions of engineers, scientists, and innovators, but its domestic architecture fails to retain them. What could have been magnetism becomes leakage. The result is a slow erosion of capability, a hollowing out of potential, and a weakening of sovereignty.

The first fault line is universities without autonomy. Constrained by outdated regulations, politicized appointments, and rigid curricula, India's higher education system fails to compete with global institutions. Students seek freedom abroad, where they find mentorship, infrastructure, and velocity. The brightest minds depart not out of disloyalty, but out of necessity.

The second fault line is research institutions trapped in bureaucracy. Scientists spend more time navigating approvals than pursuing discovery. Funding is inconsistent, priorities shift with political cycles, and breakthroughs are stifled by interference.

Innovation corridors remain unfinished, deep-tech clusters remain aspirational, and researchers migrate to ecosystems where experimentation is rewarded rather than obstructed.

The third fault line is industry-academia disconnection. Universities produce graduates, but industries fail to integrate them into meaningful pathways. Research remains trapped in journals, disconnected from factories and startups. Innovators see their work stagnate, their ideas unscaled, their careers stalled. Frustration drives them outward, where integration is seamless and impact immediate.

The fourth fault line is career pathways without longevity. Scientists and innovators face stagnant salaries, limited recognition, and unclear progression. Corporate jobs appear more attractive, while research careers appear uncertain. Without structured pathways, talent sees no future at home. The nation loses not only individuals, but generations of capability.

The fifth fault line is diaspora disconnected from domestic missions. India's global talent remains proud of its roots but finds few channels to contribute meaningfully to national projects. Networks remain fragmented, collaborations remain episodic, and circulation remains weak. The diaspora thrives abroad, while India struggles to harness its collective strength.

The philosophical diagnosis is clear: talent drain is not about departure alone—it is about disconnection. In Future B, India fails to design ecosystems that retain, return, or circulate talent. Universities remain constrained, research institutions remain politicized, industries remain disconnected, careers remain stagnant, and diaspora networks remain underutilized.

The cautionary truth is this: talent drain is not collapse—it is erosion. It weakens the nation gradually, hollowing out its capacity to innovate, compete, and lead. Sovereignty erodes not through invasion, but through leakage.

In the dependent future, India continues to produce talent but fails to retain it. The nation becomes a training ground for the world, exporting brilliance while importing dependency. Magnetism dissolves into leakage, and sovereignty dissolves with it.

25.4 — Security Fragility: From Wiring to Exposure

In the dependent future, India's sovereignty is not broken by tanks crossing borders—it is weakened by code crossing cables. The nation continues to invest in physical defense, but its digital wiring remains exposed. Security fragility becomes the fourth fault line of Future B, eroding resilience quietly, relentlessly, and invisibly.

The first weakness is cloud dependency. Government data, citizen records, and industrial flows remain hosted on foreign-controlled platforms. Sovereignty is compromised not by invasion, but by reliance on architectures India does not own. A single geopolitical shock or corporate decision can disrupt critical systems, leaving the nation vulnerable.

The second weakness is outdated governance systems. Ministries operate on obsolete software, unsecured servers, and fragmented protocols. Files are stored without encryption, communications flow through porous channels, and decision-making infrastructures remain exposed to intrusion. Governance becomes fragile not because of lack of intent, but because of lack of architecture.

The third weakness is fragmented intelligence networks. Agencies operate in silos, reluctant to share data, slow to coordinate responses. Cyberattacks unfold in milliseconds, but intelligence grids respond in weeks. Threats slip through cracks not because they are invisible, but because institutions remain disconnected.

The fourth weakness is infrastructure exposed to sabotage. Power grids, transport systems, healthcare networks, and financial flows rely on imported software and unverified components. Supply chains embed vulnerabilities that adversaries exploit. Sovereignty is compromised not by bombs, but by backdoors.

The fifth weakness is public communication without credibility. Misinformation spreads unchecked, disinformation corrodes trust, and citizens lose faith in institutions. Security is not only about protecting systems—it is about protecting coherence. In Future B, coherence collapses, leaving society fragmented and vulnerable to manipulation.

The philosophical diagnosis is clear: security fragility is not about absence of defense—it is about exposure of wiring. India may parade missiles, but if its networks are porous, its sovereignty is hollow. It may fortify borders, but if its data is compromised, its power is fragile.

In Future B, India's security remains reactive, fragmented, and outdated. Clouds are rented, governance is porous, intelligence is siloed, infrastructure is exposed, and communication is manipulated. The nation continues to defend walls but neglects wiring. Sovereignty erodes not through invasion, but through exposure.

The cautionary truth is this: security fragility is not collapse—it is erosion. It weakens the nation gradually, leaving it unable to withstand shocks. In the dependent future, India remains busy with parades and announcements, but its wiring remains exposed. And in the compute century, exposed wiring is the new vulnerability.

Chapter 26 — The Point of No Return

The year after which recovery becomes impossible

The Threshold Beyond Which Architecture Cannot Save

Every nation has turning points, but few have thresholds. A turning point can be reversed; a threshold cannot. The point of no return is not a single event—it is the year when delay hardens into dependency, when drift crystallizes into disorder, and when opportunities once available vanish permanently. After this threshold, even the most ambitious reforms cannot restore sovereignty, because the architectures required to rise have already been built elsewhere, by others, for others.

For India, this is the decisive horizon. If leadership remains fragmented, if economic depth is not secured, if talent continues to leak, and if security wiring remains exposed, the nation will cross into irreversibility. The danger is not collapse but entrapment: India will still exist, but as a dependent state, locked into architectures it does not own, governed by systems it cannot control, and vulnerable to shocks it cannot absorb.

The point of no return is not about failure—it is about foreclosure. It is the moment when the future ceases to be a choice and becomes a condition. And in the compute century, that moment arrives faster than history has ever known.

26.1 — The Nature of Irreversibility: When Delay Becomes Dependency

Irreversibility is not collapse—it is foreclosure. It is the moment when opportunities that were once open to a nation close permanently, not because of external conquest, but because of internal delay. In the compute century, irreversibility arrives faster than history has ever known. Technologies evolve in cycles measured in months, supply chains reorganize in years, and talent ecosystems shift in decades. A nation that hesitates finds itself locked out of architectures already built elsewhere.

The first dimension of irreversibility is technological foreclosure. If India delays building semiconductor ecosystems, sovereign compute clusters, and AI infrastructures, other nations will consolidate dominance. Once supply chains are secured and standards are set, latecomers cannot catch up. Dependency becomes permanent, because the architectures of power are already owned.

The second dimension is talent foreclosure. If India fails to retain or magnetize its brightest minds, they will embed themselves into foreign ecosystems. Diaspora networks may remain proud, but their loyalties will be tied to infrastructures abroad. Once talent is absorbed into other nations' architectures, it cannot be reclaimed. Leakage becomes permanent, because ecosystems elsewhere provide continuity and velocity.

The third dimension is economic foreclosure. If India delays building depth in manufacturing, research, and exports, it will remain a consumer rather than a producer. Global markets will be dominated by nations that invested early in precision industries and green technologies. India will continue to grow, but as a dependent market, not as a sovereign maker. Dependency becomes permanent, because leverage is lost.

The fourth dimension is security foreclosure. If India fails to design encrypted governance, resilient data infrastructures, and cyber-secure supply chains, adversaries will embed vulnerabilities into its wiring. Once backdoors are installed, once networks are compromised, sovereignty cannot be restored by declarations. Exposure becomes permanent, because architecture cannot be retrofitted after compromise.

The philosophical truth is stark: delay is not neutral—it is dependency. Every year of hesitation hardens into reliance, every cycle of drift crystallizes into erosion. Nations do not collapse overnight; they cross thresholds silently, gradually, until recovery becomes impossible.

In the dependent trajectory, India risks crossing this point of no return. It will still exist, still grow, still celebrate—but beneath the spectacle, sovereignty will be foreclosed. The nation will be locked into architectures it does not own, governed by systems it cannot control, and vulnerable to shocks it cannot absorb.

The cautionary insight is clear: irreversibility is not about failure—it is about foreclosure. It is the moment when the future ceases to be a choice and becomes a condition. And in the compute century, that moment arrives faster than India imagines.

26.2 — The Timeline of Collapse: How Drift Becomes Destiny

Collapse is rarely sudden. Nations do not fall overnight; they erode gradually, year by year, until the erosion hardens into destiny. The point of no return is crossed not in a single moment, but through a timeline of drift—small delays that accumulate into irreversible dependency. In the compute century, this timeline accelerates, compressing decades of decline into years of foreclosure.

The first stage is the years of delay. India continues to announce ambitious missions—semiconductors, AI, cybersecurity, green technologies—but execution lags. Ministries remain fragmented, projects stall, and reforms are diluted by political cycles. Talent continues to escape, infrastructure remains unfinished, and supply chains remain vulnerable. The nation appears busy, but beneath the surface, capability is not being built. Delay becomes the silent erosion of sovereignty.

The second stage is the years of dependency. As other nations consolidate technological dominance, India becomes a consumer rather than a producer. Chips are imported, compute is rented, and innovation is outsourced. Talent embeds itself into foreign ecosystems, diaspora networks remain disconnected, and domestic institutions stagnate. India's economy grows, but as a dependent market, not as a sovereign maker. Dependency becomes normalized, embedded into the nation's wiring.

The third stage is the years of exposure. Cyberattacks become routine, misinformation corrodes trust, and critical infrastructure is compromised through imported software and unverified components. Governance systems remain porous, intelligence networks remain fragmented, and public communication loses credibility. Sovereignty is weakened not by invasion, but by exposure. The nation defends its borders but neglects its wiring.

The fourth stage is the years of foreclosure. By this point, the architectures of power—semiconductors, AI frameworks, supply chains, security systems—are already owned by others. India cannot catch up, because the standards are set, the ecosystems are consolidated, and the talent is absorbed abroad. Even ambitious reforms cannot restore sovereignty, because the architectures required to rise have already been built elsewhere. The future ceases to be a choice and becomes a condition.

The philosophical diagnosis is clear: drift becomes destiny when delay hardens into dependency, dependency evolves into exposure, and exposure crystallizes into foreclosure. Collapse is not a sudden fall—it is a timeline of erosion.

In the dependent trajectory, India risks crossing this timeline silently. It will still exist, still grow, still celebrate—but beneath the spectacle, sovereignty will be foreclosed. The nation will be locked into architectures it does not own, governed by systems it cannot control, and vulnerable to shocks it cannot absorb.

The cautionary truth is this: collapse is not an event—it is a timeline. And in the compute century, that timeline accelerates. Drift becomes destiny faster than India imagines.

26.3 — The Year of No Return: Identifying the Threshold

Every nation faces turning points, but only a few face thresholds—the year after which recovery becomes impossible. For India, the point of no return is not a distant abstraction; it is a definable horizon. It is the year when delay hardens into dependency, when erosion crystallizes into foreclosure, and when sovereignty ceases to be a choice and becomes a condition.

The threshold is marked by technological foreclosure. If India fails to establish domestic semiconductor ecosystems and sovereign compute clusters by a certain year, the global architectures of power will already be consolidated elsewhere. Standards will be set, supply chains will be locked, and latecomers will be permanently excluded. After this horizon, India cannot catch up, because the architectures required to rise will already belong to others.

The threshold is marked by talent foreclosure. If India does not magnetize its brightest minds within the next decade, they will embed themselves permanently into foreign ecosystems. Diaspora networks may remain proud, but their loyalties will be tied to infrastructures abroad. Once absorbed into other nations' architectures, talent cannot be reclaimed. Leakage becomes permanent, and India's innovation capacity is hollowed out.

The threshold is marked by economic foreclosure. If India delays building depth in manufacturing, research, and exports, it will remain a consumer rather than a producer. Global markets will be dominated by nations that invested early in precision industries and green technologies. India will continue to grow, but as a dependent market, not as a sovereign maker. After this horizon, leverage is lost, and dependency becomes irreversible.

The threshold is marked by security foreclosure. If India fails to design encrypted governance, resilient data infrastructures, and cyber-secure supply chains, adversaries will embed vulnerabilities into its wiring. Once backdoors are installed, once networks are compromised, sovereignty cannot be restored by declarations. Exposure becomes permanent, because architecture cannot be retrofitted after compromise.

The philosophical truth is stark: the year of no return is not about collapse—it is about foreclosure. It is the moment when the future ceases to be open and becomes closed, when sovereignty ceases to be a possibility and becomes dependency.

In the dependent trajectory, India risks crossing this threshold silently. It will still exist, still grow, still celebrate—but beneath the spectacle, sovereignty will be foreclosed. The nation will be locked into architectures it does not own, governed by systems it cannot control, and vulnerable to shocks it cannot absorb.

The cautionary insight is clear: the year of no return is not distant—it is imminent. In the compute century, thresholds arrive faster than history imagines. India must act before delay hardens into destiny.

26.4 — The Consequences of Crossing: Sovereignty as Illusion

When a nation crosses the point of no return, sovereignty does not vanish overnight—it becomes an illusion. The state continues to exist, flags continue to fly, parades continue to march, and leaders continue to speak. Yet beneath the spectacle, the wiring is owned elsewhere, the architectures are controlled by others, and the nation's autonomy dissolves into dependency. Sovereignty remains visible but ceases to be real.

The first consequence is political illusion. Leaders continue to announce policies, but the infrastructures required to implement them are foreign-controlled. Decisions appear sovereign, but execution depends on external platforms, imported technologies, and rented compute. Politics becomes theater, disconnected from architecture.

The second consequence is economic illusion. GDP continues to grow, startups continue to emerge, and industries continue to expand. Yet beneath the numbers, chips are imported, supply chains are fragile, and innovation is outsourced. The economy appears vibrant, but its foundations are hollow. Growth becomes dependency disguised as progress.

The third consequence is talent illusion. Universities continue to graduate millions, diaspora networks continue to celebrate their roots, and innovators continue to emerge. Yet the brightest minds remain embedded in foreign ecosystems, breakthroughs are produced abroad, and domestic institutions stagnate. Talent appears abundant, but capability is absent. Magnetism dissolves into leakage.

The fourth consequence is security illusion. Armies continue to parade, missiles continue to be displayed, and agencies continue to operate. Yet networks remain porous, governance remains exposed, and infrastructure remains compromised. Security appears strong, but wiring is fragile. Defense becomes spectacle without resilience.

The fifth consequence is sovereignty illusion. Citizens continue to believe in independence, but their data is stored abroad, their communication flows through foreign platforms, and their industries depend on imported components. Sovereignty appears intact, but autonomy is foreclosed. The nation exists, but as a dependent state.

The philosophical diagnosis is stark: crossing the point of no return does not destroy a nation—it empties it. Sovereignty becomes a symbol without substance, a ritual without architecture, a narrative without capability. The state continues to perform independence, but beneath the performance, dependency governs reality.

The cautionary truth is this: the greatest danger is not collapse—it is illusion. A nation that collapses knows it has fallen. A nation that lives in illusion believes it is sovereign while being governed by systems it does not own. This is the true consequence of crossing the point of no return.

In the compute century, sovereignty is not defended by walls—it is defended by wiring. And once wiring is compromised, sovereignty becomes illusion.

Chapter 27 — Resetting India's Trajectory

A strategic prescription for policymakers and citizens

The Choice to Re-Architect the Future

India stands at a hinge moment. The warnings of drift, dependency, and disorder are not destiny—they are signals. The nation can still reset its trajectory, but only if policymakers and citizens treat sovereignty not as a symbol, but as a system. Resetting is not about slogans or incremental reforms; it is about re-architecting the foundations of leadership, economy, talent, and security into coherence.

This reset demands consequence-aware clarity: leaders must design operating systems that outlast personalities, industries must embed depth rather than dependence, universities must magnetize talent rather than leak it, and citizens must see sovereignty not as isolation but as alignment. The ripple view is decisive—sovereignty is the consequence of coherence, the resonance of systems moving in rhythm, the integration of openness without dependence.

The prescription is not abstract. It is strategic, actionable, and urgent. India can still ascend, but only if it chooses architecture over improvisation, depth over fragility, magnetism over leakage, and wiring over exposure. The reset is not optional—it is the only path to sovereignty in the compute century.

27.1 — Leadership Reset: Designing Systems Beyond Personalities

Resetting India's trajectory begins with leadership. Not leadership as charisma, not leadership as spectacle, but leadership as architecture. For too long, India has relied on personalities to inspire, slogans to mobilize, and improvisation to govern. This has produced motion without coherence, activity without architecture. The reset demands a decisive shift: leaders must design systems that outlast themselves, frameworks that endure beyond cycles, and architectures that sustain sovereignty across generations.

The first prescription is institutional coherence. Ministries must be re-architected into coordination platforms rather than silos. National missions—semiconductors, AI, cybersecurity, green technologies—must be orchestrated across departments with shared protocols, unified dashboards, and consequence-aware accountability. Leadership must design operating systems where ministries move in rhythm, not competition.

The second prescription is policy continuity. India's reforms cannot dissolve with elections. Long-term projects must be insulated from political volatility, embedded into national frameworks that survive transitions. Leadership must design continuity mechanisms—independent commissions, bipartisan agreements, and legally binding frameworks—that ensure missions are pursued across decades. Sovereignty requires stability, not improvisation.

The third prescription is decision velocity. Bureaucratic inertia must be replaced with agile protocols. Threats in the compute century—cyberattacks, misinformation, supply chain sabotage—unfold in milliseconds. Leadership must design decision architectures that accelerate response without sacrificing accountability. Velocity must be embedded into governance, not improvised in crisis.

The fourth prescription is talent integration. Leaders must treat governance as a magnet for brilliance. Scientists, innovators, and strategists must be embedded into policymaking, not kept at the margins. Leadership must design councils, advisory boards, and innovation corridors where talent informs architecture. Sovereignty requires intelligence embedded into systems, not slogans.

The fifth prescription is citizen alignment. Leadership must design communication systems that unify rather than fragment. Citizens must see sovereignty not as isolation, but as coherence—an alignment of leadership, economy, talent, and security. Ripple View is decisive here: sovereignty is the consequence of alignment, the resonance of systems moving in rhythm. Leaders must design architectures that empower citizens to participate in coherence, not just consume spectacle.

The philosophical reset is clear: leadership is not about personalities—it is about systems. Charisma may inspire, but architecture sustains. Leaders who design systems leave behind resilience; leaders who rely on spectacle leave behind fragility. In the reset trajectory, India's sovereignty will be powered not by speeches, but by systems.

The constructive truth is this: India can still ascend, but only if its leadership evolves from improvisation to architecture, from personality to system, from spectacle to coherence. Resetting begins here—at the level of design.

27.2 — Economic Reset: Embedding Depth into Growth

Resetting India's trajectory requires transforming its economy from surface-level growth into sovereign depth. GDP dashboards and startup headlines may signal momentum, but they do not guarantee resilience. True sovereignty emerges when economic systems embed capability—when India becomes a maker, not merely a market; a producer of architectures, not just a consumer of imports. The reset demands a decisive shift: growth must be re-architected into depth.

The first prescription is semiconductor sovereignty. India must accelerate investment in chip design, fabrication, and packaging. This is not optional—it is the backbone of every modern industry, from defense to healthcare. Without domestic semiconductors, India remains dependent on foreign supply chains. With them, India anchors sovereignty in silicon.

The second prescription is sovereign compute and AI infrastructure. India's digital economy cannot thrive on rented servers. National compute clusters, sovereign clouds, and AI frameworks designed at home must become the oxygen of innovation. Compute is the new currency of power; without it, brilliance suffocates. With it, India breathes resilience.

The third prescription is manufacturing depth. Industrial corridors must evolve into integrated ecosystems where logistics, research, and skilled labor converge. Precision manufacturing—robotics, aerospace, green technologies—must anchor resilience. India must design supply chains that are secure, verified, and globally competitive. Sovereignty requires being a maker, not just an assembler.

The fourth prescription is export leverage. India must scale industries where the world depends on its products—pharmaceuticals, electronics, aerospace, and renewable technologies. When global markets rely on India, sovereignty is reinforced. Dependency is reversed; capability becomes leverage.

The fifth prescription is research autonomy. Universities and labs must be liberated from bureaucratic micromanagement. Funding must be stable, governance must be professional, and breakthroughs must be incentivized. Indigenous intellectual property is not a luxury—it is the foundation of sovereignty. Without it, India consumes discoveries made elsewhere; with it, India produces frontier science.

The sixth prescription is policy stability. Economic architecture cannot be rebuilt every five years. Continuity mechanisms must insulate long-term projects from electoral volatility. Investors must see predictability, innovators must see stability, and industries must see credibility. Sovereignty requires depth embedded across decades, not dissolved in cycles.

The ripple view reframes this reset: economic sovereignty is not isolation, nor insulation. It is strategic integration without dependence. India must embed depth into its economy so that openness strengthens resilience rather than erodes it. Coherence across leadership, industry, research, and citizens transforms growth into architecture.

The constructive truth is clear: India can still ascend, but only if its economy evolves from surface growth to sovereign depth. Resetting begins here—at the level of capability.

27.3 — Talent Reset: From Leakage to Magnetism

Resetting India's trajectory requires transforming its talent story from leakage into magnetism. For decades, India has produced brilliance only to watch it escape—scientists migrating to foreign labs, engineers absorbed into global corporations, innovators scaling startups abroad. This leakage has hollowed out domestic capability, leaving India as a training ground for the world rather than a sovereign hub of innovation. The reset demands a decisive shift: talent must be magnetized, circulated, and embedded into India's own architectures of power.

The first prescription is university autonomy. India's higher education institutions must be liberated from political interference and outdated regulation. Curricula must evolve at digital velocity, faculty must be recruited globally, and students must be trained not just for jobs but for innovation. Universities must become magnets, rivaling the best in the world, attracting international scholars while retaining domestic brilliance.

The second prescription is research empowerment. Scientists must be freed from bureaucratic micromanagement. Funding must be stable, priorities must be long-term, and governance must be professionalized. Breakthroughs in AI, biotech, quantum computing, and green technologies must emerge not abroad but in Bengaluru, Pune, and Delhi. Research institutions must be designed as sovereign hubs of discovery, not as politicized departments.

The third prescription is industry-academia integration. Research must flow seamlessly into startups, factories, and national missions. Industries must invest in academic labs, while universities must embed students into industrial projects. Innovators must see their work translated into patents, products, and impact. Purpose must replace frustration; impact must replace stagnation.

The fourth prescription is innovation corridors and deep-tech clusters. India must design ecosystems where startups, labs, investors, and regulators co-exist. Corridors provide infrastructure, mentorship, and scale; clusters create density of ideas and talent. Together, they transform isolated ambition into collective capability. Talent thrives where ecosystems are coherent, not fragmented.

The fifth prescription is diaspora integration. India's global talent networks must be strategically connected to domestic missions. Distributed research teams, co-development labs, and entrepreneurial collaborations must transform diaspora pride into sovereign capability. Talent abroad must circulate knowledge, capital, and networks back into India's architecture of power.

The sixth prescription is career longevity. Scientists and innovators must see structured pathways—competitive funding, recognition systems, global exposure, and progression. Research careers must be as attractive as corporate careers. Talent stays where it sees not only opportunity but longevity.

The ripple view reframes this reset: talent sovereignty is not about preventing departure—it is about designing ecosystems so compelling that staying, returning, and circulating become natural choices. Magnetism is coherence; leakage is fragmentation. Sovereignty emerges when talent flows in rhythm with national architecture.

The constructive truth is clear: India can still ascend, but only if its talent ecosystem evolves from leakage to magnetism, from escape to circulation, from fragility to coherence. Resetting begins here—at the level of people.

27.4 — Security Reset: Wiring Resilience into Sovereignty

Resetting India's trajectory requires transforming security from spectacle into wiring. For too long, defense has been imagined as parades, missiles, and borders. Yet in the compute century, sovereignty is not defended by walls—it is defended by networks, data flows, and architectures of trust. India's reset must rewire its security systems so that resilience is embedded into every layer of governance, economy, and society.

The first prescription is sovereign digital infrastructure. India must design encrypted governance systems, secure citizen databases, and resilient communication platforms. Critical data cannot remain hostage to foreign-controlled clouds. Sovereignty requires owning the wiring—clouds, servers, and protocols must be built and secured at home.

The second prescription is integrated intelligence networks. Agencies must dissolve silos and operate as a coherent grid. Cyberattacks unfold in milliseconds; intelligence cannot respond in weeks. Shared dashboards, unified protocols, and consequence-aware coordination must replace fragmentation. Security is coherence, not competition.

The third prescription is supply chain verification. Every imported chip, every software module, every industrial component must be tested for vulnerabilities. Backdoors cannot be allowed to embed themselves into India's wiring. Sovereignty requires secure supply chains, verified architectures, and trusted components.

The fourth prescription is resilient infrastructure. Power grids, transport systems, healthcare networks, and financial flows must be designed with redundancy and resilience. Cyberattacks, sabotage, or misinformation campaigns must not collapse essential services. Sovereignty requires infrastructures that can absorb shocks without breaking.

The fifth prescription is citizen trust. Security is not only about protecting systems—it is about protecting coherence. Misinformation corrodes trust faster than malware corrupts code. India must design communication architectures that are credible, transparent, and consequence-aware. Citizens must see truth as resilient, not fragile.

The sixth prescription is strategic integration. Security cannot mean isolation or insulation. India must integrate with global networks strategically, aligning with allies while protecting autonomy. Ripple View reframes this: sovereignty is consequence of alignment, not isolation. Security is coherence across domestic wiring and global integration, without dependence.

The philosophical reset is clear: security is not spectacle—it is wiring. Missiles may inspire, but networks sustain. Borders may defend, but architectures protect. In the reset trajectory, India's sovereignty will be powered not by parades, but by protocols; not by charisma, but by coherence; not by isolation, but by strategic integration.

The constructive truth is this: India can still ascend, but only if its security evolves from exposure to resilience, from fragmentation to coherence, from illusion to architecture. Resetting begins here—at the level of wiring.

Final Chapter — Sovereignty as Alignment

Ripple View: Coherence as the True Architecture of Power

Beyond Symbols, Toward Systems

Sovereignty is not a flag, nor a slogan, nor a parade. It is not the illusion of independence performed on ceremonial stages. Sovereignty is consequence. It is the emergent property of coherence—when leadership, economy, talent, and security align into rhythm. In Ripple View, sovereignty is not isolation, nor insulation. It is strategic integration without dependence, openness without fragility, coherence without fragmentation.

India's future will not be decided by declarations or spectacles. It will be decided by whether its systems resonate. Whether ministries coordinate instead of compete, whether industries embed depth instead of dependence, whether talent circulates instead of leaking, and whether security wiring protects coherence instead of parading illusion. Sovereignty is not defended by walls—it is defended by wiring. And wiring is coherence.

This final chapter reframes sovereignty as alignment. It is not a possession to be defended, but a consequence to be designed. It is not a symbol to be celebrated, but a system to be sustained. Sovereignty is Ripple View made real: the resonance of architectures moving in rhythm, the coherence of fields aligned, the consequence of integration.

Leadership Alignment: Systems Beyond Personalities

Leadership in Ripple View is not charisma—it is architecture. Charisma may inspire, but architecture sustains. India's reset demands leaders who design systems that outlast themselves, frameworks that endure beyond cycles, and architectures that sustain sovereignty across generations.

Leadership alignment begins with institutional coherence. Ministries must dissolve silos and operate as orchestration platforms. National missions—semiconductors, AI, cybersecurity, green technologies—must be coordinated across departments with shared dashboards, unified protocols, and consequence-aware accountability. Leadership must design operating systems where ministries move in rhythm, not competition.

Leadership alignment requires policy continuity. India's reforms cannot dissolve with elections. Long-term projects must be insulated from political volatility, embedded into frameworks that survive transitions. Independent commissions, bipartisan agreements, and legally binding protocols must ensure missions are pursued across decades. Sovereignty requires stability, not improvisation.

Leadership alignment demands decision velocity. Bureaucratic inertia must be replaced with agile protocols. Threats in the compute century unfold in milliseconds; intelligence cannot respond in weeks. Leadership must design architectures that accelerate response without sacrificing accountability. Velocity must be embedded into governance, not improvised in crisis.

Leadership alignment integrates talent into governance. Scientists, innovators, and strategists must be embedded into policymaking, not kept at the margins. Councils, advisory boards, and innovation corridors must ensure talent informs architecture.

Sovereignty requires intelligence embedded into systems, not slogans.

Leadership alignment empowers citizen coherence. Communication systems must unify rather than fragment. Citizens must see sovereignty not as isolation, but as alignment—an architecture where leadership, economy, talent, and security resonate together. Ripple View reframes sovereignty as consequence of coherence, not spectacle.

The philosophical truth is clear: leadership is not about personalities—it is about systems. Leaders who design systems leave behind resilience; leaders who rely on spectacle leave behind fragility. Sovereignty emerges when leadership aligns architecture with consequence.

Economic Alignment: Depth as Sovereignty

Economic growth without depth is fragility disguised as progress. GDP dashboards may rise, startups may flourish, but sovereignty requires capability. India must evolve from consumer to producer, from assembler to maker, from surface growth to sovereign depth.

Economic alignment begins with semiconductor sovereignty. Chips are the backbone of every modern industry. India must accelerate investment in design, fabrication, and packaging. Without domestic semiconductors, sovereignty remains hostage to foreign supply chains. With them, India anchors sovereignty in silicon.

Economic alignment requires sovereign compute and AI infrastructure. India cannot rent its future. National compute clusters, sovereign clouds, and AI frameworks must be designed at home. Compute is the new currency of power; without it, brilliance suffocates. With it, India breathes resilience.

Economic alignment demands manufacturing depth. Industrial corridors must evolve into ecosystems where logistics, research, and skilled labor converge. Precision manufacturing—robotics, aerospace, green technologies—must anchor resilience. Sovereignty requires being a maker, not just an assembler.

Economic alignment leverages exports as power. India must scale industries where the world depends on its products—pharmaceuticals, electronics, aerospace, renewable technologies. When global markets rely on India, sovereignty is reinforced. Dependency is reversed; capability becomes leverage.

Economic alignment empowers research autonomy. Universities and labs must be liberated from bureaucratic micromanagement. Funding must be stable, governance must be professional, and breakthroughs must be incentivized. Indigenous intellectual property is not a luxury—it is the foundation of sovereignty.

Economic alignment requires policy stability. Continuity mechanisms must insulate long-term projects from electoral volatility. Investors must see predictability, innovators must see stability, industries must see credibility. Sovereignty requires depth embedded across decades, not dissolved in cycles.

Ripple View reframes economic sovereignty: it is not isolation, nor insulation. It is strategic integration without dependence. India must embed depth into its economy so that openness strengthens resilience rather than erodes it. Sovereignty emerges when economy aligns capability with coherence.

Talent Alignment: Magnetism as Architecture

Talent is India's greatest resource. Yet brilliance has leaked for decades, hollowing out domestic capability. Resetting requires transforming talent from leakage into magnetism, from escape into circulation, from fragility into coherence.

Talent alignment begins with university autonomy. Higher education must be liberated from political interference and outdated regulation. Curricula must evolve at digital velocity, faculty must be recruited globally, and students must be trained not just for jobs but for innovation. Universities must rival the best in the world, attracting international scholars while retaining domestic brilliance.

Talent alignment requires research empowerment. Scientists must be freed from bureaucratic micromanagement. Funding must be stable, priorities must be long-term, governance must be professionalized. Breakthroughs in AI, biotech, quantum computing, and green technologies must emerge not abroad but in India's own labs.

Talent alignment demands industry-academia integration. Research must flow seamlessly into startups, factories, and national missions. Industries must invest in academic labs, while universities must embed students into industrial projects. Innovators must see their work translated into patents, products, and impact.

Talent alignment designs innovation corridors and deep-tech clusters. Ecosystems where startups, labs, investors, and regulators co-exist must be built. Corridors provide infrastructure, mentorship, and scale; clusters create density of ideas and talent. Together, they transform isolated ambition into collective capability.

Talent alignment requires diaspora integration. India's global talent networks must be strategically connected to domestic missions. Distributed research teams, co-development labs, and entrepreneurial collaborations must transform diaspora pride into sovereign capability.

Talent alignment ensures career longevity. Scientists and innovators must see structured pathways—competitive funding, recognition systems, global exposure, and progression. Research careers must be as attractive as corporate careers. Talent stays where it sees not only opportunity but longevity.

Ripple View reframes talent sovereignty: it is not about preventing departure—it is about designing ecosystems so compelling that staying, returning, and circulating become natural choices. Magnetism is coherence; leakage is fragmentation. Sovereignty emerges when talent aligns with architecture.

Security Alignment: Wiring Resilience into Sovereignty

Security in Ripple View is not spectacle—it is wiring. Missiles may inspire, but networks sustain. Borders may defend, but architectures protect. India's reset requires rewiring security so resilience is embedded into every layer of governance, economy, and society.

Security alignment begins with sovereign digital infrastructure. Encrypted governance systems, secure citizen databases, and resilient communication platforms must be designed at home. Critical data cannot remain hostage to foreign-controlled clouds. Sovereignty requires owning the wiring.

Security alignment requires integrated intelligence networks. Agencies must dissolve silos and operate as a coherent grid. Cyberattacks unfold in milliseconds; intelligence cannot respond in weeks. Shared dashboards, unified protocols, and consequence-aware coordination must replace fragmentation.

Security alignment demands supply chain verification. Every imported chip, software module, and industrial component must be tested for vulnerabilities. Backdoors cannot be allowed to embed themselves into India's wiring. Sovereignty requires secure supply chains, verified architectures, and trusted components.

Security alignment designs resilient infrastructure. Power grids, transport systems, healthcare networks, and financial flows must be built with redundancy and resilience. Cyberattacks, sabotage, or misinformation campaigns must not collapse essential services. Sovereignty requires infrastructures that absorb shocks without breaking.

Security alignment empowers citizen trust. Security is not only about protecting systems—it is about protecting coherence.

Misinformation corrodes trust faster than malware corrupts code. India must design communication architectures that are credible, transparent, and consequence-aware.

Security alignment requires strategic integration. India must integrate with global networks strategically, aligning with allies while protecting autonomy. Ripple View reframes sovereignty as consequence of alignment, not isolation. Security is coherence across domestic wiring and global integration, without dependence.

The philosophical truth is clear: security is not spectacle—it is wiring. Sovereignty emerges when security aligns resilience with coherence.

Ripple View: Sovereignty as Consequence of Alignment

Ripple View reframes sovereignty as consequence. It is not defended by walls, nor sustained by isolation, nor preserved by insulation. Sovereignty is coherence—the resonance that emerges when leadership, economy, talent, and security align into rhythm. It is not spectacle, but system; not symbol, but architecture.

In Ripple View, sovereignty is alignment across fields. Leadership designs systems beyond personalities, economy embeds depth beyond dashboards, talent circulates beyond leakage, and security wires resilience beyond spectacle. Each field resonates with the others, producing coherence. Sovereignty is not the sum of fragments—it is the consequence of alignment.

Sovereignty is integration without dependence. India must remain open to global networks, but strategically integrated. Isolation weakens, insulation stagnates, dependence erodes. Integration strengthens when it is consequence-aware, when openness is designed to reinforce resilience rather than dissolve it. Sovereignty is not withdrawal—it is participation without subordination.

Sovereignty is resonance across generations. Systems must be designed to endure beyond electoral cycles, beyond personalities, beyond temporary crises. Architecture must be consequence-aware, embedding resilience across decades. Sovereignty is not improvisation—it is continuity.

Sovereignty is citizen coherence. Citizens must see independence not as a flag alone, but as a system they inhabit. Trust must be protected, misinformation must be countered, and participation must be empowered. Sovereignty is not only about leaders—it is about citizens aligned with architecture.

The philosophical truth is clear: sovereignty is not a possession to be defended, nor a symbol to be celebrated. It is a consequence to be designed. Ripple View reframes sovereignty as coherence—the emergent property of systems aligned, architectures resonant, and fields integrated.

The constructive insight is decisive: India can still ascend, but only if it treats sovereignty as consequence of alignment. Leadership must design systems, economy must embed depth, talent must circulate, and security must wire resilience. When these fields resonate, sovereignty emerges naturally, powerfully, irreversibly.

In the compute century, sovereignty is not defended by walls—it is defended by wiring. And wiring is coherence. Ripple View closes the circle: sovereignty is consequence of alignment, resonance of coherence, architecture of integration. It is neither isolation nor dependence—it is coherence made real.

Epilogue

The Last Window

A message for India in the language of consequence

The Window That Still Remains

Every civilization has windows—moments when possibility is open, when the future can still be re-architected, when destiny is not yet foreclosed. India stands at such a window now. It is not infinite. It is not permanent. It is the last window before drift hardens into dependency, before erosion crystallizes into foreclosure, before sovereignty dissolves into illusion.

This window is narrow, but it is real. It is the space between improvisation and architecture, between fragility and depth, between leakage and magnetism, between exposure and resilience. It is the moment when India can still choose coherence over fragmentation, consequence over spectacle, alignment over drift.

The last window is not about opportunity alone—it is about consequence. If India acts, sovereignty can be secured. If India delays, sovereignty will be foreclosed. The language of consequence is decisive: every choice either strengthens coherence or accelerates erosion.

The Nature of the Last Window

The last window is not a gift—it is a responsibility. It is the final horizon before irreversibility. In the compute century, technologies evolve in cycles measured in months, supply chains reorganize in years, and talent ecosystems shift in decades. Delay is not neutral—it is dependency.

The last window is defined by velocity. Nations that act now embed sovereignty into silicon, compute, and wiring. Nations that hesitate find themselves locked out of architectures already built elsewhere. India's window is closing faster than history imagines.

The last window is defined by coherence. Sovereignty cannot be secured by fragments—ministries in silos, industries without depth, universities without autonomy, security without wiring. Sovereignty emerges only when systems resonate. The window is open only if India aligns leadership, economy, talent, and security into rhythm.

The last window is defined by consequence. Every choice either strengthens resilience or accelerates erosion. Every delay either builds architecture elsewhere or forecloses sovereignty at home. The window is not about possibility—it is about consequence.

The Risks of Missing the Window

If India misses the last window, sovereignty will not collapse—it will dissolve into illusion. The nation will continue to exist, flags will continue to fly, parades will continue to march, and leaders will continue to speak. Yet beneath the spectacle, the wiring will be owned elsewhere, the architectures controlled by others, the autonomy foreclosed.

The risks are clear:

- **Leadership drift** will harden into improvisation. Ministries will remain fragmented, policies volatile, decisions sluggish. Charisma will inspire, but architecture will be absent.

Sovereignty will dissolve into spectacle.

- **Economic fragility** will harden into dependency. Chips will be imported, compute rented, innovation outsourced. GDP dashboards will rise, but capability will be hollow. Sovereignty will dissolve into consumption.
- **Talent leakage** will harden into permanent migration. Universities will stagnate, research will be politicized, diaspora networks will remain disconnected. India will continue to produce brilliance, but for others. Sovereignty will dissolve into hollow pride.
- **Security exposure** will harden into vulnerability. Clouds will be rented, governance porous, intelligence fragmented, infrastructure compromised. Armies will parade, but networks will collapse. Sovereignty will dissolve into illusion.

Missing the window does not mean collapse—it means foreclosure. Sovereignty will cease to be a choice and become a condition. India will exist, but as a dependent state.

The Possibilities of Acting Within the Window

If India acts within the last window, sovereignty can be secured—not as a symbol, but as a system. The possibilities are transformative:

- **Leadership coherence.** Ministries aligned, policies continuous, decisions agile, talent embedded, citizens empowered. Leadership becomes architecture, not spectacle.
- **Economic depth.** Semiconductors designed, compute clusters sovereign, manufacturing resilient, exports leveraged, research autonomous. Economy becomes

capability, not consumption.

- **Talent magnetism.** Universities autonomous, research empowered, industry integrated, diaspora connected, careers sustained. Talent circulates, innovates, and anchors sovereignty.
- **Security resilience.** Digital infrastructures sovereign, intelligence networks integrated, supply chains verified, infrastructures redundant, citizen trust protected. Security becomes wiring, not spectacle.

Acting within the window transforms sovereignty from illusion into coherence. It reframes independence not as isolation, but as alignment. It secures resilience not through walls, but through wiring. It anchors sovereignty not in slogans, but in systems.

The Ripple View of the Window

Ripple View reframes the last window as alignment. Sovereignty is not defended by isolation, nor preserved by insulation, nor sustained by dependence. Sovereignty is coherence—the resonance that emerges when systems align.

The window is not about isolation. India cannot withdraw from global networks. Isolation weakens, insulation stagnates, dependence erodes. Sovereignty requires strategic integration—participation without subordination, openness without fragility, alignment without dependence.

The window is not about spectacle. Sovereignty cannot be performed through parades, slogans, or charisma. It must be designed through systems, architectures, and coherence. Ripple View reframes sovereignty as consequence of alignment, not performance of independence.

The window is not about fragments. Sovereignty cannot be secured by leadership alone, or economy alone, or talent alone, or security alone. It emerges only when all fields resonate together. Ripple View reframes sovereignty as emergent property of coherence, not sum of fragments.

The Message in the Language of Consequence

The message for India is clear: sovereignty is consequence, not symbol. It is coherence, not spectacle. It is alignment, not isolation.

India must act now—within the last window—to design systems beyond personalities, embed depth beyond dashboards, magnetize talent beyond leakage, and wire resilience beyond spectacle. Sovereignty will not be secured by declarations, but by architectures.

The language of consequence is decisive: Delay is dependency. Dependency is erosion. Erosion is foreclosure. And Foreclosure is illusion.

The last window is open, but it is closing. India must act before drift hardens into destiny.

Closing Meditation: The Last Window as Choice

The last window is not infinite. It is not permanent. It is the final horizon before irreversibility. India stands at this hinge moment, with sovereignty still possible, coherence still attainable, resilience still designable.

The choice is clear: act now, and sovereignty becomes consequence of alignment. Delay now, and sovereignty dissolves into illusion.

The last window is India's final chance to re-architect its future. It is the moment when consequence becomes destiny, when coherence becomes sovereignty, when alignment becomes resilience.

The message is simple, but decisive: **India must act.**

Appendices

India at the Edge of Two Futures — Power Without Preparation in the Age of AI

Appendix A — ICDI

The India Compute Dependency Index (ICDI)

India's placement across chips, cloud, AI, and digital infrastructure

1. Purpose of ICDI

The India Compute Dependency Index (ICDI) is a strategic diagnostic tool designed to measure India's vulnerability—and readiness—in the compute century. Traditional metrics like GDP, FDI, and export volume fail to capture the new foundation of national power: compute, data infrastructure, cloud sovereignty, semiconductor depth, and algorithmic autonomy.

ICDI is not an academic exercise. It is an early-warning system. A mirror held against the architecture India must build before 2035.

2. The Four Pillars of Compute Sovereignty

Pillar 1 — Semiconductors (Chips): Measures India's position across the chip value chain:

- design capability
- fabrication access
- equipment autonomy
- packaging and testing depth
- mineral sourcing reliability

- supply chain resilience

Current Score: 2/10: Strong design talent, but weak domestic production. India remains critically dependent on Taiwan, South Korea, the U.S., Japan, and the Netherlands for core infrastructure.

Pillar 2 — Cloud Infrastructure: Cloud is the new territory of nations—the invisible landmass that stores data, runs computation, and enables digital governance.

Assessment includes:

- domestic hyperscale cloud capacity
- public-sector cloud sovereignty
- data localization reliability
- foreign provider concentration risk
- sovereign cloud R&D capability

Current Score: 3/10: AWS, Google, and Microsoft dominate. Domestic cloud remains fragmented; government cloud is improving but not yet robust enough to anchor sovereignty.

Pillar 3 — Artificial Intelligence (Algorithms): Algorithms shape everything—markets, governance, public opinion, logistics, warfare, finance, and civic behavior.

Assessment includes:

- LLM training capability
- domestic AI models
- compute availability for research
- academia–industry linkages
- talent retention
- algorithmic independence

Current Score: 2/10: India has one of the world's largest AI talent pools—but it is almost entirely plugged into U.S. and Chinese ecosystems. Domestic model capacity is constrained by compute scarcity.

Pillar 4 — Digital Infrastructure & Connectivity: Measures the strength and resilience of India's fundamental digital rails.

Assessment includes:

- broadband penetration
- fiber backbone density
- cybersecurity posture
- digital ID infrastructure
- fintech and public digital goods
- disaster resilience and redundancy

Current Score: 5/10 UPI and Aadhaar are global marvels. Yet fiber penetration and cybersecurity remain inconsistent, redundancy is weak, and rural integration incomplete.

3. India's Composite ICDI Score

Weighting by strategic importance:

- Chips — 35%
- Cloud — 25%
- AI — 25%
- Digital Infrastructure — 15%

Calculation:

$$(2 \times 0.35) + (3 \times 0.25) + (2 \times 0.25) + (5 \times 0.15)$$

= 0.70 + 0.75 + 0.50 + 0.75 = **2.70 / 10**

Composite ICDI Score: 2.7 / 10 India is in the *Strategically Vulnerable* category—ambitious, rising, but critically dependent on external architecture for continuity.

4. ICDI Interpretation Bands

Score Range	Classification	Implication
0–2	Highly Dependent	Nation fragile, reliant on external compute for core functions.
2–4	Strategically Vulnerable	Ambition present, but foundational architecture absent (India's current band).
4–6	Developing Sovereignty	Partial autonomy, but reliance persists for critical layers.
6–8	Near-Sovereign	Key compute pillars controlled; dependency risk minimal.
8–10	Full Compute Sovereignty	Nation resilient, export-capable, architecture-independent.

5. ICDI Insights: India's National Risks and Opportunities

Major Risks

- Chip chokepoints can halt defense, mobility, finance, and healthcare.
- Cloud centralization creates single-point leverage for foreign providers.
- AI dependency weakens national narratives and digital autonomy.
- Infrastructure gaps reduce resilience to cyberattacks and global shocks.

Major Opportunities

- India's talent pool is the strongest foundation for catch-up.
- Domestic cloud and compute missions can scale rapidly with policy alignment.
- Semiconductor packaging and design can accelerate

sovereignty.

- Public digital infrastructure (UPI, Aadhaar, ONDC) can become global exports.

6. The ICDI Warning for 2035

If India does not elevate its ICDI score to **6.0+ by 2035**:

- It will remain a large market, not a global power.
- It will produce talent, not architecture.
- It will consume algorithms, not govern them.
- It will depend on alliances, not shape them.
- Its sovereignty will remain conditional, not structural.

If India achieves **7.5+ by 2035**:

- It becomes a compute-era sovereign power.
- Its economic destiny shifts from services to architecture.
- Its geopolitical leverage multiplies.
- Its talent and institutions finally operate in alignment.
- Its strategic autonomy becomes irreversible.

7. Final Line

ICDI is not a score. It is a warning—and an invitation. India must choose whether 2035 becomes its launch window or its dependency trap.

Appendix B — CIIS

The Chavanian Institutional Integrity Scale (CIIS)

Measuring the Stability and Strength of India's Institutional Architecture

1. Purpose of CIIS

Nations rise on institutions, not leaders. Leaders inspire, but institutions execute.

In the compute century, institutions are not just guardians of stability—they are active engines of national power.

The **Chavanian Institutional Integrity Scale (CIIS)** measures India's institutional robustness across five critical dimensions:

- Autonomy
- Competence
- Continuity
- Accountability
- Coordination

CIIS acts as India's institutional health report, identifying where the system enables progress—and where it quietly sabotages it.

2. The Five Dimensions of CIIS

Dimension 1 — Autonomy

Does the institution operate free from political interference, partisan pressure, and arbitrary appointments?

Assessed across: judicial appointments, regulatory independence, investigative agencies, academic councils, public broadcasters, civil service operational freedom.

Score: 3/10

Pockets of excellence exist, but systemic autonomy remains fragile. Political overreach is a major structural weakness.

Dimension 2 — Competence

Does the institution have the skill, expertise, training, and modern tools required to execute its mandate?

Measured through: domain expertise at leadership levels, training ecosystems, research support, digital infrastructure, staffing ratios, professional diversity.

Score: 4/10

Competence exists in individuals, but modernization is missing. Leadership appointments often prioritize loyalty over capability.

Dimension 3 — Continuity

Can the institution maintain momentum despite political cycles, leadership changes, or administrative reshuffles?

Assessment based on: project completion consistency, long-term planning frameworks, policy stability, organizational memory retention, resistance to election-cycle disruptions.

Score: 3/10

Frequent turnover, unpredictable transfers, and politically timed policy swings weaken continuity across ministries and states.

Dimension 4 — Accountability

Is the institution accountable for outcomes—not just activity?

Measured through: performance metrics, audit and oversight mechanisms, corruption detection, internal discipline, public transparency frameworks.

Score: 2/10

Accountability remains reactive, selective, and uneven. Misconduct often goes unpunished unless politically convenient.

Dimension 5 — Coordination

Do institutions collaborate effectively across ministries, states, and agencies?

Assessed via: cross-ministry working groups, inter-state mechanisms, crisis coordination, data sharing, interoperability of systems.

Score: 3/10

Chronic fragmentation persists. Ministries guard turf, states resist alignment, agencies operate in silos. Coordination failures cost lives, money, and credibility.

3. Composite CIIS Score

Weighting:

- Autonomy — 25%
- Competence — 25%
- Continuity — 20%
- Accountability — 15%
- Coordination — 15%

Calculation:

$$(3 \times 0.25) + (4 \times 0.25) + (3 \times 0.20) + (2 \times 0.15) + (3 \times 0.15)$$

= 0.75 + 1.00 + 0.60 + 0.30 + 0.45 = **3.10 / 10**

India's CIIS Score: 3.1 / 10 Category: *Structurally Fragile* — functional but fatigued, ambitious but unstable, capable of innovation but incapable of sustaining it.

4. CIIS Institutional Integrity Bands

Score Range	Classification	Meaning
0–2.5	Fragile Systems	Institutions exist but cannot enforce, execute, or innovate.
2.5–5.0	Transitional Systems	Institutions function but remain inconsistent and vulnerable. *(India's current band)*
5.0–7.5	Resilient Systems	Institutions are stable, autonomous, coordinated, and execution-capable.
7.5–10	Sovereign Systems	Institutions anchor national power; continuity survives political cycles.

5. Key Insights From CIIS

- **India's ambition exceeds its institutional stamina.** The country is running a 21st-century race with 20th-century foundations.
- **Institutional fragility magnifies every crisis.** Pandemics, floods, cyberattacks, economic shocks—all worsen when autonomy and coordination are weak.
- **Political overreach corrodes long-term stability.** No party is exempt; every government has weakened institutions to strengthen itself.
- **India's rise depends more on institutions than leaders.** A charismatic prime minister can inspire change; only institutions can preserve it.
- **CIIS must exceed 6.5 by 2035.** Anything less, and India remains structurally vulnerable—regardless of GDP or military power.

6. The CIIS Imperative

If India wants sovereignty in the compute century:

- Autonomy must be protected.
- Competence must be rewarded.
- Continuity must be insulated from politics.
- Accountability must be uniform.
- Coordination must be engineered.

India cannot enter 2035 with fragile pillars. A century is shaped by institutions, not elections.

7. Final Line

Nations do not collapse when leaders fail. They collapse when institutions fail.

CIIS is the mirror that shows whether India is building a republic of stability—or a house of stories.

Appendix C — India's Talent Leakage Map

A systemic model of where and why India loses talent

India has one of the world's deepest reservoirs of intelligence—but one of the world's leakiest talent architectures. The tragedy is not that talent leaves; the tragedy is that the system pushes it out.

The **Talent Leakage Map** exposes the four structural drains that weaken India's long-term capability:

- **Leak 1 — Early Education Misalignment**
- **Leak 2 — Higher Education Attrition & Exodus**
- **Leak 3 — Industry Underutilization & Skill Misallocation**
- **Leak 4 — Global Absorption & National Disconnect**

These are not accidents. They are predictable outcomes of an architecture that has not been rebuilt for a compute-driven world.

Leak 1 — Early Education Misalignment (Ages 6–18)

Where talent is discovered but not cultivated.

India's first—and deepest—leak begins in childhood. A system that rewards memorization over mastery, obedience over curiosity, and uniformity over imagination cripples the intellectual spark before it becomes capability.

Symptoms:

- Exam-centric schooling that punishes creativity
- Outdated textbooks and rigid syllabi
- Teachers overburdened and under-supported
- Coaching culture replacing real learning
- No exposure to research, innovation, or systems thinking

Outcome: Potential becomes pressure. Curiosity becomes compliance. The first drain opens before talent even understands its own ability.

Leak Severity Score: 8/10 (Severe)

Leak 2 — Higher Education Exodus (Ages 18–25)

Where talent realizes its future is elsewhere.

India's universities sit at the fault line between aspiration and reality. Students enter with dreams; they leave with documents for foreign admissions.

Causes:

- Weak research ecosystems
- Outdated labs and obsolete equipment
- Political appointments in academic leadership
- Lack of funding autonomy
- Bureaucratic control over innovation
- Professors burdened with paperwork, not research

Why talent leaves: Global institutions offer freedom, funding, mentorship, and compute access. Domestic institutions offer constraint, red tape, and outdated pedagogy.

Not because students dislike India—because India's system cannot keep pace with their ambition.

Leak Severity Score: 7/10 (Severe)

Leak 3 — Industry Underutilization & Skill Misallocation (Ages 22–35)

Where talent is employed—but never empowered.

India produces world-class engineers, scientists, designers, analysts, and managers... then gives them work that requires only a fraction of their ability.

Patterns of Leakage:

- IT services valuing billable hours over innovation
- Corporate hierarchies rewarding loyalty over leadership
- Startups burning talent without building it
- Weak mentorship cultures
- No structured link between industry and academia
- Low-risk appetite for deep-tech ventures

Emotional Drain: Frustration replaces aspiration. Ambition turns into survival. Innovation becomes a side hobby instead of a career path.

Result: India does not merely lose talent abroad; it loses talent inside India through underemployment and intellectual stagnation.

Leak Severity Score: 6/10 (Moderate–Severe)

Leak 4 — Global Absorption & National Disconnect (Ages 25–50)

Where talent leaves permanently—not physically, but mentally.

Not every Indian scientist or engineer abroad is "lost" to India. What India loses is their structural contribution.

Why global systems absorb India's best minds:

- High-trust research environments

- Predictable regulatory frameworks
- Reliable institutional support
- Access to world-class compute, labs, funding, mentors, peers
- Stable governance and long-term scientific roadmaps

India offers instead:

- Bureaucratic interference
- Political volatility
- Institutional fragility
- Inconsistent policy cycles
- Weak research capital
- Professional stagnation

Outcome: Talented Indians succeed abroad—but their success does not multiply national capability at home.

Leak Severity Score: 7/10 (Severe)

The Four-Leak Flow: A Systemic Drain Diagram

Talent enters as raw potential → Schooling suppresses curiosity (Leak 1) → Universities lack architecture (Leak 2) → Industry misuses skill (Leak 3) → Global ecosystems absorb high performers (Leak 4).

The leakage is cumulative. Each stage weakens the next.

By age 30, India has often lost:

- its best researchers
- its most creative engineers
- its boldest entrepreneurs
- its most visionary thinkers
- its globally competitive scientists

National Impact of Talent Leakage

- **Economic Impact:** Loss of innovation capacity, weaker IP creation, lower industrial depth, slower compounding.
- **Technological Impact:** Dependence on foreign compute, foreign AI, foreign research.
- **Institutional Impact:** Leadership pipelines degrade; bureaucratic modernizers exit the system.
- **Geopolitical Impact:** India remains a market of talent, not a manufacturer of capability.

The Talent Leakage Index (TLI): India's Score

Leak Scores:

- Early Education — 8
- Higher Education — 7
- Industry Misallocation — 6
- Global Absorption — 7

Composite TLI Score: 7.0 / 10

Category: *High Leakage — Structural Risk Zone*

India is a nation of strong individual talent but weak talent infrastructure.

The Path Forward — From Leakage to Networks

India must shift from talent protection to talent architecture:

- Build global research corridors
- Create domestic compute hubs
- Empower universities with autonomy
- Incentivize industry-led innovation
- Establish diaspora pipelines as formal networks

- Design leadership ecosystems that attract returnees
- Institutionalize long-term research missions

Talent will not stay because of emotion. Talent will stay—and circulate—because of architecture.

Final Line

India does not suffer from brain drain. India suffers from **architecture drain.**

Fix the architecture, and the minds return—not as individuals, but as networks.

Appendix D — 10 Scenarios for India 2025–2035

From acceleration to collapse — with probability bands

This appendix presents ten strategic scenarios that define the spectrum of India's possible futures. These are not forecasts; they are architectural outcomes—determined by how India manages its capability, stability, and integration variables over the next decade.

Each scenario is assigned a probability band, not as prediction, but as a *risk–readiness indicator.*

Scenario 1 — The Sovereign Surge *(Acceleration Path)*

- **Probability: 15%**

India invests aggressively in compute, semiconductors, AI, manufacturing, and institutions. Judicial reform begins. Bureaucratic modernization accelerates. States cooperate. Talent networks—domestic and global—activate.

- **Outcome:** India enters 2035 as a near-sovereign power with rising global influence. Dependency reduces dramatically. Growth becomes architecture-driven, not narrative-driven.
- **Signal:** ICDI and CIIS scores rise sharply.

Scenario 2 — The Execution Breakthrough *(High Growth With Fragility)*

- **Probability: 20%**

India delivers major reforms—logistics, manufacturing zones, digital infrastructure—while institutions remain inconsistent. Growth surges, but vulnerability persists beneath the surface.

- **Outcome:** GDP accelerates, industries scale, startups thrive, but strategic risks remain. One shock (cyberattack, supply disruption, global recession) can derail gains.
- **Signal:** Capability grows faster than stability.

Scenario 3 — The Talent Reversal *(Brain Networks Activate)*

- **Probability: 10%**

India builds deep innovation ecosystems:

- Global Indian researchers co-develop systems with domestic teams
- Return migration of mid-career experts
- Activated diaspora pipelines
- Rise of domestic research hubs

- **Outcome:** India's talent engine becomes self-reinforcing. AI, biotech, space, and manufacturing gain momentum.
- **Signal:** Talent Leakage Index (TLI) drops below 5.0.

Scenario 4 — Strategic Multialignment Success *(The India Pivot)*

- **Probability: 15%**

India builds architecture partnerships across the U.S., Japan, EU, Taiwan, Israel, and ASEAN without overdependence on any single bloc. Supply chains realign toward India.

- **Outcome:** Sovereignty strengthens through networks, not isolation. India becomes a geopolitical balancer, not a follower.
- **Signal:** Share of diversified tech alliances rises above 60%.

Scenario 5 — The Illusion of Strength *(Narrative Outruns Capability)*

- **Probability: 25% (Most Likely)**

Political narratives overshadow technological and institutional deficits. Infrastructure is built faster than institutions can sustain. GDP optimism masks architectural weaknesses. AI and semiconductors remain largely imported.

- **Outcome:** India grows, but remains dependent. 2035 arrives with unmet potential. Strategically stable, but not sovereign.
- **Signal:** GDP rises, but ICDI and CIIS stagnate below 4.

Scenario 6 — The Domestic Turbulence Spiral *(Stability Breakdown)*

- **Probability: 15%**

Polarization, regulatory confusion, administrative fatigue, and political overreach weaken governance capability. Economic volatility interrupts reforms. States drift apart in policy direction.

- **Outcome:** Growth slows. Investors hesitate. Institutional trust erodes. Capability-building initiatives stall.
- **Signal:** CIIS < 3.0 and rising social tensions.

Scenario 7 — The Dependency Trap *(Compute Failure)*

- **Probability: 20%**

India fails to develop compute sovereignty—chips, cloud, AI infrastructure remain foreign-controlled. Algorithmic dependency deepens. Digital governance sits atop imported systems.

- **Outcome:** India remains a global services provider—but not a global power. Foreign systems shape national outcomes.
- **Signal:** ICDI remains below 4.0 through 2030.

Scenario 8 — Geopolitical Whiplash *(External Shock)*

- **Probability: 10%**

A Taiwan conflict, U.S.–China tech war escalation, or regional instability hits India's supply chains. Chip access collapses. Cloud dependence turns into exposure.

- **Outcome:** National security and economy face simultaneous stress. India scrambles to rebuild, but without foundational architecture, recovery is slow.
- **Signal:** Supply chain chokepoints dominate critical sectors.

Scenario 9 — Innovation Renaissance *(Sectoral Breakthrough)*

- **Probability: 12%**

One or more sectors experience transformative growth:

- Space tech
- Green hydrogen
- EV and battery ecosystems
- Biotech
- Fintech global exports
- Defence manufacturing

- **Outcome:** India gains pockets of sovereignty even without full architectural reform. A sector-led rise improves bargaining power globally.
- **Signal:** Sectoral export dominance increases sharply.

Scenario 10 — Institutional Saturation *(The Slow Decline)*

- **Probability: 18%**

Institutions do not collapse—they simply cannot scale. Judicial systems, regulators, and bureaucracy become too fatigued to support India's ambitions. No crisis, no crash—just slow erosion.

- **Outcome:** India enters 2035 larger but weaker relative to global peers. The world moves faster; India moves unevenly.
- **Signal:** High ambition + low bandwidth becomes a permanent pattern.

Composite Outlook: India's 2035 Trajectory

Trajectory	Probability	Outcome
Acceleration Path	25–30%	India becomes a near-sovereign power.
Middle Path	40–50%	High growth, high dependency, moderate influence.
Risk Path	20–30%	Vulnerability increases; sovereignty weakens.

Final Insight of Appendix D

Across all scenarios, one truth stands immovable: *2035 is the deadline for India to shift from ambition to architecture.*

India's future will not be decided by geopolitics, GDP, or demographics. It will be decided by whether it builds:

- **Capability** (compute, industry, research)
- **Stability** (social, economic, institutional)
- **Integration** (networks, alliances, supply chains)

Scenarios change. *Architecture decides.*

Appendix E — Glossary of New Sovereignty Terms

Architecture, capability, ripple decisions, dependency gradients, and the language of the compute century

The compute century requires a new vocabulary. Old terms—power, sovereignty, alliances, development—fail to describe the architecture-driven world emerging around us.

This glossary defines the foundational concepts introduced throughout the book. Each definition is written with precision and strategic clarity, offering readers a coherent vocabulary for India's rise.

A

Architecture Power: The strategic strength a nation derives from the systems beneath its surface—chips, cloud, algorithms, institutions, supply chains, and digital infrastructure. In the compute century, architecture—not armies—determines advantage.

Architectural Deficit: A nation's inability to convert ambition into outcomes because its foundational systems (courts, bureaucracy, compute, supply chains) are outdated or fragile. India's central weakness across Parts II and V.

Architectural Sovereignty: The ability of a nation to function, grow, innovate, and defend itself without depending on foreign-controlled systems. Measured through ICDI and CIIS.

C

Capability (National): The sum of a nation's practical power—compute depth, manufacturing resilience, talent quality, institutional maturity, and technological capacity. Capability is ambition engineered.

Capability–Ambition Gap: The distance between what a nation wants and what its systems can deliver. India's recurring challenge in Part II.

CIIS (Chavanian Institutional Integrity Scale): A five-dimensional measure (Autonomy, Competence, Continuity, Accountability, Coordination) that indicates institutional strength or fragility.

Compute Sovereignty: A nation's ability to develop, operate, and secure chips, cloud systems, and AI models without external dependency.

Coordination Tax: The economic and strategic price a nation pays due to poor inter-agency, inter-ministry, or centre–state alignment. Fragmentation is not noise—it is cost.

D

Dependency Gradient: The slope that measures how dependent a nation is across chips, cloud, AI, manufacturing, finance, and talent. A steeper gradient = weaker sovereignty.

Digital State: A governance model built on secure cloud, integrated data, algorithmic decision-making, encrypted identity systems, and cyber-resilient infrastructure.

E

Execution Bandwidth: The real-world capacity of a nation's institutions to deliver reforms, implement policies, and complete complex projects. Not ambition—capability.

Externalized Capability: When a nation's growth relies on tools, systems, algorithms, and compute owned elsewhere. India's current position across AI and cloud.

F

Fragility Window: A time period during which a nation is vulnerable due to low capability, low stability, or high dependency. For India, this window spans 2025–2035.

G

Global Architecture Map: The strategic layout of compute supply chains, semiconductor routes, cloud ecosystems, algorithmic monopolies, and network alliances. The new world map.

I

ICDI (India Compute Dependency Index): A composite score measuring India's vulnerability across four pillars: Chips, Cloud, AI, Digital Infrastructure.

Institutional Exhaustion: A condition where institutions cannot scale with population, ambition, or policy complexity—leading to slowdown even without crisis.

Integration (Strategic): Partnerships built on compute, supply chains, research, and capability—not ideology. Foreign policy becomes architecture.

M

Multialignment: A foreign policy strategy rooted in diversification across global architectures (U.S., EU, Japan, Taiwan, ASEAN), enabling strategic autonomy. India's best path between the U.S. and China.

N

Narrative Sovereignty: A nation's control over the story it tells about itself—free from algorithmic manipulation or external influence. A hidden battlefield in the compute century.

Network Power: Advantage derived from being embedded in multiple global networks—technological, economic, research, and talent.

P

Pillar Industries: Sectors that shape sovereignty in the compute era—semiconductors, AI, advanced manufacturing, green tech, biotech, defence tech.

Policy Volatility: The instability caused by sudden regulation changes, political U-turns, and inconsistent enforcement. A major drain on stability.

R

Ripple Decisions: Small structural reform choices that create large long-term consequences—positive or negative. Borrowed from Chavanian systems thinking.

Ripple Vulnerability: The compounding effect of small institutional weaknesses that eventually lead to large national crises.

S

Sovereignty Index: A composite measure of a nation's independence across capability, stability, and integration.

Stability (National): The multiplier variable that amplifies or destroys capability. Includes economic predictability, social cohesion, political maturity, regulatory consistency, and institutional continuity.

T

Talent Infrastructure: The full architecture required to cultivate, retain, and deploy talent—education, research ecosystems, industry depth, global networks, leadership pathways, and compute availability.

Talent Leakage Map: A structural model documenting where and why India loses talent at every stage—from schools to global markets.

W

Wiring Sovereignty: Control over the nation's digital plumbing—cloud, data pipelines, encryption, cybersecurity, identity systems, and compute nodes.

Z

Zero-Sovereignty Zones: Areas where a nation has no domestic capability—fully dependent on external technologies or systems. Examples: advanced chips, cloud hyperscale, frontier AI labs.

Final Line

The future will belong to nations fluent in the language of architecture. This glossary is the dictionary of India's next century.

References and Further Reading

This curated list highlights books, papers, and reports that illuminate the deeper themes explored in *Sovereignty 2035: The India Equation*. These works are not endorsements; they are contextual signals—ideas, frameworks, and research that help readers understand the architecture shaping global power in the 21st century.

1. The Compute Century: Chips, Cloud, and AI

Semiconductors & Supply Chains

- Chris Miller — *Chip War: The Fight for the World's Most Critical Technology*
- Willy Shih — "Restoring American Competitiveness" (*Harvard Business Review*)
- RAND Corporation — *Semiconductor Supply Chain Security*
- McKinsey & Co. — *The Future of Microelectronics*

Cloud, Cybersecurity & Digital Infrastructure

- Nicole Perlroth — *This Is How They Tell Me the World Ends*
- Carnegie Endowment — *Cybersecurity and India's Digital Future*

- World Bank — *Digital Public Infrastructure: A Framework for Countries*

AI, Algorithms & Compute Power

- Kai-Fu Lee — *AI Superpowers*
- Stuart Russell — *Human Compatible*
- OECD — *AI Policy Observatory Reports*
- Allen Institute — *AI Model Scaling & Compute Economics*

2. Power, Sovereignty & Geopolitical Architecture

Geopolitics in the Compute Era

- Henry Kissinger, Eric Schmidt & Daniel Huttenlocher — *The Age of AI*
- Parag Khanna — *Connectography*
- National Bureau of Asian Research — *Emerging Technologies and Great Power Competition*

Comparative Models: U.S., China, Russia

- Graham Allison — *Destined for War*
- Elizabeth Economy — *The Third Revolution*
- Dmitri Trenin — *What Is Russia Up To in the Middle East?*
- CSIS — *Strategic Technologies and the Global Order*

3. India — Economy, Governance & Institutions

Indian State Capacity & Governance

- Arun Maira — *Transforming Systems*

- T.N. Ninan — *The Turn of the Tortoise*
- Pratap Bhanu Mehta — Essays on institutions and democracy
- Devesh Kapur — *Public Institutions in India*

Economy & Industrial Capability

- Raghuram Rajan & Rohit Lamba — *Breaking the Mould*
- Ashok Gulati & Shweta Saini — *The Indian Agricultural Ecosystem*
- NITI Aayog — *India's Manufacturing Vision 2030*
- ICRIER — *India and Global Value Chains*

Talent, Education & Innovation

- Andreas Schleicher (OECD) — *Learning for Life*
- Jitendra Singh — *India's Innovation Landscape*
- UNESCO — *Science Reports on Research & Development Trends*

4. Technology, Society & Stability

Institutional Fragility & Reform

- Francis Fukuyama — *Political Order and Political Decay*
- Daron Acemoglu & James A. Robinson — *Why Nations Fail*
- Lant Pritchett — *The State, Capability, and Development*

Digital Society & Social Stability

- Shoshana Zuboff — *The Age of Surveillance Capitalism*

- Yuval Noah Harari — *21 Lessons for the 21st Century*
- Brookings Institution — *The Future of Digital Citizenship*

5. Reports, Indices & Global Data Signals

These publications offer ongoing updates relevant to the ICDI, CIIS, TLI, and broader architectural analysis:

- World Economic Forum (WEF) — *Global Competitiveness Report*
- UNDP — *Human Development Report*
- World Bank — *Governance Indicators*
- ITU — *ICT Development Index*
- OECD — *AI & Digital Economy Policy Reports*
- IMF — *World Economic Outlook*
- IPR India — *Innovation & Patent Landscape*

6. Suggested Readings to Understand the Architecture Lens

These works help readers internalize the shift from old metrics (GDP, military, demographics) to new ones (compute, supply chains, institutions, networks):

- Geoffrey West — *Scale*
- Thomas Friedman — *The World is Flat* (concept evolution)
- Joseph Nye — *Soft Power*
- Niall Ferguson — *The Square and the Tower*
- Dan Breznitz — *Innovation in Real Places*

7. The Author's Intellectual Foundations *(Implicit Influences)*

Although this book stands apart from conventional frameworks, it intersects with the broader themes studied by:

- Systems theorists (Donella Meadows)
- Network scientists (Albert-László Barabási)
- Institutional economists (Douglass North)
- Technology strategists (Ben Thompson)
- Futurists and geopolitical analysts worldwide

These works are not referenced directly but provide intellectual context for readers exploring the deeper currents behind this worldview.

Final Note

This curated list is not comprehensive—it is directional. Its purpose is simple: to point readers toward the global literature that complements the architectural doctrine of this book.

The future belongs to readers who study systems, not slogans; architecture, not ideologies; capability, not stories.

Quote Bank from the Book

A reservoir of distilled clarity—each line a signal, each phrase a mirror. These quotes are not ornaments; they are anchors, capturing the architecture of sovereignty in words designed to endure.

1. On Modern Power

- "In the compute century, nations don't win by size—they win by structure."
- "Power no longer grows from the barrel of a gun; it grows from the density of a country's architecture."
- "A nation may have territory, population, and history—but without compute, it has no future."

2. On Capability

- "Ambition without capability is not a plan; it is a national illusion."
- "India does not lack talent. It lacks the architecture to hold talent."
- "Capability is not what a country dreams of—it is what it can deliver at scale."

3. On Stability

- "Chaos is the tax India pays for refusing to confront its own dysfunction."

- "When institutions tire, nations stall. When institutions collapse, nations decline."
- "Stability is not silence—it is the discipline that turns potential into acceleration."

4. On Integration

- "Sovereignty today is not independence—it is intelligent interdependence."
- "No nation rises by avoiding the world; nations rise by wiring themselves into it."
- "The future won't belong to blocs or camps—it will belong to the networks that execute."

5. On India's Reality

- "India is not weak; India is unstructured."
- "We celebrate ambition as if it were achievement—and lose years correcting the confusion."
- "Every Indian generation has carried potential. Only a few built systems. The next decade must do both."

6. On U.S.–India Dynamics

- "The U.S. can accelerate India's rise—or quietly define it. Integration is power; dependence is surrender."
- "America is not the enemy. Illusion is."

7. On China

- "China shows what scale can achieve; India must show what freedom can."

- "Competing with China does not require confrontation—it requires coherence."

8. On Russia

- "Russia did not fall because the world attacked it—it fell because its architecture could not stand alone."
- "Isolation is not sovereignty. It is slow suffocation."

9. On India's Strategic Equation

- "National Power = Capability × Stability × Integration. One weak variable turns the entire equation to zero."
- "Narratives can win elections. Only institutions can win centuries."
- "Strength performed is not strength possessed."

10. On the 2035 Moment

- "Windows of opportunity don't close loudly. They close quietly—while nations argue."
- "2035 is not destiny. It is a deadline."

11. On Leadership

- "The next India cannot be built by icons. It must be built by architectures."
- "Leadership is not charisma; it is coherence."

12. On Sovereignty

- "Sovereignty is no longer a flag on land—it is control over the rails your nation runs on."
- "A country that borrows its architecture will rent its future."

13. On National Choices

- "India does not need more slogans. It needs systems."
- "Nations don't fail because they lack potential—they fail because they ignore the variables that convert potential into power."

Closing Note

When I began writing this book, I did not set out to praise or to condemn. I set out to understand. To hold a mirror to a nation that often celebrates its ambition while ignoring the scaffolding that must hold that ambition upright. To decode the architecture of power in a world that no longer rewards size, sentiment, or slogans—but structure.

If this book has one message, it is this: **India is not weak. India is unstructured.** And structure—not emotion—decides who rises in the compute century.

Through these chapters, I have watched India's contradictions unfold: a billion dreams sprinting ahead while institutions lag behind; world-class minds leaking out of broken pipelines; governments performing strength instead of building it; a nation pulled between integration and dependence, between ambition and preparation. Yet beneath all of this lies something extraordinary: **potential that refuses to die.**

India is not a story of failure. India is a story of incompleteness.

The next decade will decide whether that incompleteness becomes a foundation... or a ceiling.

Real progress will not come from one leader, one party, one election, or one reform. It will come from a country willing to confront its own illusions, strengthen its institutions, protect its talent, invest in capability, and embed itself intelligently into global architectures. It will come from the discipline to redesign the systems we inherited and the courage to build the systems we need.

As a teacher, I see every day what India could become. As a researcher, I see what India must fix. As a citizen, I see what India must choose.

2035 is not a prophecy. It is a window. A narrow one.

If we step through it with clarity, discipline, and architectural intent, India will not just rise—it will redefine the meaning of national power itself. If we hesitate, the window will close quietly, without drama, without announcement, and the world will move forward while we continue debating the past.

This book is my invitation—to policymakers, thinkers, entrepreneurs, educators, and every Indian who believes this nation deserves more than narratives.

Let us build the India we keep imagining. Not someday—now. Not in words—in architecture. Not for applause—but for the century that awaits us.

— **Sandeep Chavan**

Acknowledgements

Books of this nature are never written by a single mind. They are shaped, challenged, sharpened, and sometimes rescued by the people, institutions, conversations, and contradictions that surround us.

This work was born from years of teaching, observing, debating, and questioning India's trajectory—often in classrooms filled with anxious students, in quiet corridors of institutions wrestling with their purpose, and in late-night reflections about what this country could become if its brilliance ever aligned with its architecture.

I am deeply grateful to the students who kept asking the uncomfortable questions, forcing me to look beyond narratives and into the mechanics of national power. Their curiosity was not just academic—it was a daily reminder that India's future belongs to those who refuse to accept what is broken.

My sincere thanks to colleagues, friends, and well-wishers who challenged my assumptions, argued with me, corrected me, and encouraged me through each stage of this work. Many of our debates—across tea shops, classrooms, and living rooms—quietly shaped the contours of this book. Their honesty strengthened my conviction; their disagreements sharpened my clarity.

I am grateful to the thinkers, researchers, policymakers, diplomats, technologists, and everyday citizens whose ideas and lived experiences form the invisible scaffolding of this work. This book stands on the collective dialogue of a nation that is constantly searching for its next breakthrough.

I want to acknowledge my family—whose patience and understanding fuel every page I write. Their quiet support anchors me when the world becomes too loud. Every late night, every manuscript draft, and every moment of self-doubt was held by their belief in me.

A special note of appreciation goes to the global and domestic voices—past and present—who continue to explore the evolving idea of national power. Their work forms the intellectual environment within which this book took shape.

Finally, I want to acknowledge the readers. This book is written for those who refuse to accept simplifications, who understand that real progress requires difficult conversations, and who believe that India's destiny must be built—not declared.

If this book contributes even slightly to India's collective capacity to think more clearly, act more intelligently, and build more deliberately, then every word has been worth it.

About the Author

Sandeep Chavan is an independent researcher, educator, and author whose work spans physics, national strategy, institutional architecture, human behaviour, and the emerging science of sovereignty in the compute century. Over the years, he has written extensively on the intersections of energy, intelligence, institutions, and leadership—building a unique intellectual framework that challenges conventional narratives and redefines how nations understand power.

As a physics teacher by training and a systems thinker by instinct, Sandeep has spent more than two decades observing India's talent pipeline, institutional machinery, and structural contradictions from the ground up. His insights emerge not from distant commentary but from daily engagement with students, researchers, policymakers, and working professionals who live within the Indian ecosystem.

He is the author of numerous books across science, philosophy, governance, and strategy—many of which have shaped conversations on Universal Energy Dynamics (UED), institutional integrity, and the evolving nature of human capability. His work combines analytical rigour with a narrative clarity that makes complex ideas accessible to diverse audiences.

Driven by a belief that India's rise requires more than optimism—that it demands architecture—Sandeep writes to provoke deeper reflection, sharper debate, and more deliberate nation-building. *Sovereignty 2035: The India Equation* continues his effort to decode the forces shaping modern power and to illuminate the choices India must make before the window closes.

He lives his life as a teacher first, researcher second, and student forever.

Also by Sandeep Chavan

The journey does not end here. Each book is a ripple in a larger continuum — a field of ideas that challenge assumptions, reframe realities, and open new pathways of thought. Explore these Chavanian works to step deeper into the architecture of consequence, energy, and human possibility.

Series

A Monk on World Tour

- The Making of the Monk

Chavanian Philosophy

- The Law of Consequences
- Ethics & Morale: Shades of Consequence
- The Human Mind: Ripple of Awareness
- Universal Skill: Navigating Consequences

Chavan's UED Research

- CMGED Research Report

Chavan's Cosmic Continuum (C^3)

- Frequency
- Ripples of Reality
- Reality Realigned
- The Great Realignment
- I – The Cosmic Leverage
- Chavan's Cosmic Theory of Relativity (CTR)
- Chavan's Theory of Light
- Feeling Like a Physicist
- TIME – The New Definition
- $E \neq mc^2$: The Collapse of Classical Assumptions
- The Chavan Codex
- Chavan's Atomic Model
- Chavan's Theory of Everything

Doctor AI

- The Diagnosis of Data

Echoes of War: The Russia–Ukraine Conflict and Its Global Ripples

- Shattered Lives
- The War Economy
- Borders Redrawn
- Arms and Allies
- Collateral Damage
- Justice in the Ashes

Somewhere in the Darkness of the Cosmos

- The Blueprint of the Universe
- The Cosmic Breath
- From the Edge of the Universe
- The Old Sky & the New Language

The AI Transition

- The Human Upgrade
- The Jobless Future

The Eternal Sage Chronicles

- The Sage and the Sovereign
- The Family Pillar
- The People's Flame
- The Warrior's Soul
- The Bridging Mentor
- The Guiding Light

The Exodus

- The Last Cycle: 2075

The Fundamental Theory of Life & Existence

- Energy in Action: The Soul Demystified
- The Active Mind
- Energy in Connection
- Death: The Disconnection
- Subconsciousness: The Chosen Disconnection

- Desires: The Engine of Life

The Harmony Codex

- The Unwritten Code
- The Silent Algorithm
- The Equation of Life

The Moral Archetypes of Humanity

- Dhritarashtra: The Blindness Within

The Restoration of Human Knowledge

- Restoring Bhagavad Gita

The War of Thoughts

- Cracks in the Known
- The Human Game
- The Divine Dilemma
- The Original Intent
- The Answers

Ultra Modern Life Philosophy

- The Duality of Laughter and Tears
- Take It Easy
- Compare to Accept

Universal Energy Dynamics Canon (UED 2.0)

- The Structure of Reality

Standalone Works

- It's Not AI, It's AHI – Amplified Human Intelligence
- The Decision Paradox
- The Four Sapiens
- Malicious Script of Indian Polity
- The IIT Legacy & Global Impact
- You Are Just a Version of Your Original
- Win the Game You Didn't Choose
- Always Keep Your Bags Packed
- Reveal to Shield – Learn the Game of Facades
- Engage Beyond Elections
- Culture, Identity & Change: The Evolution of Indian Society
- The Triangular Dynamics
- Never Trust Without Doubt
- If You Can't Change the Country, Leave the Country
- Live Fearless with Fear
- India: The Investment Magnet
- Realignment
- Powering a Billion Dreams
- Universal Skill
- Extension: From Brush to Algorithm
- Human Side of Einstein
- The Future Knows No Lines
- Let's Bring the Generations to the Table
- Unified Energy Dynamics
- A Beat That Never Dies

- Strategic Horizons
- Right From Scratch
- The Forgotten Innovators
- Physics Fixing
- The Savior Illusion
- The Selfish Side
- The Age of the Weakest Sapiens
- Neural Wars
- The Absorption: There Is No Death
- Strange Therapist
- Bubbles: Become a Drop
- Beyond the Blue
- Half-Scholar
- The Law of Truth
- Failure
- Philosophy 2.0: A Structural Manifesto
- Chaos: A Gentle Guide to the Unresolvable
- Self-Help: New Syllabus
- Rippling
- Game: How to Play the Share Market
- Out of Syllabus
- Saffronized: The Code Behind the Crown
- The Anger
- Moksha: The Liberation
- Chavan vs Einstein: The Universe Was Never Curved
- Rocket Science: The Ripple Gambling
- The Cosmos: The Still Universe
- The Taste of Silence
- Chavan's Post-Materialist Human Model
- 10-Second Rule
- Chavan vs Hawking
- It Was Never a Wave Signal

- Quantum Courtroom: The Trial of a Century
- Chavan–Heisenberg Ripple Uncertainty Principle
- The Great Disruption
- Dark ≠ Hidden
- Breath
- Calculus of Life
- The Earth Doesn't Move
- Black Hole Don't Exist
- Chavan vs Kant
- Naked Truth: Everything and Else
- The Moon: Co-Author of Life's Script
- World War-3
- Aham Brahmasmi
- Chavan's Declaration
- Light: Neither a Wave, Nor a Photon
- Chavan vs Plato
- Good Morning
- Myth Wrapped in Math
- Our Story
- Rethinking Energy: Ripple Tension, Not Substance
- Statue vs Scaffold: MODI vs RAHUL
- Chavan's Universal Framework for Everything
- Heraclitus: A Chavanian Interpretation
- The Clear View: Living Through Universal Lenses
- Conspiracy of Convenience & Profit
- The Happiness Scam
- The Last Quantum Book
- Vedanta Reimagined
- Intelligence: It's Not What You Think
- Let's Meet the GOD
- The Question That Won't Go Away
- The Return Journey

- Mandatory Reset
- Ripple Centrism: From Copernicus to Chavan
- Aligned Father, Misaligned Dad
- Not Yet, But Becoming
- The Fumes of Deeper Fire
- The Nobel for Accidents
- What It Meant to Be an Author
- The Nation Splitting Within
- 3.17 Hz: The Consequence of Silence
- The Real Story of AI
- Politics @ Coffee Machine
- The Middle Guard
- Chavanian Psychology
- Synthetic Prostitution
- The End of Particle Age
- Stop Acknowledging AI
- Nationalism
- Intelligent Before AI: The American Advantage
- The Russian Dilemma

Don't miss out!

Visit the website below and you can sign up to receive emails whenever Sandeep Chavan publishes a new book. There's no charge and no obligation.

https://books2read.com/r/B-A-EPGPC-JBBOI

BOOKS 2 READ

Connecting independent readers to independent writers.

Did you love *Sovereignty 2035: The India Equation*? Then you should read *Nationalism*[1] by Sandeep Chavan!

[2]

Nationalism: A Consequence of Shared Intelligence is a groundbreaking redefinition of what a nation truly is — not a political idea, not an emotional myth, but an emergent phenomenon of **collective resonance**. In this transformative and deeply original work, Sandeep Chavan reframes nationalism through the lens of **field dynamics**, revealing how consciousness, awareness, intelligence, systems, and ethics interact to produce the rise or decline of nations.

Drawing upon the Chavanian interpretation of Universal Energy Dynamics (UED), the book argues that nationalism is not a cause of unity — it is **the outcome of aligned human fields**

---

1. https://books2read.com/u/mBq2Ry

2. https://books2read.com/u/mBq2Ry

operating across layers: emotional, professional, and ethical. When these layers harmonize, nations achieve stability, progress, and coherence. When they drift apart, societies fracture, systems decay, and national identity collapses from within.

This book moves in eight sweeping parts, guiding the reader from the foundations of human fields to the construction of national identity, from the oscillations between emotion and institutions to the emergence of ethical nationalism as the stabilizing layer. The narrative expands outward into global field interactions — how nations influence each other, amplify or distort one another's ripples, and co-evolve in a planetary resonance.

The book delivers a powerful framework for interpreting geopolitics, public policy, education, leadership, AI, technological acceleration, and civilizational cycles through the alignment lens. It positions nationalism not as ideology but as a **living field phenomenon** measurable through emotional coherence, institutional capability, and ethical integrity — culminating in the **Chavanian Field Resonance Index**, a tool for diagnosing national health.

In the final section, the book steps beyond nations, exploring how civilizations emerge, evolve, collapse, and converge. It closes with a bold thesis: humanity's destiny is the gradual alignment of human and machine intelligence into a unified planetary field, where consequence-awareness becomes the guiding force of civilization.

Written in a narrative, reflective, and profoundly philosophical tone, this book is accessible to thinkers, policymakers, students, leaders, and citizens seeking clarity in an increasingly complex world. It replaces slogans with science, myth with intelligence, and fear with consequence-awareness — offering a new blueprint for the 21st century: **Chavanian Nationalism**, a myth-free, ethics-driven, alignment-centric model of national identity.

This is not another book on nationalism.This is a new grammar for understanding nations themselves — not as borders or governments, but as **evolving ripples of shared intelligence**.

Read more at https://www.sandeepjchavan.com/.

www.ingramcontent.com/pod-product-compliance
Lightning Source LLC
Chambersburg PA
CBHW031335230926
51848CB00002B/241
9788199541498